JIHAD

Bin Laden in His Own Words

Declarations, Interviews and Speeches

JIHAD

Bin Laden in His Own Words

Declarations, Interviews and Speeches

Brad K. Berner

PEACOCK BOOKS

Published by
PEACOCK BOOKS
B-2, Vishal Enclave, New Delhi-110 027
Phones : 2541 3460, 2542 9987, 2546 6842

Distributed by
ATLANTIC PUBLISHERS AND DISTRIBUTORS (P) LTD.
7/22, Ansari Road, Darya Ganj, New Delhi-110 002
Phones : 2327 3880, 2327 5880, 2328 0451
Fax : 91-11-2328 5873
E-mail : info@atlanticbooks.com
Web : www.atlanticbooks.com

Peacock Books is an imprint of
Atlantic Publishers and Distributors (P) Ltd.

ISBN 81-248-0112-6

Printed in India at Nice Printing Press, Delhi

For Zetun, Lucky, Masha and Luba

Preface

Born into a very wealthy family in Saudi Arabia in 1957, Osama bin Laden, who founded Al Qaeda in 1988, has come to epitomize contemporary Islamist fundamentalist terrorism. A lauded hero upon his return to Saudi Arabia from Afghanistan, after having fought against the Soviets in the 1980s, Bin Laden stridently criticized the Saudi government for having invited Western forces, led by the U.S., into Saudi Arabia to force Saddam Hussein out of Kuwait and for its failure to rule under Islamic law.

Bin Laden soon left for Sudan, where Al Qaeda began operations against the U.S. in its 1992 failed bombing in Aden, Yemen and its bombings in Saudi Arabia in 1995. Forced to leave Sudan in 1996, he returned to Afghanistan, where he supported the Taliban regime. His organization bombed the U.S. embassies in Kenya and Tanzania in 1998, attacked the USS *Cole* in Aden in 2000, and undertook the 9/11 operations in the U.S.

In his public statements, Bin Laden justified these actions as a defensive response to Western attacks on the Islamic world, and the West's support for contemporary 'apostate' regimes in Muslim countries and of Israel.

For much of the world he is the public face of contemporary Islamist fundamentalist terrorism. However, for a significant Islamist fundamentalist minority, he is a hero, representing a violent resistance to Western encroachment on Islamic societies and the 'apostate' regimes currently ruling Muslim countries. Consequently, his words are important.

When Bin Laden speaks, the Western media usually asks: Is he really alive? Where is he? Hardly ever does it ask: What did he say? This brief compilation of his declarations, speeches and interviews is meant to give the reader an opportunity to ask, and hopefully answer, the last question.

Definitions of significant terms and individuals are listed at the end of the book, with Arabic terms in *italics*. Words in brackets are meant to clarify the preceding term or terms, while parenthesis are used for standardized terms used in Arabic in referring to God, Muhammad, etc. A few changes have been made to achieve uniformity in spelling and in the use of terms.

Finally, special thanks to PBS Frontline, MEMRI (Middle East Research Institute), *Dawn* (Pakistan), *Ummat* (Karachi, Pakistan), islamicawakening.com, and the *BBC* for permission to reprint their respective translations. These are cited at the end of the declarations, speeches and interviews. Those without sources listed have been independently translated.

BRAD K. BERNER

Contents

1

An Open Letter to King Fahd

(3 August 1995)

> Angered by the Saudi royal family's permitting U.S. troops to be stationed in Saudi Arabia, Bin Laden, in a lengthy public letter, outlined his major grievances against the regime and called for the regime's resignation.

Praise be to God, and blessings and peace be upon the Messenger of God, his family, Companions, those who follow His guidance.

To the King of Najd and al-Hijaz [Saudi Arabia], *Fahd bin Abdul-Aziz*

Peace be upon those who follow the Guidance [of God].

We send to you this open letter, far removed from royal complimentary titles and words of glorification. It shall be a frank manifesto to make apparent that which you, and those around you, have committed against God and Islam, against the land of Islam and the Muslims, and against the Sacred City [Mecca] and the Muslim community. We hope that our frankness in displaying the glaring truth to you will tear through the barriers you have set up between you and it.

O King, this letter is in response to the roguery and mind-games you and your implementer Princes have played on people, so that you may suppress their anger upon you and your ways. Your marginal and deceiving 'rectifications' are nothing but short-term sedatives to ease this anger. Examples of the former would be the Consultation Council that you have set up, which the Muslim community has awaited for a long time, and to their disappointment, it was born dead. Now you have made these marginal ministerial changes that didn't have any effect on the sources of all evil—namely you, your Defense Minister, Internal Affairs Minister, Prince of Riyadh, and the likes of all of you.

The main reason for writing this letter to you is not your oppression of people and their rights, especially the scholars, the callers to righteousness, the merchants, and the senior chiefs of tribes. It's not your insult to the dignity of our nation, your desecration of its sanctuaries, and your embezzlement of its wealth and riches. It's not what has been spread during your reign of bribery, forging, and disintegration of management and morals. It's not the economic breakdown that has hit the country and almost made it reach the level of bankruptcy. These things are all important, but we shall discuss them at another time after we expose to you the quintessence of our dispute with you. The quintessence of our dispute is the fact that your ruling system has transgressed "*There is no god except God and Muhammad is the Messenger of God*," and that is the basis on which the belief in the oneness of God differentiates between belief and disbelief. All the aforementioned problems are a result of your transgression against the basic tenets of the belief in the oneness of God. Since we are, God willing, going to soon release detailed research about your transgressions, we will confine our letter to two main aspects:

Ruling By and Legislating Other than That Which God Has Sent

It has recurred in *Qur'an*ic verses, the Prophetic traditions, and the sayings of the scholars of the Muslim community, that whosoever vindicates for himself or others to follow a positivistic legislature or a man-made law that transgresses the laws of God, then he, in fact, is a disbeliever and is out of our creed. God—the Exalted—says: "*Have you seen those hypocrites who claim that they believe in that which has been sent down to you, and that which was sent down before you, and they wish to go for judgment* [in their disputes] *to the false judges while they have been ordered to reject them. But Satan wishes to lead them far astray*" [Qur'an 4:60].

Sheikh Abdul-Rahman bin Hassan al-Sheikh—may God have mercy on him—has said in the interpretation of this verse: Whosoever calls to arbitrating other than God and His Messenger, he has then left what the Messenger (PBUH) brought, refuted it, and has ascribed partners in his obedience to God, and he has gone against what the Prophet (PBUH) taught us when the following verses were revealed to him: "*And so judge* [you Muhammad] *between them by what God has revealed and follow not their vain desires, but beware of them lest they turn you* [Muhammad] *far away from some of that which God has sent down to you. And if they turn away, then know that God's will is to punish them for some sins of theirs. And truly, most of men are disobedient* [to God]" [Qur'an 5:49]. And: "*But no, by your Lord, they can have no faith, until they make you* [Muhammad] *judge in all disputes between them, and find in themselves no resistance against your decisions and accept* [them] *with full submission*" [Qur'an 4:65].

Whosoever contradicts that which God and His Messenger have ordered and arbitrates between people by other than that which God has sent, or ordered that so as to fulfil his desires; he indeed has disbelieved and expelled himself from the folds of Islam—even if he says that he's a believer. God—Exalted be He—has disavowed their belief and refuted it in the verse mentioned above when He used the word 'claim'—referring to the false claim of them still believing—for they were 'ordered to reject them' [false judges]. The disbelief in false judges is an essential basis for believing in monotheism and the oneness of God, as mentioned in the verse: "*Whoever disbelieves in false judges and believes in God, he has grasped the most trustworthy handhold that will never break*" [Qur'an 2:256]. If this pillar is not fulfilled, the person is not a monotheist, and monotheism is the base of belief. Its presence helps a man's deeds and its absence hinders them. [From the book *Fath al-Majeed, Sharh Kitaab al-Tawheed*, pp. 392-93.]

Sheikh Muhammad bin Ibraheem aal al-Sheikh—may God have mercy on him—said in regards to the interpretation of the verse: "*Have you seen those hypocrites who claim that they believe in that which has been sent down to you, and that which was sent down before you, and they wish to go for judgment* [in their disputes] *to the false judges while they have been ordered to reject them. But Satan wishes to lead them far astray*" [Qur'an 4:60].

God has disavowed the belief of those hypocrites who arbitrate between people by other than that which the Messenger (PBUH) brought from God—Exalted be He—used the word "claim"—referring to the false claim of believing, for belief and arbitration by other than that which the Messenger (PBUH) brought cannot be combined in the heart of a believer. In fact, they annul each other. The word *taghut* [false judges] is derived from "the transgression of boundaries." Whosoever rules by other than that which the Messenger (PBUH) brought, he has, in fact, ruled by the false judges. [From the letter *Tahkeem al-Qawaneen* by Sheikh Muhammad bin Ibraheem aal al-Sheikh] God says: "*Do they then seek the judgment of* [the Days of] *Ignorance? And who is better in judgment than God for a people who have firm faith*" [Qur'an 5:50].

Ibn Katheer says with regards to the interpretation of this verse: Whosoever disregards the laws of God, the laws that comprise all goodness and forbid all evil, and takes on man-made laws, views, and desires, which were put in place without any reference to the laws of God—as is the case in the times of ignorance, when people would rule by laws laid out to satisfy their whims and desires. Or like the Tatars who ruled by laws derived from the doctrine the *Yaasiq* put for them by their King Genghis Khan. The *Yaasiq* is a collection of rules he derived from Judaism, Christianity, Islam and other creeds, as well as things he put from his own self to suit his whims. This became prioritized legislation to be followed and implemented before the Book of God [the *Qur'an*] and the traditions of His Messenger (PBUH). Such a person is to be regarded as a disbeliever and should be killed, unless he returns to ruling by the laws of God and His Messenger in all matters, big or small. Is this *Yaasiq* but a modern example of the rules that you and your ruling system go by and those like you?

The arbitration of positivistic laws and judging by them is, without doubt, a form of worship to the author of these laws, and a form of distancing those who follow these legislations from the ones set by God. This meaning has been clarified by the Messenger (PBUH) to Adyy bin Haatim in the *Hadith* related by at-Tirmithy and others: While Adyy bin Haatim was still a Christian, he heard the Prophet (PBUH) reciting the verse: "*They* [Jews and Christians] *have taken as lords besides God their rabbis and their monks and the Messiah son of Mary, when they were bidden to worship only One God. There is no god save Him. Be He glorified from all that they ascribe as partner* [unto Him]" [Qur'an 9:31]. He said: "O Messenger of God, we did not worship them." The Messenger (PBUH) said: "Did they not make forbidden that which God has made lawful for you, and so you forbade it? And they made lawful what God has forbidden, and you then legitimized it?" He said: "They did." The Messenger replied: "That is a form of worshipping them."

Adyy bin Haatim used to think that worship was confined to the religious rituals such as prayers and the like, and when the Christians didn't pray to their rabbis and priests, he thought that they, therefore, were not worshipping them. But the Prophet (PBUH) cleared up Adyy's misconception and clarified that, by obeying them in legitimizing and forbidding matters in a way that is contradictory to the legislation of God, they have then taken them as gods besides God. This concept of worship that the Messenger (PBUH) has clarified and explained to Adyy bin Haatim—may God be pleased with him—is the concept that the Muslim community has agreed upon. And it has recurred in the explanations of the scholars, which we shall mention below in brief:

Ibn Hazm says about the verse: "*They* [Jews and Christians] *have taken as lords besides God their rabbis and their monks and the Messiah son of Mary, when they were bidden to worship only One God. There is no god save Him. Be He glorified from all that they ascribe as partner* [unto Him]" [Qur'an 9:31]. When the Jews and Christians used to forbid what their rabbis and priests would declare unlawful and enjoin what they legitimized, that was a form of taking them as their lords and a form of worship to those rabbis and priests. God has called their act a form of taking them as lords besides Him, and that certainly is a form of ascribing partners to God [*The Fasi* 3/66].

The Sheikh al-Islam, Ibn Taymiyah, may God have mercy on him, after mentioning the above saying of the Prophet (PBUH) about Adyy bin Haatim, said: "And so has said Abu al- Bakhtary: 'Even though they didn't direct their prayers to them, they obeyed them in legitimizing the unlawful and forbidding the lawful; thus, they have taken them as lords besides God. The Prophet (PBUH) has clarified that their worship to the rabbis and priests was in obeying them in the aforementioned matter, and not necessarily by directing prayers and fasts to them. Obeying them is a form of associating partners with Him in worship.' God says: "*There is no god except God, praise and glory be to Him,* [far above is He] *from having the partners they associate* [with Him]" [Qur'an 9:31] [*The Fatwa* 7/67].

Sheikh Muhammad bin Abdul Wahhab—may God have mercy on him—quoted the aforementioned saying of the Prophet and said: "Whosoever obeys the scholars and princes in forbidding what God has made legitimate and enjoying that which God has forbidden, has taken them as lords besides God" [From the side notes in the book *Monotheism*, p. 146].

The Sheikh al-Islam, Ibn Taymiyah—may God have mercy on him—said: "It is known from resolution from the sources of the religion of Islam, and by agreement of all Muslims, that whosoever vindicates the following of a religion other than Islam, and a legislature other than the legislation brought by Muhammad (PBUH), he is a disbeliever" [*Fatawa*, part 12/524]. He also said—may God have mercy on him—"Islam encompasses the submission to God alone, so whosoever submits to God and someone else, he therefore is an idol worshipper. And whosoever doesn't submit to God, he therefore is too proud to worship God. So the idol worshiper and the too proud are disbelievers. Submission to God requires that one submits fully and solely to the worship and obedience of Him alone" [*Fatawa* 3/91].

Sheikh Muhammad bin Ibrahim aal al-Sheikh [The former interpreter of Islamic law in the Kingdom of Saudi Arabia]—

may God have mercy on him—said: "It is a major and clear disbelief—that of putting the wicked laws at the level of the laws that descended through the angel Gabriel unto the heart of Muhammad (PBUH), who was sent as a warner, in a clear Arabic tongue, with rulings to judge between people, and to serve as a guide and a reference for settling disputes.

In a letter directed to the Prince of Riyadh at the time, the Sheikh said with regards to the man-made laws that are applied in the trading rooms in Riyadh: "Considering any of the man-made rules or ruling by them—even in the slightest manner—is, without no doubt, dissatisfaction with the rules of God and His Messenger. And it reflects a person's belief that the rules of God and His Messenger are inadequate for solving matters, returning rights to people, and ruling justly between them. Believing that is an apostasy that expels one from the Islamic creed—and that is a serious matter, not one that is unclear and needing clarification. Deploying the legislations of God alone is the twin half of the worship of Him alone. For the gist of the declaration of faith is that the only deity worthy of worship is God alone with no partners ascribed, and that His Messenger would be the example to follow. The rules that have been revealed to him by God are the rules to be followed. Have the swords of *jihad* been put to action except for that cause—to restore the laws of God among mankind?" [*Fatawa* 12/251].

The prominent scholar Sheikh Muhammad al-Ameen al-Shanqeetee says in the book *Adwaa' al-Bayaan*: "Deploying a system of ruling to judge between people and take care of their matters, that is contradictory to the legislations of the Creator of the heavens and the earth, is disbelief in the Creator of the heavens and the Earth. And it is a rebellion against the divine system which was revealed to the best of creation [Muhammad]. He [God] knows best about that which is of benefit to the creation. Exalted be He from ever having a competitor in legislating laws for His creation: *Say* [O Muhammad to these polytheists]: "*Tell me, what provision God has sent down to you! And you have made of it lawful and unlawful.*" *Say* [O Muhammad]: "*Has God permitted you* [to do so], *or do you invent a lie against God?*" [Qur'an 10:59] [*Adwaa' al-Bayaan* 4/84].

Sheikh Muhammad Mahed al-Faqyy—may God have mercy on him—says in his commentary on the book of *Monotheism*, on the topic of deploying man-made laws: "He who does that and insists upon it, refusing to rule by that which God has sent down, with no doubt, is a disbeliever and an apostate. His title as a Muslim and all his deeds [prayers and fasting] shall not avail him" [From *Fath al-Majeed*—the explanation of the book of *Monotheism*—side note 3/296].

Sheikh Ahmad Muhammad Shakir—may God have mercy on him—with regards to deploying man-made laws: "This is revolt against the rules of God and His religion, and is a preference to the rules of the disbelievers over the rules of God the Almighty. It is an act of disbelief, which no Muslim doubts, despite their difference on whether or not the person himself becomes an apostate" [From *Omdat al-Tafseer* 4/157].

These are authentic evidences from revelation and straight forward quotations of Islamic scholars that lie at the heart of the matter, and that are designed to end disagreement, put bickering to rest, and silence arrogance. But for avoidance of lengthiness, we would have cited more evidence and quotations, as this issue constitutes the principal theme in the entire *Qur'an*. Nonetheless, we believe that it is sufficient for any that has a heart and understanding or who gives ear and earnestly witnesses the truth.

It remains to remind you [King Fahd] of what you and your regime are doing by enforcing these non-Islamic laws and abrogating God's legitimate rulings. The average man, let alone the punctilious researcher, will not have to labor long in order to prove that you, as well as your regime, are legislating and enforcing secular laws which you are making binding on the people.

In point of fact, a quick glance at the statutes of commercial courts and laws that legalize usurious transactions in banks and so forth, as well as at work and workers' law, Saudi Arabia's army's regulations, and similar non-Islamic laws, will underscore the extent to which these non-Islamic laws have expanded and taken hold in the country. Further, the *Memorandum of Advice* [Drawn up by a group of scholars to recommend to the king that he enact reforms in the kingdom] mentioned the existence of dozens of legal committees that adjudicate between citizens by means of secular laws, with which you rule the country and the people within, let alone such laws that govern foreign relations abroad.

An example is your submission to the decisions of the committee for conflict resolution between the countries of the Gulf Council for Cooperation. Without doubt, this Council, headquartered in Saudi Arabia, the main member, is a secular non-Islamic legislative organization. This committee provides in article 9 of its principal charter: "The committee shall issue its recommendations and rulings in accordance with:

1. The provisions of the main constitution of the Council of Cooperation.
2. International law.
3. International norms.
4. Principles of Islamic law. Its reports with regards to the issue shall then be submitted to the Supreme Council so that the latter may decide that which is appropriate."

What a mockery of God's religion and what disdain of His law!

You have put Islamic law only at the very end of the above-mentioned list of legislative sources, even after the garbage of human thoughts, norms and traditions of the disbelieving nations and the laws of the disbelieving regimes!!! Is all this not enough disbelief and straying for you that you finally even subjugated God's law to the condescension of your Supreme Council, which is free to pick and choose which laws to honor at the Council's whims and desires?

What do the protectors of religion, guardians of the creed and callers to monotheism, say to submission to such committees and courts, O 'Servant of the Two Sacred Mosques'? The answer, as we have indicated on previous occasions, is so evident that it is comparable to the sun at high noon, admitting no hesitancy, nor stammering, or dodging, or evasiveness, or appeasement. It is clear that disbelief is taking you out of the fold of Islam according to the Noble Book [*Qur'an*], and the traditions of the Prophet and the consensus of the Islamic nation.

Here are some statements by notable scholars which speak to these non-Islamic laws and express the pertinent Islamic rulings:

Sheikh Muhammad bin Ibrahim, may God have mercy upon him, wrote in a letter he sent to Riyadh's Prince concerning the laws of the commercial courts: "We have received a copy titled the *Charter of the Commercial Court of Saudi Arabia*. Upon perusing half of it, we have found it consisting of non-Islamic secular illegal systems.... The implementation of any of these [non-Islamic] laws, however trifling, is undoubtedly tantamount to displeasure with the judgment of God and His Prophet...and that is clear disbelief, which takes one outside the realm of the Islamic nation" [Excerpted from the *Fatawa* of the Sheikh, 12/251].

The Sheikh, may God have mercy upon him, in a letter he addressed to the chair of the Supreme Court in Riyadh regarding the rules and regulations issued by the Office of Work and Workers, and the duty of Islamic courts with respect to that office, says:

From Muhammad bin Ibrahim to his Excellency, Chair of the Supreme Council in Riyadh.

"Peace be upon you, and may God's mercy and blessings be upon you, we have received your memorandum on the transactions that we get from the Office of Work and Workers. The appropriate procedures in this case fall into two categories:

1. As to that transaction which is referred to the court for deliberation and finalization, the court should take it up, as that is the core of its mission.
2. As for that transaction which is submitted for mere approval and afterwards to be returned to the Office of Work for finalization through directives from this office, that which is unjustifiable by what God sent

> down, it is the duty of the court to ignore it. If not, then such action will be regarded as approval and complicity in stripping the authority of God's law" [10/23/1379 A.H., Excerpted from the *Fatawa* of the Sheikh 12/251].

Also, on the issue of the Charter of Work and Workers, Supreme Justice Abdallah bin Hamid, may God have mercy upon him, wrote that referral to the laws of the Charter is disbelief, which places one outside the pale of Islam. The aforementioned *fatwa* proves the existence of such laws, as well as expressing the Islamic rulings on these laws. Hence, we need not elaborate further as the matter is clear and evident.

It is also known that there is a clear difference between those who commit such aggravated sins like usury, all the while believing it prohibited, and those that legislate laws that give license to indulge in all types of aggravated sins. One who engages in usury, though admitting it is prohibited, is a perpetrator of one of the most egregious aggravated sins, from which we seek protection in God, whereas one who legislates and passes laws that sanction usury is an apostate disbeliever. We need only point to the towers of usurious banks that crowd the minarets of the Two Sacred Mosques and that put into execution your [Fahd's] secular rulings.

The statement of God, most high—"*But no, by your Lord, they can have no faith until they make you, O Muhammad, judge in all disputes between them, and find in themselves no dislike against your decisions, and accept with full submission.*" [Qur'an 4:65]—asserts that he is a disbeliever who does not resign to His law in complete surrender and submission. God stresses this fact using various syntaxes expressive of emphasis, foremost of which is an oath on His exalted and majestic name.

This verse along with the explanation by the Prophet (PBUH) to Adyy ibn Hatim of the verse—"*They* [Jews and Christians] *have taken as lords besides God their rabbis and their monks and the Messiah son of Mary, when they were bidden to worship only One God*" [Qur'an 9:31]—clears away any misconception and washes away any ground a dissenter may stand on.

Taking Disbelievers as Allies and Antagonizing Believers

There is not a more striking example in your foreign policy than your partnership to the interests of Western, militant, crusading Christian countries and the disbelieving regimes in the Muslim world. The verification of this truth does not need a great deal of labor, as everyone realizes the extent of these affiliations. In point of fact, while your regime gloats over protecting the creed and serving the Two Sacred Mosques, it declared in 1991 payment of $4 billion to the ex-Soviet Union, which at the time had not even washed its hands of the blood of the Muslim people of Afghanistan.

Furthermore, it was your regime, O 'guardian' of the tolerant creed, that gave billions of dollars to the Nusairis [non-Muslim minority ruling Syria] in 1982, as a reward for slaughtering tens of thousands of Muslims in Hamah [in Syria], as well as supporting the Christian Maronite Phalanges against Muslims in Lebanon. It was your 'wise' regime that lavished billions of dollars on that disbelieving regime which is fighting Islam and grinding under its heels the Muslims in Algeria. Your very regime is the one shoring up Christian rebels in southern Sudan with money and weapons.

Numerous as these great crimes against the religion and the Islamic nation are, and notwithstanding that your regime had managed for a while to fool some people and steer them away from these facts, God made certain to reveal the truth during the recent events in Yemen, which tore off the last mask you had been camouflaged under while you misled the people. Your political and military support to the Communists in Yemen dealt you a devastating blow, as it nullified your Islamic credibility. The events of Yemen threw you into the dreadful contradiction which revealed that your support for the Afghan *mujahideen* was not for the sake of Islam but rather to protect Western interests which were under threat of a Russian victory there. For the Afghan Communist is certainly no different from the Yemeni Communist, as the Muslim

Yemeni is no different from the Muslim Afghan. So, how do you justify your simultaneous support for Muslims against Communists in Afghanistan and your support for the Communists against Muslims in Yemen?!

No one can decipher this contradiction except those who are aware that your policy is dictated upon you by the Western crusading world to which you have linked your destiny. Your sporadic support for some Muslim causes is not motivated, as we have made clear, by a sincere embrace of Islamic causes and the strengthening of its respective principles, but is actually driven by a motive to protect the interests of the Western disbelieving countries, which may in some instances advocate Islamic causes, as was the case in Afghanistan.

In fact, you have always acted against those Islamic causes which oppose Western interests and to the detriment of Muslims. For example, with respect to the Muslim people of Somalia, you were against their interests and worked in tandem with the United States, providing resources stolen from the Islamic nation, including men bound by duty.

And on top of all, there is the Palestinian cause, the mother of all causes. You have blessed the march toward humiliation, normalization and bewilderment, and continued the farce of peace, which in fact is forced submission. Volunteering to pay for a great share of the expenses of the process, despite the economic hardship besetting the country, you donated $100 million to Yasser Arafat's secular authority, which was formed to do what the Jewish occupational forces had failed to achieve—the oppression of the Muslim Palestinian people and the war on its *jihad* movements, chief among which is the Islamic resistance movement, Hamas. You did not refrain from supporting Arafat's authority and greeted him in Riyadh, even after his hostility during the Gulf War and his ostentatious support for Saddam Hussein. You swallowed this insult in order to indulge America's sponsorship of this false peace process.

Yet, all that does not really surprise us. Even if you yourself are not convinced of the alleged peace process, you will have no recourse but to submit to your U.S. warden. Was not U.S. President Clinton the one who, upon visiting the country, refused to call on you in Riyadh and insisted that you come to him in humiliation to the U.S. bases in Hafr al-Batin?

The U.S. president underscored two points:

1. To emphasize that his visit was primarily to see his stationed troops at those bases.
2. To teach you a lesson of humiliation and your doom to failure so that you understand that he is your true guardian, even inside your kingdom, which in all truthfulness is a U.S. state, subject to U.S. jurisdiction.

There is neither doubt nor disagreement among Muslim scholars that taking the disbelievers as allies and supporting them against Muslims is regarded as an absolute nullifier of Islam. This fact was expounded by Sheikh al-Islam, Ibn Taymiyah, as well as Muhammad bin Abdul Wahhab in his *Ten Negators of Islam*. God, most high, indeed says: "*O you who believe! Take not the Jews and the Christians as protectors; they are but protectors to one another. And if any among you takes them as protectors, then surely he is one of them. Verily, God guides not those people who are the wrongdoers*" [Qur'an 5:51]. He also says: "*You will not find people who believe in God and the Last Day befriending those who oppose God and His Prophet, even if they are their fathers, progeny, brothers, or tribesmen*" [Qur'an 58:22].

In fact, God informs us that taking the disbelievers as protectors in order to gain power is a characteristic of hypocrites, as He says: "*Give to the hypocrites the tidings that there is for them a painful torment; those who take disbelievers for protectors instead of believers, do they seek honor, power and glory with them? Verily, then to God belongs all honor, power and glory*" [Qur'an 4:138-139].

Taking the disbelievers for protectors consists, according to the scholars, in honoring, praising, supporting and aiding them against the believers, as well as sharing one's life with them and not dissociating oneself from them openly. All of this is regarded as apostasy. Whoever engages in it becomes subject to the ruling relevant to apostates, as borne out by the

Noble Book [the *Qur'an*], the Prophet's tradition, and the statements of the Islamic nation's exemplary scholars.

A poet, may God bless his heart, said:

> "Whoever takes disbelievers for protectors is like them....
>
> There's not doubt about his disbelief to the least sensible person.
>
> And those who love aid or support them....
>
> And openly approve their actions,
>
> Are like them as far as disbelief is concerned....
>
> This is the discourse of someone who knows truth from error."

So, what do those who adhere to the pure creed and crystal clear monotheism say, O King, as to your disbelieving deeds? On what grounds would those falsely argue who debate on your behalf? "*Lo! You are those who have argued for them in the life of this world, but who will argue for them on the Day of Resurrection against God, or who will then be their defender?*" [Qur'an 4:109].

Having established that your regime does not meet the necessary conditions of the word of monotheism—"*There is no god except God and Muhammad is the Messenger of God*"—and its tolerant creed, which you boastfully claim to protect. Having exposed your true nature through Islam's criteria, let us now evaluate with full objectivity your achievements in the worldly domain. We will indeed discuss with you the following points:

There is no doubt that you realize, along with us, that the country sits on a lake of oil that comprises one-fourth of the world's reserves, whose importance is no secret. That the country's average daily income from oil revenues used to equal $100 million a day, in addition to savings that we put at $140 million when you acceded to the throne. This surpassed those of the U.S., the U.K. and France lumped together, and the country produced one-third of OPEC's output. Under the economic factors of the past years and with the population having been low, the country witnessed a phenomenon that flew in the face of sensible economics. Some held the opinion that there would never come a day when the economy would collapse and that the country would be one of the most indebted in the world.

However, your suicidal policies disappointed those and others, for not a decade had elapsed since you assumed power before the situation was turned upside down and inconsistency set in. The country subsequently became indebted to the tune of 80% of its income, and the average citizen was transformed from one who possessed the largest savings into one who is buried in debt. The collapsing economic situation has been dropped, with all its weight, on the lives of the citizens and residents who have a lot of pressure on their shoulders due to taxes and fines. Their pockets have been strangled by increasing prices of water, electricity and food, which has led to an insane inflation which has never been witnessed before.

The educational situation didn't help to further this disaster either. Schools suffer from immense overcrowding in classrooms, which is affecting students, teachers and parents alike. This matter has been worsened by the Ministry's inability to take action in order to maintain the classes and to build new schools. The situation of the hospitals isn't any better than the schools, as the government has failed to even maintain them. They are transforming many of its wings to what resemble human slaughterhouses, without the much needed medicine, treatment and care, which is further compounded by the Ministry's inability to build new hospitals. What has also made the situation worse is the spread of unemployment in the ranks of the young and the graduates who possess university degrees. The number of those who haven't found jobs has reached 150,000 and continues to increase year after year. Due to the worsening current economic crisis, the job market keeps waning and constantly shrinking in front of them.

With the intensity of this crisis and with the aggravation of the situation, neither you nor your governors have hesitated to ask people to save in power consumption and other matters at a time when your behavior was a horrible example for the people, encouraging them to become even more extravagant.

So, how can you ask people to save power when everyone can see your enchanting palaces lit up night and day? And how can anyone accept a call from you to cut spending when everybody can see your palaces and your homes, which fill the lands and horizons, and when people hear about the big accounts you possess, using the nation's wealth in and outside the country?

The amount of spending you do from the nation's wealth on these palaces and homes all over the world is indeed estimated to be within thousands of millions of dollars. Discussing it will certainly take long and the narrator wouldn't know where to begin—the industrial and chanting cities of Jeddah and Ajzar, where you build your most grandiose palaces, right in the middle of the land on the seafront. Or shall the narrator begin with lands where you weren't satisfied in building palaces but had to go as far as building them underneath the surface? Or shall he begin with your palaces in Mina, Taif, Huda, Shifa, Holy Mecca and Holy Medina and the rest of the cities in the country? Or shall the narrator leave them all and begin with the palaces you have built in various Western resorts and cities? Palaces you haven't even stepped inside of very often during your entire life, and you probably never will with what's remaining of it.

If these words came from someone else, you probably wouldn't believe them. But you know the people you speak with, and you know that they are the wisest people when it comes to these realities, which are no longer hidden from the public anymore and certainly not from notable citizens. And who can warn you better than an expert?

Your loved ones and your entourage have built palaces, treasured wealth and competed with everyone. This is indeed the main thing you have spent most of your time and effort on. Internal quarrels have torn your relations apart and raised the wrath of some. Their anger has been fueled by you and your possessions. The Prophet's (PBUH) saying was true when he said: "Miserable is indeed the slave of the dinar [a gold coin], and miserable is the slave of the dirham [a silver coin, about one-tenth of a dinar], miserable is indeed the slave of the luxurious clothes, for he is pleased if these things are given to him, and if not, he is displeased! Let there be no one to help him in as much as pulling a thorn that he would step on" [Narrated by al-Bukhari].

Indeed, this extravagance and excessive spending from the general wealth of the nation, combined with the interest and competition in your personnel matters, has been one of the main reasons that has lead the country to the precipice of bankruptcy under the shadows of your wise policy! Indeed, the squanderers are the brothers of devils.

The current crisis in the economy, combined with the dangers it is warning of and the results it is causing, didn't arise without initial signs or reasons. It was the outcome of a series of fatal actions and policies you and your ruling family are responsible for. The most important acts, in addition to the extravagance and squandering we have mentioned, that you have committed are:

The Deterioration of Oil Prices

The oil prices started crashing in the 1980's; however, the effect of these prices didn't start affecting the country's economy in an overt manner until the 1990's, when you repeatedly took refuge in the country's financial reserves to cover up the constant impotence of the budget with a stupid policy that has consumed the country's monetary reserves. This policy hasn't put forward any plan to solve this crisis, which is worsening day by day.

And as a reminder, you surely recall your full subjection to the polices of Western states and their instructions to back your old friend Saddam Hussein with $25 billion, combined with the increase in oil production to reduce prices in order to make up for Iran's damages during their war with him. This had a big role in the decline of oil prices to their current levels, which serves the Western consumers. Even though the West is careful not to kill the Saudi goose which lays eggs made of black gold, they are very careful indeed in making sure the price of those eggs is at the lowest possible level.

The Lack of Serious Work in Order to Find an Alternative Source of Income

Even though it is well-known that oil is a source of income that is subjected to depletion and to fuctuation in price, and even though the country is qualified for alternative sources of income that are numerous and readily available, your system has failed, without exception, in developing these sources and has kept the country relying almost fully on oil.

The Insane Spending on the Allied Forces during the Gulf War

Even with the financial stress through which the country was passing during the Gulf War, and even with the destruction of the Muslim forces and the Muslim people of Iraq, which was a goal for the Western states before anything else, these Western states found the opportunity of a lifetime by blackmailing you and by exploiting your cowardly feelings of fear. So, they insisted that you pay almost the whole amount of the war bill. You spent on this war approximately $60 billion, out of which $30 billion went to the pockets of the Americans, and approximately half of that amount to the pockets of the remaining allies. The remainder was spent on commissions, deals and local bribes.

The costs of the war didn't stop at this point either, but your solidarity with the allied states has pushed you to strike more deals that were beneficial to them after the war. Those deals cost more than $40 billion, an imaginary price for military and civilian deals with the Americans alone. Additionally, the purchase of Tornado airplanes from the British, which was done as a compliment to the [former] British Prime Minister John Major, was carried out without even having the necessary manpower in the country to utilize these airplanes, as was proven during the Gulf War, in addition to their lack of efficiency which was witnessed by the engineering committee in the army, a point which will be dissected later.

Instead of putting into place a successful policy that would have avoided the current situation and instead of rectifying the degrading financial situation, you and your ruling system have adopted a suicidal financial policy which has worsened the situation. Among these policies:

The Termination of the Country's Offshore Accounts

It was previously mentioned that the balance of the country's offshore accounts was estimated to be $140 billion when you first started ruling, and its yearly income estimate during that time was around $97 billion. You only have to imagine, like us, the foolishness in squandering, after remembering that these reserves were completely washed out after only seven years.

High-Interest Loans from Local and Foreign Banks

Even with the severe threats and the war with God (SWT) that are found in usury—"*And if you do not do it, then take a notice of war from God and His Messenger*" [Qur'an 2:279]—Even with the proven reality that bank loans which deal in usury are only doomed to make the poor poorer day after day. Even with all of this, you and your ruling system have drowned the country in a sea of debt. There are no signs whatsoever on the horizon that indicate there is a possibility of at least getting rid of the interest, as opposed to the country's inability to even pay back the interest charges. As an example of the size of this debt, in the year 1411 A.H. [1991] alone, you have resorted to borrowing tens of billions of dollars from local and foreign banks.

This debt has been frozen by its composed interest since the year 1414 A.H. [1994], when the government was unable to fulfil its commitment to the proprietors. This means that the simple fact of paying back the interest will keep on adding more weight on the shoulders of the state's budget. This will prohibit you from even paying back the original debt. It also means you will leave the future of the country and future generations pawned off to the hands of international corporations. Their control doesn't end at the economic domain of indebted countries, but it has to exceed it and control the political decision-making of this country. And this in addition to 200 billion riyals in debt by the government to more than 3,000 businessmen and contractors whose payments keep getting deferred.

You have destroyed, with this behavior, all records of squandering and lavishness from the general funds. This was caused by you to distance yourself, so congratulations over this deed! This is not strange coming from someone like you, the likes of which don't care about the future of their own country and their own people; compared to the amount of care you spend on fulfilling your personal desires and your constant caprices.

You have forgotten, while being distracted by these actions, what became of the Shah of Iran, or Marcos from the Philippines, or Ceausescu of Romania, and others who suck their people's blood and who don't pay attention to the outcome of their country.

Indeed, this country is going through the most dangerous economic crisis in its history. The first crisis was in 1384/1385 A.H. [1964/1965], due to the disorder in King Saud's administration, which ended with his demise. The second crisis was in 1406 A.H. [1986], caused by the surprising fall of oil prices.

The first crisis was solved with the King and his entourage being deposed, and the second was overcome when the country resorted to its huge monetary reserves at that time. Indeed, it appears, in light of the total loss of the country's financial accounts and from the loss of its financial credibility, both inside and outside of the Kingdom, that this current crisis won't be resolved in the near future.

Your failure to heal the situation, when the country wasn't in debt and had reserves which were estimated at $140 billion, is indeed the strongest indication of your failure to treat it, particularly after having wasted all the reserves and having drowned the country in a sea of debt. Like the poet said:

> "Whoever lacked feats when times were compliant
> Won't improve his exploits when times turn defiant."

Your media outlets are certainly not being beneficial when they mislead people and trick them. They deceive people by saying that the crisis is about to end soon. The lying and cheating committed by these media outlets can no longer deceive this awakened nation that no longer believes these exposed lies.

After wasting the nation's wealth, and after your extravagance in their luxuries and lying to them afterwards, indeed all of these are the characteristics which God (SWT) has ruled on their owner by saying: "*Verily, God guides not one who is a liar*" [Qur'an 40:28].

This is directed to the common people. The lying King's punishment is indeed much more severe at the hands of God (SWT), like is mentioned in the following authentic saying of the Prophet, which is narrated by *Imam* Muslim ibn al-Hajjaj: "Three of whom God does not speak with at the Day of Judgment, nor praise them, and they will have a painful torture: an adulterous man, a lying king, and a proud sustainer."

In light of the information stated previously, it seems that the course of action to be taken should correspond with an ending of King Saud's first crisis. Deposing the king from his throne is the best radical solution presented.

Prior to all of this, bitter and hard work remains in front of you on the one hand, and on the other, it will lack efficiency and effectiveness. Will this push you to resort to the reduction of the Riyal for example? This course of action will only help temporarily, aside from the fact that it will have political repercussions which will be much more dangerous than its financial ones. Will you risk your ambitious status by leading the Council of Cooperation and by reducing the value of the Riyal proportionately to foreign currencies?

Your love for politics and your love for authority will prevent you from doing so, especially when your rule over this country is the only thing you have left from your dream of supreme power, which met its demise when you failed to attain any considerable position in the Arab and Muslim world. There was a time when the country spoke in His name and when they supported His authority during the reign of King Faisal.

Will you raise taxes and increase the fines on the citizens and residents in order to save more money in the bankrupt state treasury? This will without a doubt increase the cash flow, but its political repercussions won't allow you to complete this plan. The citizen has been forcefully kept quiet when he saw you squandering the nation's wealth, but he won't keep quiet when he sees the taxes and fines he paid and earned with his sweat being spent on the desires and necessities of the reckless ruling family.

The Military Situation

You probably agree with us that for several decades one-third of the country's budget has been allocated to the armed forces. It is worth mentioning that a country with nuclear capacity, such as France, allocates only 4% of its budget to its armed forces. You also probably agree with us that, despite the enormous expenditure on the armed forces, the result has been no more than piles of weapons and no manpower to utilize them.

This comes as no surprise because the real purpose for spending this kind of money has not been to prepare a strong and able army. The real purpose has been to generate a source of income for those Princes in charge. Another reason for the unjustified spending mentioned above was to compensate the Western allies and protectors for helping you to defend your throne. Many transactions were approved and processed just to show your appreciation for allowing you to be their loyal servant. For example, 70 F-15 fighter jets were purchased to support George Bush's re-election campaign after the Gulf War. The deal to purchase aircraft for the Saudi Airlines fleet and the deal to expand the telephone network was a favor to Clinton, and the purchase of 48 Tornado fighter planes from the U.K. are just more examples of your spending policy.

The embarrassing performance of the Defense Ministry during the Gulf War tells a lot about what was behind all those weapons' deals. The air force had possession of 500 fighter jets, and yet their only accomplishment was shooting down two Iraqi planes that had no air cover. As for the navy, despite the possession of 30 war vessels, 20 of them with missile launching capability, not a single shot was fired during the war. The army did not fare any better either. The country had to bring in technical personnel from Pakistan just to put together one armored infantry division. Hundreds of billions of dollars were wasted. It is astonishing to know that Prince Sultan, who is the most senior Defense Minister in the world, accomplished nothing but failure during that war. Prince Sultan had been Defense Minister for 32 years with nothing to show for it.

To put the magnitude of defense spending into perspective, let it be known that the financial burden on each Saudi citizen exceeds the financial burden on citizens of ten countries put together: U.S., Germany, Italy, Egypt, Romania, Poland, Spain, Ecuador, Uruguay and Ireland. Some of these countries have nuclear capability and some of them are active members of NATO. It is also mind-boggling to know that what Saudi Arabia spends on each person in its military exceeds what is spent on military persons in nine countries put together: U.S., Germany, Belgium, Argentina, China, Iran, the Zionist enemy Israel, South Korea and Tanzania.

Do we not have the right to ask you, O King, where has all the money gone? Never mind answering—one knows how many bribes and commissions ended in your pocket, Prince Sultan's pocket, and the pockets of those Princes in charge of arranging deals with arms dealers and construction companies. It is a known fact that you and your Princes pocketed between 40-60% of the value of every transaction. Most of what was left was spent on construction of military bases and facilities, the size of which far exceeds the size and the quality of the country's armed forces. It appears that those facilities were built for the U.S. and other Western armies. U.S. army personnel are indeed occupying those facilities in many cities.

Do we not have the right to ask why foreign military forces with enormous fire power and equipment still remain on our holy land? Does Iraq, after the destruction of its armed forces and the subjecting of its Muslim people to starvation, still pose a threat to your throne?

The presence of a foreign power on the holy land is not to defend the country against the already destroyed and starved nation of Iraq when all the facts and observation suggest otherwise. The truth is that a foreign power is there to protect your throne from the inevitable and growing threat of Islam. The country is experiencing a blessed Islamic awakening that is on the rise in many military and civilian sectors in the country, causing you a great deal of concern.

The country's army has a duty to protect the entire Muslim population and to defend their interests everywhere, let alone to defend the holy land. Therefore, there is no justification for keeping the national army in a state of weakness that hinders its enormous responsibility. It is unconscionable to let the country become an American colony with American soldiers, with their filthy feet roaming everywhere, for no reason other than protecting your throne and oil sources for their own use. Those filthy, infidel Crusaders must not be allowed to remain in the holy land.

In light of current events, does our Islamic nation not have the right to ask "Who is causing our security to be compromised? Who is the culprit behind all the unrest in the region?" Is it not the governmental system that has allowed the deterioration of the military strength which led to bringing armies from the infidel Christians and Jews to fill our pure holy land with their filth? Or is it the man who is calling for preparing the Islamic nation spiritually and militarily for the honor of defending itself, its religion, its holy places and the dignity of its own citizens?

The truth of the matter is that you have no one to blame but yourself and your Defense Minister. No one should blame members of the armed forces or National Guard, many of whom are judged to be honorable and brave. Their hands are tied, however, and they cannot do anything to change the situation. In fact, you have marginalized many leaders in case they call for changes. You even planted spies among the rank and file to abort any attempt for a change. You even went further than that. You have disallowed any form of cooperation and coordination between the three branches of the military. Such cooperation and coordination is vital to any successful military campaign. However, protecting your throne was more important than the dignity of the entire Islamic nation.

Conclusions

It has been proven that your system has committed the kind of violations that invalidate its legitimacy according to God's law. The widespread corruption and total failure of your system is mandated to be ousted. You have legislated and ruled by man-made laws. You have forced people to be governed by man-made laws in total rejection to God's principles. God is the only law giver. You have also taken the disbelievers as allies and protectors against Muslims. These violations clearly make you an apostate, making your system invalid and one that must be toppled. Even without violating any Islamic law, your inability to implement a sound and successful economic and defense policy justifies your removal.

You have brought to our people the two worst calamities, which are blasphemy and poverty. One can clearly see from what we have indicated in this letter that the disagreement between you and your system of government and Muslim scholars, business leaders and tribal leaders is not a temporary or minor disagreement. Rather, it is the kind of disagreement that is fundamental and deep-rooted. It is simply a struggle between the Lord's complete Islamic system that is based on submitting to God's principles in everything we do, and the man-made system, that only serves the interest of those who created it. The Lord's system is beautifully illustrated in the following verse of the Holy *Qur'an*: "*Say, my prayer, religious act of worship, my life and death all belong to God, the Lord of all creation and creatures. That was what I was mandated to do and I am the first to declare being Muslim*" [Qur'an 6:162-163].

The Lord's system is the system of "*There is no god except God and Muhammad is the Messenger of God*", with all that it entails in terms of what conduct is acceptable and unacceptable. The man-made system is also illustrated in the following verses from the Holy *Qur'an*: "*Do you believe and accept some parts of the Holy Scripture and reject other parts?*" [Qur'an 2:85]. "*They* [think to] *deceive God and those who believe, while they only deceive themselves, and perceive it not*" [Qur'an 2:9].

Therefore, based on what we have described herein, any action taken by this Islamic nation's religious, business, and tribal leaders against your system does not constitute unlawful disobedience, for it is your system that is unlawful. Furthermore, it is the general consensus of this Islamic nation that an apostate ruler must be toppled. This, of course, does not mean that every action committed by anybody and everybody is necessarily correct. Each stage on the road to change has its own requirements, means and goals. In other words, things cannot and should not be decided based on hasty individual decisions or unfair rulings. The decision to take any action is taken after full consultation with those faithful and trusted leaders of this Islamic nation and only those leaders who through trials have proved to be worthy of handling the critical task at hand.

O King, aside from all we have described here, it is incumbent upon you to do everything you can to end the suffering of this Islamic nation. It is in the best interest of you, your family, and everyone else around you to put an end to all these domestic and international problems and conflicts that have plagued this nation for a long time. You have reached an old age and your health is deteriorating; therefore, your ability to maintain control is diminishing. Our best advice to you now is to submit your resignation in order that this nation may appoint those who can lift it from the hole you have dug for it. There is no realistic chance that you have the means to carry out the needed change, especially in view of your old age and poor health. Let me remind you with what a poet has said once in years past: "Once an old man becomes a fool, he will no longer be forbearing. And a youth can only dream after becoming a fool."

You may recall that King Saud was removed for actions that were far less serious than yours. At that time, you yourself were one of the leading lobbyists for his removal. What you did then was correct and justified. It is now time for a repeat performance. We hope that not only will you resign but that you will also call for the resignation of everyone in your government who has played a role in the current state of affairs of the country. It is only fair to ask you to undo the damage you have done. Take for example your Defense Minister. He has never handled any political or administrative matter with any degree of success. He has escalated the border problem with Qatar and almost started a war with Yemen. That, of course, was on top of his total failure in running the Defense Ministry and the Saudi Airlines Company. It is worth mentioning that the airlines company went bankrupt as a result of his poor management.

The changes and shuffling of positions in various ministries have been useless. The new appointees have always been from those having strong ties to the corrupted system and therefore have had a conflict of interest. Even in the event that some of them meant to do what is right, your total control over them would have made it impossible for them to implement any change. 'The shadow of a bent object will never be straight.'

Let us remind you again that what we are asking you to do is the very same thing that you demanded of King Saud. You were able to do it; therefore, it is not an impossible task or demand.

Before we put down our pen to end this letter, we want you to think hard and search your soul in light of all the facts we have put forth here. We hope you do that before you act arrogantly and reject tour advice. We also ask you to think hard before you decide to punish whoever attempts to deliver this letter to you as you have done many times in the past. Time after time, faithful scholars have forwarded memos that were full of advice. The most famous is the one that detailed all the required actions, identified all the problems and their causes and provided a detailed, workable plan to remedy the situation. This was put together in a format reflecting the highest level of care, respect, politeness, and sincere desire to do what is best for the nation. Your response has always been one of rejection and punishment. You not only have rejected all attempts for corrective actions, but you have punished those who tried to steer you in the right direction. You have used your agents, soldiers, supporters and those who were fooled by you to punish and humiliate the sincere ones. You went as far as using your influence to have *fatawa* issued to indict those scholars. They are still in your jails and have not lost their patience.

We ask God to set them free, facilitate their mission, and help us and them to stay the course. The course of carrying out God's message and mandate in order for Islam to become the only religion on earth and until God alone is worshipped.

We ask God to help us fulfil our pledge to Him. We pledge to take revenge for any aggression against God's religion [Islam], punish whoever harms God's servant and allies, and punish those who torture our Muslim brothers in various jails in your kingdom.

Our last call is all praise and thanks are to God, the Lord of the Universe.

Osama bin Muhammad bin Laden

5/3/1416 A.H. [3 August 1995]

2

Declaration of Jihad Against the Americans Occupying the Land of the Two Sacred Mosques

(23 August 1996)

This declaration of war by Osama bin Laden was first published in *Al Quds Al-Arabi*, a London-based newspaper, in August 1996 and later on various Islamist websites. It was entitled "Message from Osama bin Muhammad bin Laden to His Muslim Brothers in the Whole World and Especially in the Arabian Peninsula. Declaration of Jihad against the Americans Occupying the Land of the Two Holy Mosques: Expel the Heretics from the Arabian Peninsula."

Praise be to God, we seek His help and ask for His pardon. We take refuge in God from our wrongs and bad deeds. Whoever has been guided by God will not be misled, and whoever has been misled, he will never be guided. I bear witness that "*There is no god except God and Muhammad is the Messenger of God.*"

"*O you who believe! Be careful of your duty to God with the proper care which is due to Him, and do not die except as a Muslim*" [Qur'an 3:102].

"*O people! Be careful of your duty to your Lord, Who created you from a single being and created its mate of the same kind, and spread from these two, many men and women; and be careful of your duty to God by whom you demand one of another your rights, and* [be careful] *to the ties of kinship; surely God ever watches over you*" [Qur'an 4:1].

"*O you who believe! Be careful of your duty to God and speak the right word; He will put your deeds into a right state for you, and forgive you your faults; and whoever obeys God and His Messenger, he indeed achieves a mighty success*" [Qur'an 33:70-71].

Praise be to God, reporting the saying of the prophet Shu'aib: "*I desire nothing but reform so far as I am able, and with none but God is the direction of my affair to the right and successful path; in Him do I trust and to Him do I turn*" [Qur'an 11:88].

Praise be to God, saying: "*You are the best of the nations raised up for the benefit of men; you enjoin what is right and forbid what is wrong and believe in God*" [Qur'an 3:110].

God's blessing and salutations on His servant and Messenger who said: "The people are close to an all-encompassing punishment from God if they see the oppressor and fail to restrain him."

It should not be hidden from you that the people of Islam have suffered from aggression, iniquity and injustice imposed on them by the Zionist-Crusaders' alliance and their collaborators; to the extent that the Muslims' blood has become cheap and their wealth has become as loot in the hands of the enemies. Their blood has been spilled in Palestine and Iraq. The horrifying pictures of the massacre of Qana, in Lebanon, are still fresh in our memory. Massacres in Tajikistan, Burma, Kashmir, Assam, the Philippines, Patani [Thailand's Muslim-dominated province], Ogadin, Somalia, Eritrea, Chechnya and in Bosnia-Herzegovina took place, massacres that send shivers through the body and shake the conscience. All of this the world watched and heard, yet not only didn't respond to these atrocities, but also, with a clear conspiracy between the U.S. and its allies and under the cover of the iniquitous United Nations, the dispossessed people were even prevented from obtaining arms to defend themselves.

The people of Islam have awakened and realized that they are the main target for the Zionist-Crusaders' aggression. All the false claims and propaganda about 'Human Rights' have been torn down and exposed by the massacres that have taken place against Muslims in every part of the world. The latest and greatest of these aggressions, the greatest incurred by the

Muslims since the death of the Prophet (PBUH), is the occupation of the Land of the Two Sacred Mosques—the foundation of the House of Islam, the place of the revelation, the source of the message and the place of the Noble *Ka'ba*, the *qibla* of all Muslims—by the armies of the American Crusaders and their allies. We bemoan this and can only say: "*There is neither power nor strength except from God.*"

In the present circumstances and under the banner of the blessed awakening which is sweeping the world in general and the Islamic world in particular, I meet with you today. And after a long absence imposed on the scholars and preachers of Islam by the iniquitous Crusaders' movement under the leadership of the U.S., who fears that they, the scholars and preachers of Islam, will instigate the Islamic nation against its enemies as did previous scholars, may God be pleased with them, like Ibn Taymiyah and Al'iz ibn Abd es-Salaam, did. Therefore, the Zionist-Crusader alliance resorted to killing and arresting the truthful scholars and the working preachers. We are not praising or sanctifying them; God sanctifies with whom He is pleased. They killed the *Mujahid* Sheikh Abdullah Azzam, and they arrested the *Mujahid* Sheikh Ahmad Yaseen and the *Mujahid* Sheikh Omar Abd ur-Rahman [in America].

By orders from the U.S., a large number of scholars, preachers and young people were arrested in the Land of the Two Sacred Mosques, among them the prominent Sheikh Salman al-Oud'a and Sheikh Safar al-Hawali and their brothers. We bemoan this and can only say: "*There is neither power nor strength except from God.*" We, I and my group, have suffered some of this injustice ourselves. We have been prevented from addressing the Muslims. We have been pursued in Pakistan, Sudan and Afghanistan, hence this long absence on my part. But by the grace of God, a safe base is now available in the high Hindu Kush Mountains in Khurasan [Afghanistan], where, by the grace of God, the largest infidel military force in the world was destroyed, and the myth of the superpower withered in front of the *mujahideen*'s cries of "God is greatest."

Today we work from the same mountains to lift the iniquity that has been imposed on the Islamic nation by the

Zionist-Crusader alliance, particularly after they have occupied the blessed land around Jerusalem, route of the journey of the Prophet (PBUH), and the Land of the Two Sacred Mosques. We ask God to bestow us with victory. He is our Patron and He is the Most Capable. From here, today we begin the work of discussing the ways of correcting what has happened to the Islamic world in general, and the Land of the Two Sacred Mosques in particular. We wish to study the means we can follow to return the situation to its correct path, and to return to the people their own rights, particularly after the large damages and the great aggression on the life and the religion of the people. An injustice has affected every section and group of the people: civilians, military and security men, government officials and merchants, young and old people, as well as schools and university students. Hundreds of thousands of unemployed graduates, who have become the broadest section of society, were also affected.

Injustice has affected the people of industry and agriculture. It has affected the people of rural and urban areas, and almost everybody has complained about something. The situation in the Land of the Two Sacred Mosques has become like a huge volcano on the verge of an eruption that will destroy disbelief and corruption and their sources. The explosions at Riyadh and Al-Khobar are a warning of this volcanic eruption emerging as a result of the severe oppression, suffering, excessive iniquity, humiliation and poverty.

People are fully concerned about their everyday lives. Everybody talks about the deterioration of the economy, inflation, ever-increasing debts, and jails full of prisoners. Government employees with limited incomes talk about debts of tens of thousands and hundreds of thousands of Saudi Riyals. They complain that the value of the Riyal is greatly and continuously deteriorating among most of the major currencies. Great merchants and contractors speak about hundreds and thousands of millions of Riyals owed to them by the government. The government owes more than 340 billion Riyals to the people, in addition to the daily accumulated interest, let alone the foreign debt. People wonder, are we the largest oil exporting country? They even believe this situation is a curse put on them by God for not objecting to the oppressive and illegitimate behavior and measures of the ruling regime: ignoring divine Islamic law, depriving people of their legitimate rights, allowing the Americans to occupy the Land of the Two Sacred Mosques, and the unjust imprisonment of the sincere scholars.

All the honorable scholars, as well as merchants, economists and eminent people of the country, have been alerted by this disastrous situation. Quick efforts were made by each group to contain and to correct the situation. All have agreed that the country is heading toward a great catastrophe, the depth of which is not known except by God. One big merchant commented: "The king is leading the state into 'sixty-six' folded disaster." We bemoan this and can only say: "*There is neither power nor strength except from God.*" Numerous Princes have shared their feelings with the people, privately expressing their concerns and objecting to the corruption, repression and the intimidation taking place in the country. But the competition between influential Princes for personal gain and interest has destroyed the country.

Through its course of action, the regime has torn off its mantel of legitimacy:

1. Suspension of Islamic law and replacing it with man-made civil law. The regime entered into a bloody confrontation with the truthful scholars and the righteous youth. We sanctify nobody; God sanctifies whom He pleases.
2. The inability of the regime to protect the country, and allowing the enemy of the Islamic nation—the American Crusader forces—to occupy the land for many years. The Crusader forces have become the main cause of our disastrous condition, particularly economically, due to the unjustified heavy spending on these forces and as a result of the policy imposed on the country, especially in the field of the oil industry, where production is restricted or expanded and prices are fixed to suit the American economy, ignoring the economy of the country. Expensive deals were imposed

> on the country to purchase arms. People have been asking: Then, what is the justification for the very existence of the regime?

Rapid efforts were made by individuals and by different groups of society to contain the situation and to prevent the danger. They have advised the government, both privately and openly. They have sent letters and poems, report after report, and reminder after reminder. They have explored every avenue and enlisted every influential man in their movement of reform and correction. They have written with passion, diplomacy and wisdom, asking for corrective measures and repentance from the 'great wrong-doings and corruption' that have engulfed even the basic principles of the religion and the legitimate rights of the people. But to our deepest regret, the regime has refused to listen to the people, accusing them of being ridiculous and imbecilic. Matters have gotten worse as previous wrong doings have been followed by corruption of greater magnitude. All of this taking place in the Land of the Two Sacred Mosques! It is no longer possible to be quiet. It is not acceptable to turn a blind eye to this matter.

As the extent of these infringements reached the highest levels and evolved into destructive forces threatening the very existence of Islamic principles, a group of scholars who could take no more, supported by hundreds of retired officials, merchants, prominent and educated people, wrote to the King asking for the implementation of corrective measures. In 1411 A.H. [May 1991], at the time of the Gulf War, a letter, the famous letter of *Shawwaal*, with over 400 signatures, was sent to the King demanding the lifting of oppression and the implementation of corrective actions. The King humiliated those people and chose to ignore the content of their letter; and the very bad situation of the country became even worse.

People, however, tried again to send more letters and petitions. One particular report, the *Glorious Memorandum of Advice*, was handed over to the King on *Muharram*, 1413 A.H. [July 1992], which tackled the problems, pointed out the illness, and prescribed the medicine in an original, righteous and scientific style. It described the gaps and the shortcomings in the philosophy of the regime and suggested the required course of action and remedy. The report gave a description of:

1. The intimidation and harassment suffered by the leaders of society, the scholars, heads of tribes, merchants, academic teachers and other eminent individuals.
2. The situation of the law within the country and the arbitrary declaration of what is lawful and unlawful, regardless of the Islamic law instituted by God.
3. The state of the press and the media, which became a tool of truth-hiding and misinformation. The media carried out the plan of the enemy of an idolizing cult of certain personalities and spreading scandals among the believers to repel people away from their religion, as God, the Exalted said: "*Those who love to see scandal circulate among the believers will have a grievous penalty in this life and in the hereafter.*" [Qur'an 24:19]
4. Abuse and suspension of human rights.
5. The financial and economic situation of the country and the frightening future in view of the enormous amount of debt and interest owed by the government. This situation is being left unresolved at a time when the wealth of the Islamic nation is being wasted to satisfy the personal desires of certain individuals, while imposing more custom duties and taxes on the Islamic nation. The Prophet (PBUH) said about the woman who committed adultery and brought herself to be stoned: "She repented in such a way sufficient to bring forgiveness to a custom collector!"
6. The miserable situation of the social services and the infrastructure, especially the water service and supply, the basic requirement of life.
7. The state of the ill-trained and ill-prepared army and the impotence of its Commander-in-Chief, despite the incredible amount of money that has been spent on the army. The Gulf War clearly exposed the situation.

8. Islamic law was suspended and man-made law has been used instead.
9. And as far as foreign policy is concerned, the report exposed not only how this policy has disregarded Islamic issues and ignored Muslims, but also how help and support have been provided to the enemy against the Muslims. The cases of Gaza-Ariha and the Communists in southern Yemen are still fresh in the memory, and more can be said.

As stated by people of knowledge, it is not a secret that to use man-made law instead of Islamic law and to support the infidels against the Muslims is one of the ten acts that annul religion and strip a person of his Islamic status. The Almighty said: "*And whoever did not judge by what God revealed, those are the unbelievers*" [Qur'an 5:44], and "*But no! By your Lord! They do not believe* [in reality] *until they make you a judge of that which has become a matter of disagreement among them, and then do not find the slightest misgiving in their hearts as to what you have decided and submit with entire submission*" [Qur'an 4:65].

In spite of the fact that the report was written with soft words and in a very diplomatic style, reminding of God, giving truthful sincere advice, and despite the importance of advice in Islam being absolutely essential for those in charge of the people and the large number who signed this document, as well as the large number of their supporters, all of that was not an intercession for the *Memorandum*. Its content was rejected, and those who signed it and their sympathizers were ridiculed, prevented from travel, punished and even jailed.

Therefore, it is very clear that the advocates of the correction and reform movement were very keen on using peaceful means in order to protect the unity of the country and to prevent bloodshed. Why is it then the regime closed all peaceful routes and pushed the people toward armed action, which is the only choice left for them to implement righteousness and justice? For whose benefit do Prince Sultan and Prince Nayeff push the country into a civil war that will destroy everything? And why do the *amirs* consult those who ignite internal feuds, playing the people against each other and instigating the policemen, the sons of the Islamic nation, to abort the reform movement, yet leave in peace and security such traitors who implement the policy of the enemy in order to bleed the financial and human resources of the Islamic nation, and leaving the main enemy in the area—the American-Zionist alliance—to enjoy peace and security?!

The advisor [Zaki Badr, the Egyptian ex-Minister of the Interior] to Prince Nayeff—the Saudi Minister of the Interior—was not acceptable even to his own country. He was fired from his position there due to the filthy attitude and aggression he exercised on his own people, yet he was warmly welcomed by Prince Nayeff to assist in sins and aggression. He unjustly filled the prisons with the best sons of this Islamic nation and caused misery to their mothers. Does the regime want to play the civilians against their military personnel and *vice versa*, like what had happened in some of the neighboring countries?!! No doubt this is the policy of the American-Israeli alliance, as they are the first to benefit from this situation.

But with the grace of God, the majority of the Islamic nation, both civilian and military individuals, were aware of the wicked plan. They have refused to be played against each other and to be used by the regime as a tool to carry out the policy of the American-Israeli alliance through their agent in our country: the Saudi regime. Therefore, everyone has agreed that the situation cannot be rectified unless the root of the problem is tackled. ['The shadow cannot be straightened when its source, the rod, is not straight either.'] Hence, it is essential to hit the main enemy who has divided the Islamic nation into small and little countries, and pushed it, for the past few decades, into a state of confusion. The Zionist-Crusader alliance has moved quickly to contain and abort any 'corrective movement' appearing in the Islamic countries. Different means and methods have been used to achieve their target, and on occasion the 'movement' has been dragged into an armed struggle at a predetermined unfavorable time and place. Sometimes officials from the Ministry of Interior, who are also graduates of the colleges of Islamic law, have been leased out to mislead and confuse the Islamic nation [By wrong *fatawa*] and to circulate false information about the movement. On other occasions some righteous people have been tricked into a war of words against the scholars and the leaders of the movement, wasting the energy of the nation in discussing minor issues and ignoring the main one; that is, the unification of the people under the divine law of God.

In the shadow of these discussions and arguments truthfulness has been covered by falsehood, and personal feuds and partisanship created among the people have increased the division and weakness of the Islamic nation. The priorities of the Islamic work have been lost while blasphemy and polytheism have continued their grip and control over the Islamic nation. We should be alert to these atrocious plans carried out by the Ministry of Interior. The right answer is to follow what has been decided by the people of knowledge, as was said by Ibn Taymiyah (PBUH): "People of Islam should join forces and support each other to get rid of the main disbelief that is controlling the countries of the Islamic world, even to bear the lesser damage to get rid of the major one—the great disbelief."

If there is more than one duty to be carried out, then the most important one should receive priority. Clearly after Belief, there is no more important duty than pushing the American enemy out of the sacred land. No other priority, except Belief, can be considered before it. The people of knowledge, as Ibn Taymiyah said, stated: "To fight in defense of religion and Belief is a collective duty. There is no other duty after Belief than fighting the enemy who is corrupting the life and the religion. There is no precondition for this duty, and the enemy should be fought with one's best abilities" [Supplement of *Fatawa*].

If it is not possible to push back the enemy except by the collective movement of the Muslim people, then there is a duty on the Muslims to ignore the minor differences among themselves. The ill effect of ignoring these differences, at a given period in time, is much less than the ill effect of the occupation of the Muslims' land by the main disbelief. Ibn Taymiyah explained this issue and emphasized the importance of dealing with the major threat at the expense of the minor one. He described the situation of the Muslims and the *mujahideen* and stated that even the military personnel who are not practicing Islam are not exempted from the duty of *jihad* against the enemy.

Ibn Taymiyah, after mentioning the Mongols and their behavior in changing the law of God, stated that the ultimate aim of pleasing God, raising His word, instituting His religion and obeying His Messenger (PBUH) is to fight the enemy in every aspect and in a complete manner. If the danger to the religion from not fighting is greater than that of fighting, then it is a duty to fight them, even if the intention of some of the fighters is not pure, *i.e.* they are fighting for the sake of leadership [personal gain], or if they do not observe some of the rules and commandments of Islam. To repel the greater of the two dangers at the expense of the lesser one is an Islamic principle which should be observed.

It was the custom of the people of the Prophet's traditions to join, invade, and fight with the righteous and non-righteous men. God may support this religion by righteous and non-righteous people as told by the Prophet (PBUH). If it is not possible to fight except with the help of non-righteous military personnel and commanders, then there are two possibilities: Either fighting will be ignored and the others, who are the greater danger to this life and religion, will take control; or to fight with the help of non-righteous rulers, thereby repelling the greater of the two dangers and implementing most, though not all, of the Islamic laws. The latter option is the right duty to be carried out in these circumstances and in many other similar situations. In fact, many of the fights and conquests that took place after the time of Rightly Guided *Caliphs* [Immediate successors to Muhammad] were of this type [*Majmoo' al Fatawa*, 26/506].

No one, not even a blind or a deaf person, can deny the presence of the widely spread mischief or the prevalence of great sins that have reached the grievous iniquity of polytheism and to share with God in His sole right of sovereignty and making of the law. The Almighty stated: "*And when Luqman said to his son while he admonished him: O my son! Do not associate ought with God; most surely polytheism is a grievous iniquity*" [Qur'an 31:13]. Humanly fabricated laws have been put forward permitting what has been forbidden by God, such as usury and other matters. Banks dealing in usury are competing for land with the Two Sacred Mosques and declaring war against God by disobeying His order: "*God has allowed trading and forbidden usury*" [Qur'an 2:275]. All this is taking place in the vicinity of the Sacred Mosque in the Sacred Land!

God (SWT) stated in His Holy Book [the *Qur'an*] a unique promise [that had not been promised to any other sinner] to the Muslims who deal in usury: "*O you who believe! Be careful of your duty to God and relinquish what remains* [due] *from usury, if you are believers. But if you do* [it] *not, then be appraised of WAR from God and His Messenger*" [Qur'an 2:278-279]. This is for the Muslim who deals in usury [believing that it is a sin]. What is it then to the person who makes himself a partner and equal to God, legalizing [usury and other sins] what has been forbidden by God? Despite all of the above we see the government has misled and dragged some of the righteous scholars and preachers away from the issue of objecting to the greatest of sins and disbelief. We bemoan this and can only say: "*There is neither power nor strength except from God.*"

Under such circumstances, to push the enemy—the greatest disbelief—out of the country is a prime duty. No other duty after Belief is more important than the duty of at hand [*jihad*]. Utmost effort should be made to prepare and instigate the Islamic nation against the enemy, the American-Israeli alliance occupying the Land of the Two Sacred Mosques and the route of the Messenger (PBUH) to the furthest mosque [Al-Aqsa Mosque]. Also to remind the Muslims not to be engaged in an internal war among themselves, as that will have grave consequences, namely:

1. Consumption of the Muslims' human resources, as most casualties and fatalities will be among the Muslims people.

2. Exhaustion of the economic and financial resources.

3. Destruction of the country's infrastructure.

4. Dissociation of the society.

5. Destruction of the oil industries. The presence of the U.S. Crusader military forces on the land and sea, and in the air of the states of the Islamic Gulf is the greatest danger threatening the largest oil reserve in the world. The existence of these forces in the area will provoke the people of the country and induce aggression on their religion, feelings and pride, and push them to take up armed struggle against the invaders occupying the land. Therefore, the spread of fighting in the region will expose the oil wealth to the danger of being burned up. The economic interests of the Gulf States and of the Land of the Two Sacred Mosques will be damaged, and an even greater damage will be caused to the economy of the world.

I would like here to alert my brothers, the *mujahideen*, the sons of the Islamic nation, to protect this [oil] wealth and not to include it in the battle, as it is a great Islamic wealth and a large economic power essential for the soon to be established Islamic state, by God's permission and grace. We also warn the aggressors, the U.S., against burning this Islamic wealth, a crime which they may commit in order to prevent it, at the end of the war, from falling into the hands of its legitimate owners and to cause economic damages to the competitors of the U.S. in Europe or the Far East, particularly Japan, which is a major consumer of the region's oil.

6. Division of the Land of the Two Sacred Mosques and annexing of the northern part of it by Israel. Dividing the Land of the Two Sacred Mosques is an essential demand of the Zionist-Crusader alliance. The existence of such a large country with its huge resources under the leadership of the forthcoming Islamic state, by God's grace, represents a serious danger to the very existence of the Zionist state in Palestine. The Nobel *Ka'ba*—the *qibla* of all Muslims—makes the Land of the Two Sacred Mosques a symbol for the unity of the Islamic world. Moreover, the presence of the world's largest oil reserve makes the Land of the Two Sacred Mosques an important economic power in the Islamic world.

The sons of the Two Sacred Mosques are directly related to the tradition of their forefathers, the Companions, may God be pleased with them. They consider the tradition of their forefathers as a source and an example for re-establishing the greatness of this Islamic nation and to raise the word of God again. Furthermore, the presence of a population of fighters in southern Yemen, fighting in the cause of God, is a strategic threat to the Zionist-Crusader alliance in the area. The Prophet (PBUH) said: "Around twelve thousand will emerge from Aden/Abian helping the cause of God and His Messenger; they are the best, in the time between me and them" [Narrated by Ahmad with a correct trustworthy reference].

7. An internal war is a great mistake, no matter what reasons there are for it. The occupier, the U.S. forces, will control the outcome of the battle for the benefit of the international disbelief.

I now address my brothers of the security and military forces and the National Guard, may God preserve you for Islam and the Muslim people:

O you protectors of unity and guardians of Faith. O you descendants of the ancestors who carried the light [torch] of guidance and spread it all over the world. O you grandsons of Sa'd ibn Abi Waqqaas, Al-Mothanna ibn Haritha Ash-Shaybani, Al-Ga'ga ibn Amroo al-Tameemi and those pious Companions who fought *jihad* alongside them; you competed to join the army and the guard forces with the intention to carry out *jihad* in the cause of God, raising His word, and to defend the faith of Islam and the Land of the Two Sacred Mosques against the invaders and the occupying forces. That is the ultimate level of believing in this religion. But the regime has reversed these principles and their understanding, humiliating the Islamic nation and disobeying God. Half a century ago the rulers promised the Islamic nation that they would regain the first *qibla*, but fifty years later a new generation arrived and the promises were changed. The Al-Aqsa Mosque was handed over to the Zionists, and the wounds of the Islamic nation are still bleeding there.

At this time, when the Islamic nation has not regained the first *qibla* and the route of the journey of the Prophet (PBUH), and despite all that has been mentioned, the Saudi regime has harmed the Islamic nation in the remaining sanctuaries, the sacred city of Mecca, and the mosque of the Prophet, by calling the Christian army to defend the regime. The Crusaders were permitted to be in the Land of the Two Sacred Mosques. Not surprisingly, the King himself wore the Cross on his chest. The country was opened wide from north to the south and from east to west for the Crusaders. The land was filled with the military bases of the U.S. and its allies. The regime became unable to keep control without the help of these bases. You know more than anybody else about the size, intention and the danger of the presence of the U.S. military bases in the area.

The regime betrayed the Islamic nation and joined disbelief, assisting and helping them against the Muslims. It is well known that this is one of the ten acts that annul Islam. By opening the Arabian Peninsula to the Crusaders, the regime disobeyed and acted against what has been enjoined by the Messenger of God (PBUH), who said while on his death bed: "Expel the polytheists from the Arabian Peninsula," [Narrated by al-Bukhari] and: "If I survive, God willing, I will expel the Jews and the Christians out of the Arabian Peninsula" [Saheeh al-Jame As-Sagheer].

It is out of date and no longer acceptable to claim that the presence of the Crusaders is a necessity and only a temporary measure to protect the Land of the Two Sacred Mosques. Especially when the civil and the military infrastructures of Iraq were savagely destroyed, showing the depth of the Zionist-Crusader hatred of the Muslims and their children, and the rejection of the idea of replacing the Crusader forces by an Islamic force composed of the sons of the country and other Muslim people. Moreover, these excuses and the claim itself were demolished and wiped out by the sequence of speeches given by the leaders of the disbelievers in America. The latest of these speeches was the one given by William Perry, the Defense Secretary, after the explosion in Al-Khobar, saying that the presence of the American solders there is to protect the interests of the U.S. The imprisoned Sheikh Safar al-Hawali, may God hasten his release, wrote a book of seventy pages. In it he presented evidence and proof that the presence of the Americans in the Arabian Peninsula is a pre-planned military occupation.

The regime wants to deceive the Muslim people in the same manner as the Palestinian *mujahideen* were deceived, causing the loss of the Al-Aqsa Mosque. In 1304 A.H. [1936] the awakened Muslim nation of Palestine started their great struggle, *jihad*, against the British occupying forces. Britain was impotent to stop the *mujahideen* and their *jihad*, but their devil inspired that there is no way to stop the armed struggle in Palestine unless through their agent King Abdul Aziz, who managed to deceive the *mujahideen*. King Abdul Aziz carried out his duty to his British masters. He sent his two sons to meet the *mujahideen* leaders and to inform them that King Abdul Aziz would guarantee the promises made by the British government of leaving the area and responding positively to the demands of the *mujahideen* if the latter stopped their *jihad*. And so King Abdul Aziz caused the loss of the first *qibla* of the Muslim people. The King supported the Crusaders against the Muslims, and instead of supporting the *mujahideen* in the cause of God to liberate the Al-Aqsa Mosque, he disappointed and humiliated them.

Today, his son, King Fahd, is trying to deceive the Muslims for the second time, so as to lose what is left of the sanctuaries. When the Islamic world resented the arrival of the Crusader forces in the Land of the Two Sacred Mosques, the King told lies to the scholars, who issued *fatawa* about the arrival of the Americans, and to the gathering of the Islamic leaders at the conference of the union [*Rabitah*], which was held in the sacred city of Mecca. The King said: "The issue is simple. The American and the alliance forces will leave the area in few months." Today, it has been seven years since their arrival, and the regime is not able to move them out of the country. The regime has made no confession about its ineffectiveness and carries on lying to the people, claiming that the Americans will leave. But never—never again. A believer will not be bitten twice from the same hole or snake! Happy is the one who takes note of the sad experience of others!

Instead of motivating the army, the guards, and the security men to oppose the occupiers, the regime uses these men to protect the invaders, further deepening the humiliation and the betrayal. We bemoan this and can only say: "*There is neither power nor strength except from God.*" To those little groups of men within the army, police and security forces, who have been tricked and pressured by the regime to attack the Muslims and spill their blood, we would like to remind them of the narration: "I promise war against those who take my friends as their enemy" [Narrated by al-Bukhari]. And his saying of: "On the Day of Judgment, a man comes holding another, complaining about being slain by him. God, blessed be His Names, asks: 'Why did you slay him?' The accused replies: 'I did so that all exaltation may be Yours.' God, blessed be His Names, says: 'All exaltation is indeed mine!' Another man comes holding a fourth with a similar complaint. God, blessed be His Names, asks: 'Why did you kill him?' The accused replies: 'I did so that exaltation may be for Mr. X!' God, blessed be His Names, says: 'Exaltation is mine, not for Mr. X, carry all the slain man's sins and proceed to the Hell fire!'" In another wording of An-Nasa'i: "The accused says: for strengthening the rule or kingdom of Mr. X."

Today your brothers and sons, the sons of the Two Sacred Mosques, have started their *jihad* in the cause of God, to expel the occupying enemy from the Land of the Two Sacred Mosques. And there is no doubt you would like to carry out this mission too, in order to re-establish the greatness of this Islamic nation and to liberate its occupied sanctuaries. Nevertheless, it must be obvious to you that, due to the imbalance of power between our armed forces and the enemy forces, a suitable means of fighting must be adopted, *i.e.* using fast moving, light forces that work under complete secrecy. In other words, to initiate a guerrilla war where the sons of the Islamic nation, and not the military forces, take part in it. And as you know, it is wise, in the present circumstances, for the armed military forces not to be engaged in conventional fighting with the forces of the Crusader enemy, unless a big advantage is likely to be achieved. The exceptions are the bold and forceful operations carried out by the members of the armed forces individually, that is, without the movement of the formal forces in its conventional shape; and hence, the responses will not be directed strongly against the army. And by this war, great losses will be induced on the enemy side that would shake and destroy its foundations and infrastructure, helping to expel the defeated enemy from the country.

The *mujahideen*, your brothers and sons, request that you support them in every possible way by supplying them with the necessary information, materials and arms. Security men are especially asked to cover up for the *mujahideen* and to assist them as much as possible against the occupying enemy, and to spread rumors, fear and discouragement among the members of the enemy forces. We bring to your attention that the regime, in order to create friction and feuding between the *mujahideen* and yourselves, might resort to taking deliberate action against the personnel of the security guards and military forces, and blame the *mujahideen* for these actions. The regime should not be allowed to have such opportunity.

The regime is fully responsible for what has been incurred by the country and the Islamic nation; however, the occupying American enemy is the principle and main cause of the situation. Therefore, efforts should be concentrated on destroying, fighting, and killing the enemy until, by the grace of God, it is completely defeated. The time will come, by the permission of God, when you'll perform your decisive role so that the word of God will be supreme and the word of the infidels will be the inferior. You will hit with iron fists against the aggressors. You'll re-establish the normal course, give the people their rights, and carry out your true Islamic duty. God willing, I'll have a separate talk about these issues.

My Muslim Brothers, particularly those of the Arabian Peninsula:

The money you pay to buy American goods will be transformed into bullets and used against our brothers in Palestine and in the future against our sons in the Land of the Two Sacred Mosques. By buying these goods we are strengthening their economy, while our dispossession and poverty increases.

Muslims Brothers of the Land of the Two Sacred Mosques:

It is incredible that our country is the world's largest buyer of arms from the U.S. and the area's biggest commercial partner of the Americans, who are assisting their Zionist brothers in occupying Palestine and in evicting and killing the Muslims there, by providing arms, men and financial support. To deny these occupiers the enormous revenues of their trading with our country is a very important aid for our *jihad* against them. To express our anger and hate to them is a very important moral gesture. By doing so we will take part in the process of cleansing our sanctuaries from the Crusaders and the Zionists, and forcing them, by the permission of God, to leave disappointed and defeated.

We expect the women of the Land of the Two Sacred Mosques and other countries to carry out their role in boycotting American goods. If economic boycotting is combined with the military operations of the *mujahideen*, defeating the enemy will be even nearer, by the permission of God. However, if Muslims don't cooperate and support their *mujahideen* brothers, then, in effect, they are supplying the army of the enemy with financial help, extending the war, and increasing the suffering of the Muslims. The security and the intelligence services of the entire world cannot force a single citizen to buy the goods of his/her enemy. The economic boycotting of American goods is a very effective weapon for hitting and weakening the enemy, and it is not under the control of the security forces of the regime.

Before closing my talk, I have a very important message to the youth of Islam, men of the brilliant future of the Islamic nation of Muhammad (PBUH). Our talk with the youth is about their duty in this difficult period in the history of our Islamic nation—a period of time in which the youth and no one else has come forward to carry out the variable and different duties. While some well-known individuals have hesitated in their duty of defending Islam and saving themselves and their wealth from the injustice, aggression and terror exercised by the government, the youth, may God protect them, have been forthcoming and raised the banner of *jihad* against the American-Zionist alliance occupying the sanctuaries of Islam. Others who have been tricked into loving this materialistic world, and those who have been terrorized by the government, have chosen to give legitimacy to the greatest betrayal, the occupation of the Land of the Two Sacred Mosques. We bemoan this and can only say: "*There is neither power nor strength except from God.*" We are not surprised by the action of our youth. The youth were the Companions of Muhammad (PBUH), and was it not the youth themselves who killed Aba Jahl, the Pharaoh of this Islamic nation? Our youth are the best descendants of the best ancestors.

Abd ur-Rahman ibn Awf, may God be pleased with him, said: "I was at Badr where I noticed two boys, one to my right and the other to my left. One of them asked me quietly, so as not to be heard by the other: 'O uncle, point out Abu Jahl to me.' 'What do you want him for?' I asked. The boy answered: 'I have been informed that he, Abu Jahl, abused the Messenger of God. I swear by God, who has my soul in His hand, that if I see Abu Jahl, I'll not let my shadow depart his shadow till one of us is dead.' 'I was astonished,' said Abd ur-Rahman. Then the other youth said the same thing as the first one. Subsequently, I saw Abu Jahl among the people. I said to the boys: 'Do you see? This is the man you are asking me about.' The two youths hit Abu Jahl with their swords till he was dead."

God is the greatest, praise be to Him: Two youths of a young age but with great perseverance, enthusiasm, courage and pride for the religion of God, each one of them asking about the most important act of killing that should be imposed on the enemy. That is the killing of Abu Jahl, the Pharaoh of this Islamic nation, the leader of the unbelievers at the battle of Badr. The role of Abdul Rahman ibn Awf, may God be pleased with him, was to direct the two youths toward Abu Jahl. That was the perseverance and the enthusiasm of the youth of that time, and that was the perseverance and the enthusiasm of their fathers. It is this role that is now required from the people who have expertise and knowledge in fighting the enemy. They should guide their brothers and sons in this matter. Once that has been done, then our youth will repeat what their forefathers had said before: "I swear by God, who has my soul in His hand, that if I see Abu Jahl, I'll not let my shadow depart his shadow till one of us is dead."

And the story of Abd ur-Rahman ibn Awf about Ummayyah ibn Khalaf shows the extent of Bilal's, may God be pleased with him, persistence in killing the head of the disbelief: "The head of disbelief is Ummayyah ibn Khalaf.... I shall not live if he survives," said Bilal.

A few days ago the news agencies reported that the Defense Secretary of the crusading Americans had said that the explosions at Riyadh and Al-Khobar had taught him one lesson: Not to withdraw when attacked by cowardly terrorists. We say to the Defense Secretary that his talk can induce a grieving mother to laughter! It shows the fears that have enveloped you all. Where was your courage when the explosion in Beirut took place in 1403 A.H. [1983]? You were turned into scattered bits and pieces; 241 soldiers, mostly Marines, were killed. And where was this courage of yours when two explosions made you to leave Aden in less than twenty-four hours!

But your most disgraceful case was in Somalia, where, after vigorous propaganda about the power of the U.S. and its post-Cold War leadership of the New World Order, you moved tens of thousands of an international force, including 28,000 American soldiers, into Somalia. However, when tens of your soldiers were killed in minor battles and one American pilot was dragged in the streets of Mogadishu, you left the area carrying disappointment, humiliation, defeat, and your dead with you. Clinton appeared in front of the whole world threatening and promising revenge, but these threats were merely a preparation for withdrawal. You had been disgraced by God and you withdrew. The extent of your impotence and weakness became very clear. It was a pleasure for the heart of every Muslim and a remedy to the chests of believing nations to see you defeated in the three Islamic cities of Beirut, Aden and Mogadishu.

I say to the Secretary of Defense: The sons of the Land of the Two Sacred Mosques came out to fight against the Russians in Afghanistan, the Serbs in Bosnia-Herzegovina, and today they are fighting in Chechnya and, by the permission of God, they have been made victorious over your partner, the Russians. By the command of God, they are also fighting in Tajikistan.

I say: Since the sons of the Land of the Two Sacred Mosques know and strongly believe that fighting [*jihad*] against the disbelievers in every part of the world is absolutely essential, then they would be even more enthusiastic, more powerful and even larger in number upon fighting in their own land—the place of their birth—defending the greatest of their sanctuaries, the Noble *Ka'ba*, the *qibla* of all Muslims. They know that the Muslims of the world will assist and help them to victory. To liberate their sanctuaries is the greatest of issues concerning all Muslims. It is the duty of every Muslim in this world.

I say to you William (Defense Secretary): These youths love death as you love life. They pass the traits of dignity, pride, courage, generosity, truthfulness and sacrifice from father to father. They are most delivering and steadfast at war. They inherit these values from their ancestors, even from the Time of the Ignorance before Islam. These values were approved and completed by the arrival of Islam, as stated by the Messenger of God (PBUH): "I have been sent to perfect the good values" [Saheeh al-Jame As-Sagheer].

When, the pagan King Amroo ibn Hind tried to humiliate the pagan Amroo ibn Kulthoom, the latter cut off the head of the King with his sword, rejecting aggression, humiliation and indignation. If the king oppresses the people excessively, we reject submitting to humiliation. By which legitimacy, or command, O Amroo bin Hind, do you want us to be degraded?! By which legitimacy, or command, O Amroo bin Hind, do you listen to our foes and disrespect us? Our toughness has, O Amroo, tired the enemies before you, never giving in!

Our youth believe in paradise after death. They believe that taking part in fighting will not bring their day nearer and staying behind will not postpone their day either. God, the Exalted, said: "*And a soul will not die but with the permission of God, the term is fixed*" [Qur'an 3:145]. Our youth believe in the saying of the Messenger of God (PBUH): "O boy, I am going to teach you a few words. Preserve God, He will protect you. Preserve God, you will find Him before you. If you ask for something, ask God. If you seek help, seek help from God. And know that if all people come together to help you, they will not help you except with something that God has preordained for you. And if they assemble to harm you, they will not harm you except with something that God has preordained for you. The pen has been lifted and the sheets have dried. It is fixed. Nothing in these truths can be changed" [Saheeh al-Jame As-Sagheer].

Our youth take note of the meaning of the poetic verse: "If death is a predetermined must, then it is a shame to die cowardly."

And the other poet saying: "Who do not die by the sword will die by other reason; many causes are there, but only one death."

These youth believe in what has been told by God and His Messenger (PBUH) about the greatness of the reward for the *mujahideen* and martyrs; God, the most Exalted, said: "*And as for those who are slain in the way of God, He will by no means allow their deeds to perish. He will guide them and improve their condition, and cause them to enter the garden of paradise which He has made known to them*" [Qur'an 47:4-6]. God, the Exalted, also said: "*And do not speak of those who are slain in God's way as dead; nay, they are alive, but you do not perceive*" [Qur'an 2:154].

His Messenger (PBUH) said: "For those who strive in His cause, God prepared a hundred degrees [levels] in paradise. The difference between two degrees is as the distance between heaven and earth" [Saheeh al-Jame As-Sagheer]. He (PBUH) also said: "The best of the martyrs are those who do not turn their faces away from the battle till they are killed. They are in the high level of paradise. Their Lord smiles at them, and when your Lord smiles to a servant of His, He will not hold him to an account" [Narrated by Ahmad with correct and trustworthy reference].

And: "A martyr will not feel the pain of death except like how you feel when you are pinched" [Saheeh al-Jame As-Sagheer]. He also said: "A martyr's privileges are guaranteed by God; forgiveness with the first gush of his blood, he will be shown his seat in paradise, he will be decorated with the jewels of belief, married off to the beautiful ones, protected from the test in the grave, assured security in the Day of Judgment, crowned with the crown of dignity, a ruby of which is better than this whole earthly world and its entire content, wedded to seventy-two of the pure, beautiful ones of paradise and his intercession on the behalf of seventy of his relatives will be accepted" [Narrated by Ahmad and At-Tirmithi with the correct and trustworthy reference].

Those youth know their reward in fighting you, the U.S., is double the reward of fighting someone not from the People of the Book [Christians and Jews]. They have no intention except to enter paradise by killing you. An infidel, an enemy of God like you, cannot be in the same heaven with his righteous executioner.

Our youth chant and recite the word of God, the most Exalted: "*Fight them; God will punish them by your hands and bring them to disgrace, and assist you against them and heal the heart of a believing people*" [Qur'an 9:14]. And the words of the Prophet (PBUH): "I swear by Him, who has my soul in His hand, that the man who gets killed fighting them today, patiently attacking and not retreating, surely God will let him into paradise." And His (PBUH) saying to them: "Get up to a paradise as wide as heaven and earth." The youth also recite the Almighty's words: "*So when you meet in battle those who disbelieve, then smite the necks*" [Qur'an 47:19]. Those youth will not ask you [William Perry] for explanations. They will tell you, singing, that nothing between us needs to be explained; there is only killing and neck smiting.

And they will say to you what their grandfather, Harun al-Rashid, Commander of the Faithful, replied to your grandfather, Nagfoor, the Byzantine emperor, when he threatened the Muslims: "From Harun al-Rashid, Commander of the Faithful, to Nagfoor, the dog of the Romans: The answer is what you will see, not what you hear." Harun al-Rashid led the armies of Islam to the battle and handed Nagfoor a devastating defeat.

The youth you call cowards are competing among themselves in fighting and killing you, reciting what one of them said: "The Crusader army became dust when we detonated Al-Khobar, with the courageous youth of Islam fearing no danger." If [they are] threatened that the tyrants will kill them, they reply: "My death is a victory." "I did not betray that king, he did betray our *qibla*, and he permitted in the holy country the filthiest sort of humans." "I have made an oath by God, the Great, to fight whoever rejects the faith."

For more than a decade, they carried arms on their shoulders in Afghanistan, and they have made vows to God that, as long as they are alive, they will continue to carry arms against you until you are, God willing, expelled, defeated and humiliated. They will carry on as long as they live saying: "O William, tomorrow you will know which young man is confronting your misguided brethren!" A youth smiling while fighting, returning with the spear colored red, stated: "May God keep me close to knights, humans in peace, demons in war. Lions of the jungle, their teeth are spears and Indian swords. The horses witness that I push them hard forward in the fire of battle. The dust of the battle bears witnesses for me, so also the fighting itself, the pens and the books!"

So, to abuse the grandsons of the Companions, may God be pleased with them, by calling them cowards and challenging them by refusing to leave the Land of the Two Sacred Mosques shows the insanity and the imbalance from which you are suffering. Its appropriate remedy, however, is in the hands of the youth of Islam, as the poet said:

> "I am willing to sacrifice self and wealth for the knights who never disappointed me.
>
> Knights, who are never fed up or deterred by death, even if the mill of war turns.
>
> In the heat of battle they do not care and cure the insanity of the enemy by their 'insane' courage."

Terrorizing you, while you are carrying arms on our land, is a legitimate and morally demanded duty. It is a legitimate right, well-known to all humans and other creatures. Your example and our example are like a snake which entered into a house of a man and got killed by him. The coward is the one who lets you walk on his land, carrying arms freely, and provides you with peace and security.

Those youth are different from your soldiers. Your problem will be how to convince your troops to fight, while our problem will be how to restrain our youth to wait for their turn in fighting and in operations. These youth are commendable and praiseworthy.

They stood up tall to defend the religion at the time when the government misled the prominent scholars and tricked them into issuing *fatawa* that have no basis, neither in the Book of God, nor in the tradition of His Prophet (PBUH), in opening the Land of the Two Sacred Mosques to the Christian armies and handing the Al-Aqsa Mosque to the Zionists. Twisting the meanings of the holy text will not change this fact at all. They deserve the words of the poet:

> "I reject all the critics, who chose the wrong way.
>
> I reject those who enjoy fireplaces in clubs discussing eternally.
>
> I reject those, who despite being lost, think they are at the goal.
>
> I respect those who carried on, not asking or bothering about the difficulties.
>
> Never letting up from their goals, despite all hardships of the road.
>
> Whose blood is the oil for the flame which guides in the darkness of confusion.
>
> I feel still the pain of the loss of Al-Quds in my internal organs.
>
> That loss is like a burning fire in my intestines.
>
> I did not betray my covenant with God, when even states did betray it!

As their grandfather Assim bin Thabit said, rejecting a surrender offer of the pagans:

What excuse do I have to surrender, while I am still able, having arrows and my bow having a tough string?

Death is truth and ultimate destiny, and life will end anyway.

If I do not fight you, then my mother must be insane!"

The youth hold you responsible for all of the killings and evictions of the Muslims and the violation of the sanctuaries carried out by your Zionist brothers in Lebanon. You openly supplied them with arms and finance. More than 600,000 Iraqi children have died due to lack of food and medicine, and as a result of the unjustifiable aggression [sanctions] imposed on Iraq and its people. The children of Iraq are our children. You, the U.S., together with the Saudi regime, are responsible for the shedding of the blood of these innocent children. Due to all of that, whatever treaty you have with our country is now null and void.

The treaty of Hudaybiyah (1) was cancelled by the Messenger of God (PBUH) once Quraysh had assisted Bani Bakr against Khuzaah, the allies of the Prophet (PBUH). The Prophet (PBUH) fought Quraysh and conquered Mecca. He (PBUH) considered the treaty with the Bani Qainuqa void because one of their Jews publicly hurt one Muslim woman, one single woman, at the market. When we compare this to your killing of hundreds of thousands of Muslims and occupying their sanctuaries, it is now clear that those who claim that the blood of the American soldiers, the enemy occupying the land of the Muslims, should be protected are merely repeating what is imposed on them by the regime, fearing aggression and interested in saving themselves.

It is a duty now on every tribe in the Arabian Peninsula to fight *jihad* in the cause of God and to cleanse the land from those occupiers. God knows that their blood is permitted to be spilled and their wealth is considered booty; their wealth is booty to those who kill them. The most Exalted said in 'The Verse of the Sword': "*So when the sacred months have passed away, then slay the idolaters wherever you find them, and take them captive and besiege them and lie in wait for them in every ambush*" [Qur'an 9:5]. Our youth know that the humiliation suffered by the Muslims as a result of the occupation of their sanctuaries cannot be removed except by explosions and *jihad*.

As the poet said:

> "The walls of oppression and humiliation cannot be demolished except in a rain of bullets.
>
> The freeman does not surrender leadership to infidels and sinners.
>
> Without shedding blood, no degradation and branding can be removed from the forehead."

I remind the youth of the Islamic world—who fought in Afghanistan and Bosnia-Herzegovina with their wealth, pens, tongues and selves—that the battle has not yet finished. I remind them about the talk between Gabriel and the Messenger of God (PBUH) after the battle of Ahzab (2) when the Messenger of God (PBUH) returned to Medina, and before putting his sword aside, Gabriel (PBUH) descended saying: "Are you putting your sword aside? By God, the angels haven't dropped their arms yet; march with your Companions to Bani Quraydah. I am going ahead of you to throw fear in their hearts and to shake their fortresses." Gabriel marched with the angels (God's Blessings and Salutations be upon them all), followed by the Messenger of God (PBUH) marching with the immigrants [*Muhajirun*], and supporters [*Ansar*] [Narrated by al-Bukhari].

These youth know that if one is not to be killed one will die [anyway], and the most honorable death is to be killed in the way of God. They are even more determined after the martyrdom of the four heroes who bombed the Americans in Riyadh. (3) Those youth raised high the head of the Islamic nation and humiliated the Americans, the occupier, by their operation in Riyadh.

They remember the poetry of Jafar, the second commander in the battle of Mutah (4), in which 3,000 Muslims faced over 100,000 Romans:

> "How good is the Paradise and its nearness, good with cool drink.
>
> But the Romans are promised punishment [in Hell], if I meet them.
>
> I will fight them."

And the poetry of Abdullah bin Rawaha, the third commander in the battle of Mutah, after the martyrdom of Jafar, when he felt some hesitation:

> "O my soul, if you do not get killed, you are going to die anyway.
>
> This is the death pool in front of you!
>
> You are getting what you have wished for [martyrdom] before, and you follow the example of the two previous commanders, you are rightly guided!"

As for our daughters, wives, sisters and mothers, they should take prime example from the Prophet's (PBUH) pious female Companions, may God be pleased with them; they should adopt the lifestyle of the female Companions, of courage, sacrifice and generosity in the cause of the supremacy of God's religion. They should remember the courage and the personality of Fatima, daughter of al-Khatab, when she accepted Islam and stood up in front of her brother, Omar ibn al-Khatab and challenged him, before he became a Muslim, saying: "O Omar, what will you do if the truth is not in your religion?!" And to remember the stand of Asma, daughter of Abu Bakr, on the day of migration [*Hijra*], when she attended the Messenger [Muhammad] and his Companion in the cave and split her belt in two pieces for them. And to remember the stand of Naseeba Bint Kab, striving to defend the Messenger of God (PBUH) on the day of Uhud (5), in which she suffered twelve injuries, one of which was so deep it left a deep, lifelong scar! They should remember the generosity of the early women of Islam who raised finances for the Muslim army by selling their jewelry.

Our women have set a tremendous example of generosity in the cause of God. They motivated and encouraged their sons, brothers and husbands to fight in the cause of God in Afghanistan, Bosnia-Herzegovina, Chechnya and in other countries. We ask God to accept from them these deeds, and may He help their fathers, brothers, husbands and sons. May God strengthen the belief of our women in the way of generosity and sacrifice for the supremacy of the word of God. Our women weep not, except over men who fight in the cause of God. Our women instigate their brothers to fight in the cause of God.

Our women bemoan only fighters in the cause of God, as said: 'Do not moan on anyone except a lion in the woods, courageous in the burning wars. Let me die dignified in wars, an honorable death is better than my current life.'

Our women encourage *jihad* saying: 'Prepare yourself like a struggler; the matter is bigger than words! Are you going to leave us for the wolves of disbelief eating our wings?! The wolves of disbelief are mobilizing all evil persons from everywhere! Where are the free men defending free women by arms?! Death is better than life in humiliation! Some scandals and shames will never be otherwise eradicated.'

My Muslim Brothers of the World:

Your brothers in Palestine and in the Land of the Two Sacred Mosques are calling upon your help and asking you to take part in fighting against your enemy and their enemy—the Americans and the Israelis. They are asking you to do whatever you can, with one's own means and ability, to expel the enemy, humiliated and defeated, out of the sanctuaries of Islam. God, the Exalted, said in His book: "*And if they ask your support, because they are oppressed in their faith, then support them*!" [Qur'an 8:72].

O you soldiers of God, ride and march on. This is the time of hardship, so be tough. And know that your gathering and cooperation in order to liberate the sanctuaries of Islam is the right step toward unifying the Islamic nation under the banner of "*There is no god except God and Muhammad is the Messenger of God.*" From our place, we raise our palms humbly to God, asking Him to bestow on us His guidance in every aspect of this issue.

Our Lord, we ask you to secure the release of the truthful scholars of Islam and the pious youth of the Islamic nation from their imprisonment. O God, strengthen them and help their families.

Our Lord, the people of the Cross have come with their soldiers and occupied the Land of the Two Sacred Mosques. And the Zionist Jews fiddle as they wish with the Al-Aqsa Mosque, the route of the ascent of the Messenger of God (PBUH). Our Lord, shatter their gathering, divide them among themselves, shake the earth under their feet and give us control over them. Our Lord, we take refuge in you from their deeds and take you as a shield between us and them.

Our Lord, show us a black day for them!

Our Lord, show us the wonderment of your ability in them!

Our Lord, You are the Revealer of the Book, Director of the clouds.

You defeated the allies; defeat them and make us victorious over them.

Our Lord, You are the one who helps us, and You are the one who assists us. With Your Power we move and by Your Power we fight. On You we rely and You are our cause.

Our Lord, those youth got together to make Your religion victorious and raise Your banner. Our Lord, send them Your help and strengthen their hearts.

Our Lord, make the youth of Islam steadfast and descend patience on them and guide their shots!

Our Lord, unify the Muslims and bestow love in their hearts!

O Lord, pour down upon us patience, make our steps firm and assist us against the unbelieving people!

Our Lord, do not lay on us a burden as You did lay on those before us. Our Lord, do not impose upon us that which we have no strength to bear, and pardon us and grant us protection and have mercy on us. You are our patron, so help us against the unbelieving people.

Our Lord, guide this Islamic nation, and make the right conditions by which the people of Your obedience will be in dignity and the people of disobedience in humiliation, and by which the good deeds are enjoined and the bad deeds are forbidden.

Our Lord, bless Muhammad (PBUH), Your servant and Messenger, his family and descendants, and Companions and salute him with a [becoming] salutation.

And our last supplication is: All praise is due to God, the Lord of the Universe.

Osama bin Laden, 9/4/1417 A.H. (8/23/1996) Hindu Kush Mountains, Khurasan, Afghanistan.

1. The Treaty of Hudaybiyyah: 628 A.D., between Muhammad and the Quraysh.
2. Battle of Ahzab: 627 A.D., Muslims repulse forces of Mecca.
3. Riyadh bombing: 13 November 1995 car bombing of joint U.S.-Saudi training facility.
4. Battle of Mutah: 629 A.D., Muslims survive against overwhelming Roman [Byzantine] force; therefore, considered a victory.
5. Battle of Uhud: 625 A.D., Muslims initially defeat Quraysh and then lose.

3

Interview with *Nida'ul Islam*

(October-November 1996)

Nida'ul Islam is a militant-Islamic magazine published in Australia. The following are excerpts of an interview with Osama bin Laden.

How do you evaluate the Saudi regime's foreign policy towards the Muslim world in the past years?

Bin Laden: The external policy of the Saudi regime towards Islamic issues is a policy which has been tied to the British outlook from the establishment of Saudi Arabia until 1364 A.H. [1945]. Then it became attached to the American outlook after America gained prominence as a major power in the world after the Second World War. It is well-known that the policies of these two countries bear the greatest enmity towards the Islamic world…the regime does not cease to cry in the open over the matters effecting the Muslims without making any serious effort to serve the interests of the Muslim community, apart from small efforts in order to confuse people and throw some dust into their eyes.

The confrontation between the Islamic movement and the apostate Saudi regime recorded a historical turning point following the latest attacks against the American occupiers' targets. How did these attacks reflect on the internal front, and how did they affect the Saudi-American relations?

Bin Laden:…There were important effects to the two explosions in Riyadh on both the internal and external aspects. Most important amongst these is the awareness of the people to the significance of the American occupation of the Land of the Two Sacred Mosques, and that the original decrees of the regime are a reflection of the wishes of the American occupiers.

So the people have become aware that their main problems have been caused by the American occupiers and their puppets in the Saudi regime.... This movement—with the grace of God—is increasing in power and in supporters day after day at the expense of the regime. The sympathy with these missions at the civil and military levels has been great, as also the sympathies of the Muslim world with the struggle against the Americans.... These missions also paved the way for the raising of the voices of opposition against the American occupation from within the ruling family and the armed forces; in fact we can say that the remaining Gulf countries have been effected to the same degree, and that the voices of opposition to the American occupation have begun to be heard at the level of the ruling families and the governments of the Cooperative Council of Gulf countries. The differences in outlooks between the Americans and the Gulf States have appeared for the first time since the Second Gulf war....

It was observed that the American and Saudi officials tried to link the latest operations to some foreign countries. What is behind these attempts?

Bin Laden: A result of the increasing reaction of the people against the American occupation and the great sympathy with the *jihad* missions against the Americans is the eagerness of the Americans and the Saudis to propagate false information to disperse these sympathies. This can be witnessed in their statements that some of the countries in the region were behind the *jihad* missions inside the Land of the Two Sacred Mosques; however, the people are aware that this is an internal Islamic movement against the American occupation which is revealing itself in the most clear picture after the killing of the four champions who performed the Riyadh operation, the ones concerning whom, we ask God to accept among the martyrs.

It has become routine policy for countries upon facing an internal calamity to lay the responsibility on an external country. Before the puppetry of the Arabic countries to America became plainly obvious, the security sections never hesitated to accuse any rectifying Islamic movement to be a puppet to America and Israel.

As a part of the furious international campaign against the *jihad* movement, you were personally the target of a prejudiced attack, which accused you of financing terrorism and being part of an international terrorist organization. What do you have to say about that?

Bin Laden: After the end of the Cold War, America escalated its campaign against the Muslim world in its entirety, aiming to get rid of Islam itself. Its main focus in this was to target the scholars and the reformers who were enlightening the people to the dangers of the Judeo-American alliance, and they also targeted the *mujahideen*. We also have been hit with some of the traces of this campaign as we were accused of funding terrorism, and being members of an international terrorist organization. Their aims in making these allegations were to place psychological pressure on the *mujahideen* and their supporters so that they would forsake the obligation of *jihad* and the resistance of oppression and American-Israeli occupation of Islamic sacred lands. However, thanks to God, their campaign was not successful, as terrorizing the American occupiers is a religious and logical obligation. We are grateful to God, Most Exalted, in that He has facilitated *jihad* in His cause for us, against the American-Israeli attacks on the Islamic sanctuaries.

As for their accusations of terrorizing the innocent, the children, and the women, these are in the category 'accusing others with their own affliction in order to fool the masses.' The evidence overwhelmingly shows America and Israel killing the weaker men, women, and children in the Muslim world and elsewhere.... Despite the continuing American occupation of the Land of the Two Sacred Mosques, America continues to claim that it is upholding the banner of freedom and humanity, while these deeds which they have done, you would find that the most ravenous of animals would not descend to.... Our encouragement and call to Muslims to enter *jihad* against the Americans and the Israeli occupiers are actions which we are engaging in as religious obligations....

What is the responsibility of the Muslim populations towards the international campaign against Islam?

Bin Laden: What bears no doubt in this fierce Judeo-Christian campaign against the Muslim world, the likes of which has never been seen before, is that the Muslims must prepare all the possible might to repel the enemy on the military, economic, missionary, and all other areas. It is crucial for us to be patient and to cooperate in righteousness and piety, and to raise awareness to the fact that the highest priority, after faith, is to repel the incursive enemy which corrupts the religion and the world. Nothing deserves a higher priority after faith, as the scholars have declared, for this cause, it is crucial to overlook many of the issues of bickering in order to unite our ranks so that we can repel the greater infidelity....

4

Declaration of the World Islamic Front for Jihad Against the Jews and Crusaders

(23 February 1998)

Published under the title "Kill Americans Everywhere" by *Al-Quds al-Arabi*, a London-based newspaper, the declaration was faxed to the newspaper.

Praise be to God, who revealed the Book [the *Qur'an*], controls the clouds, defeats factionalism, and says in His Book: "*But when the sacred months are past, then fight and slay the pagans wherever you find them, seize them, beleaguer them, and lie in wait for them in every stratagem* [of war]" [Qur'an 9:5]; and peace be upon our Prophet, Muhammad bin Abd-Allah, who said: "I have been sent with the sword between my hands to ensure that no one but God is worshipped, God who put my livelihood under the shadow of my spear and who inflicts humiliation and scorn on those who disobey my orders."

The Arabian Peninsula has never—since God extended it, created its desert, and encircled it with seas—been stormed by any forces like the Crusader armies spreading in it like locusts, consuming its riches and destroying its plantations. All this is happening at a time when nations are attacking Muslims, like people fighting over a plate of food. In light of the grave situation and the lack of support, we and you are obliged to discuss current events, and we should all agree on how to settle the matter.

No one argues today about three facts that are known to everyone. We will list them in order to remind everyone:

First, for over seven years the United States has been occupying the lands of Islam in the most sacred of places, the Arabian Peninsula, plundering its riches, dictating to its rulers, humiliating its people, terrorizing its neighbors, and turning its bases in the Peninsula into a spearhead through which to fight the neighboring Muslim peoples.

If some people have formerly debated the fact of the occupation, all the people of the Peninsula have now acknowledged it. The best proof of this is the continuing American aggression against the Iraqi people, using the Peninsula as a staging post. Even though all its rulers are against their territories being used to that end, still they are helpless.

Second, despite the great devastation inflicted on the Iraqi people by the Crusader-Zionist alliance, and despite the huge number of those killed, in excess of one million. Despite all this, the Americans are once again trying to repeat the horrific massacres, as though they are not content with the protracted blockade imposed after the ferocious war or the fragmentation and devastation. So, now they come to annihilate what is left of this people and to humiliate their Muslim neighbors.

Third, if the Americans' aims behind these wars are religious and economic, their aim is also to serve the Jews' petty state and divert attention from its occupation of Jerusalem and the murder of Muslims there. The best proof of this is their eagerness to destroy Iraq, the strongest neighboring Arab state, and their endeavor to fragment all the states of the region—such as Iraq, Saudi Arabia, Egypt, and Sudan—into paper statelets and through their disunion and weakness to guarantee Israel's survival and the continuation of the brutal Crusader occupation of the Peninsula.

All these crimes and sins committed by the Americans are a clear declaration of war on God, his Messenger and Muslims. Scholars have throughout Islamic history unanimously agreed that *jihad* is an individual duty if the enemy destroys the Muslim countries. This was revealed by Imam ibn Qadamah in *Al-Mughni*, Imam al-Kisa'i in *Al-Bada'i*, al-Qurtubi in his interpretation [of the meanings of the *Qur'an*], and the Sheikh al-Islam [Ibn Taymiyah] in his books, where he said: "As for the militant struggle, it is aimed at defending sanctity and religion, and it is a duty as agreed [by the scholars]. Nothing is more sacred other than belief itself except repulsing an enemy who is attacking religion and life."

On that basis, and in compliance with God's command, we issue the following *fatwa* to all Muslims:

> The ruling to kill the Americans and their allies—civilians and military—is an individual duty for every Muslim who can do it in any country in which it is possible to do it, in order to liberate the Al-Aqsa Mosque and the sacred mosque [Mecca] from their grip, and in order for their armies to move out of all the lands of Islam, defeated and unable to threaten any Muslim. This is in accordance with the words of Almighty God: "*And fight the pagans all together as they fight you all together,*" [Qur'an 9:36] and "*Fight them until there is no more tumult or oppression, and there prevail justice and faith in God.*" [Qur'an 8:39]

This is in addition to the words of Almighty God: "*And what is it with you that you do not fight in the path of God, while the weak among the men, and the women, and the children who say: Our Lord, rescue us from this town, whose people are oppressive, and make for us from You a protecting friend and make for us from You a succorer*" [Qur'an 4:75].

We—with God's help—call on every Muslim who believes in God and wishes to be rewarded to comply with God's order to kill the Americans and plunder their money wherever and whenever they find it. We also call on Muslim scholars, leaders, youth, and soldiers to launch the raid on Satan's U.S. troops and the devil's supporters allying with them, and to displace those who are behind them so that they may learn a lesson.

Almighty God said: "*O you who believe, give your response to God and His Apostle, when He calls you to that which will give you life. And know that God comes between a man and his heart, and that it is He to whom you shall all be gathered*" [Qur'an 8:24].

Almighty God also says: "*O you who believe, what is the matter with you, that when you are asked to go forth in the cause of God, you cling so heavily to the earth! Do you prefer the life of this world to the hereafter? But little is the comfort of this life, as compared with the hereafter. Unless you go forth, He will punish you with a grievous penalty, and put others in your place; but Him you would not harm in the least. For God has power over all things*" [Qur'an 9:38].

Almighty God also says: "*So lose no heart, nor fall into despair. For you must gain mastery if you are true in faith*" [Qur'an 3:139].

Signed by Sheikh Osama bin Muhammad bin Laden, Ayman al-Zawahiri (*Amir* of the Jihad Group in Egypt), Abu-Yasir Rifa'i Ahmad Taha (Egyptian Islamic Group), Sheikh Mir Hamzah (Secretary of the Jamait-ul-Ulema, Pakistan); and Fazlul Rahman (*Amir* of the Jihad Movement in Bangladesh).

5

Interview with John Miller of *ABC*

(28 May 1998)

John Miller of ABC television interviewed Bin Laden in the mountains of southern Afghanistan. The interview aired on the "Nightline" program on 10 June 1998. In the first part of this interview, Bin Laden answers questions posed to him by some of his followers. In the latter part, ABC reporter John Miller is asking the questions.

What is the meaning of your call for Muslims to take arms against America in particular, and what is the message that you wish to send to the West in general?

The call to wage war against America was made because America has spearheaded the Crusade against the Islamic nation, sending tens of thousands of its troops to the Land of the Two Sacred Mosques over and above its meddling in its affairs and its politics, and its support of the oppressive, corrupt and tyrannical regime that is in control. These are the reasons behind the singling out of America as a target. And not exempt of responsibility are those Western regimes whose presence in the region offers support to the American troops there. We know at least one reason behind the symbolic participation of the Western forces and that is to support the Jewish and Zionist plans for expansion of what is called the Greater Israel. Surely, their presence is not out of concern over their interests in the region.... Their presence has no meaning save one and that is to offer support to the Jews in Palestine who are in need of their Christian brothers to achieve full control over the Arab Peninsula which they intend to make an important part of the so-called Greater Israel....

Many of the Arabic as well as the Western mass media accuse you of terrorism and of supporting terrorism. What do you have to say to that?

There is an Arabic proverb that says "she accused me of having her malady, then snuck away." Besides, terrorism can be commendable, and it can be reprehensible. Terrifying an innocent person and terrorizing him is objectionable and unjust, also unjustly terrorizing people is not right. Whereas, terrorizing oppressors and criminals and thieves and robbers is necessary for the safety of people and for the protection of their property. There is no doubt in this. Every state and every civilization and culture has to resort to terrorism under certain circumstances for the purpose of abolishing tyranny and corruption. Every country in the world has its own security system and its own security forces, its own police and its own army. They are all designed to terrorize whoever even contemplates to attack that country or its citizens. The terrorism we practice is of the commendable kind for it is directed at the tyrants and the aggressors and the enemies of God, the tyrants, the traitors who commit acts of treason against their own countries and their own faith and their own Prophet and their own nation. Terrorizing those and punishing them are necessary measures to straighten things and to make them right. Tyrants and oppressors who subject the Arab nation to aggression ought to be punished. The wrongs and the crimes committed against the Muslim nation are far greater than can be covered by this interview. America heads the list of aggressors against Muslims. The recurrence of aggression against Muslims everywhere is proof enough. For over half a century, Muslims in Palestine have been slaughtered and assaulted and robbed of their honor and of their property. Their houses have been blasted, their crops destroyed. And the strange thing is that any act on their part to avenge themselves or to lift the injustice befalling them causes great agitation in the United Nations, which hastens to call for an emergency meeting only to convict the victim and to censure the wronged and the tyrannized whose children have been killed and whose crops have been destroyed and whose farms have been pulverized....

In today's wars, there are no morals, and it is clear that mankind has descended to the lowest degree of decadence and oppression. They rip us of our wealth and our resources and our oil. Our religion is under attack. They kill and murder our brothers. They compromise our honor and our dignity, and dare we utter a single word of protest against the injustice, we are called terrorists. This is compounded injustice. And the United Nations' insistence to convict the victims and support the aggressors constitutes a serious precedent which shows the extent of injustice that has been allowed to take root in this land....

What is your relationship with the Islamic movements in various regions of the world like Chechnya and Kashmir and other Arab countries?

Cooperation for the sake of truth and righteousness is demanded from Muslims. A Muslim should do his utmost to cooperate with his fellow Muslims. But God says of cooperation that it is not absolute, for there is cooperation to do good, and there is cooperation to commit aggression and act unjustly. A Muslim is supposed to give his fellow Muslim guidance and support. He [Muhammad] said: "Stand by your brother be he oppressor or oppressed." When asked how were they to stand by him if he were the oppressor, He answered them, saying "by giving him guidance and counsel." It all goes to say that Muslims should cooperate with one another and should be supportive of one another, and they should promote righteousness and mercy. They should all unite in the fight against polytheism, and they should pool all their resources and their energy to fight the Americans and the Zionists and those with them. They should, however, avoid side fronts and rise over the small problems for these are less detrimental. Their fight should be directed against unbelief and unbelievers....

We heard your message to the American government and later your message to the European governments who participated in the occupation of the Gulf. Is it possible for you to address the people of these countries?

As we have already said, our call is the call of Islam that was revealed to Muhammad. It is a call to all mankind. We have been entrusted with good cause to follow in the footsteps of the Messenger and to communicate his message to all nations. It is an invitation that we extend to all the nations to embrace Islam, the religion that calls for justice, mercy and fraternity among all nations, not differentiating between black and white or between red and yellow, except with respect to their devotedness. All people who worship God, not each other, are equal before Him. We are entrusted to spread this message and to extend that call to all the people. We, nonetheless, fight against their governments and all those who approve of the injustice they practice against us. We fight the governments that are bent on attacking our religion and on stealing our wealth and on hurting our feelings. And as I have mentioned before, we fight them, and those who are part of their rule are judged in the same manner....

In your last statement, there was a strong message to the American government in particular. What message do you have for the European governments and the West in general?

Praise God and praises and peace upon Muhammad. With respect to the Western governments that participated in the attack on the Land of the Two Sacred Mosques regarding it as ownerless, and in the siege against the Muslim people of Iraq, we have nothing new to add to the previous message. What prompted us to address the American government in particular is the fact that it is on the head of the Western and the Crusading forces in their fight against Islam and against Muslims. The two explosions that took place in Riyadh and in Khobar recently were but a clear and powerful signal to the governments of the countries which willingly participated in the aggression against our countries and our lives and our sacrosanct symbols. It might be beneficial to mention that some of those countries have begun to move towards independence from the American government with respect to the enmity that it continues to show towards the Muslim people. We only hope that they will continue to move in that direction, away from the oppressive forces that are fighting against our countries. We, however, differentiate between the Western governments and the people of the West. If the people have elected those governments in the latest elections, it is because they have fallen prey to the Western media which portray things contrary to what they really are. And while the slogans raised by those regimes call for humanity, justice and peace, the behavior of their governments is completely the opposite. It is not enough for their people to show pain when they see our children being killed in Israeli raids launched by American planes, nor does this serve the purpose. What they ought to do is change their governments which attack our countries. The hostility that America continues to express against the Muslim people has given rise to feelings of animosity on the part of Muslims against America and against the West in general. Those feelings of animosity have produced a change in the behavior of some crushed and subdued groups who, instead of fighting the Americans inside the Muslim countries, went on to fight them inside the United States of America itself.

The Western regimes and the government of the United States of America bear the blame for what might happen. If their people do not wish to be harmed inside their very own countries, they should seek to elect governments that are truly representative of them and that can protect their interests.... The enmity between us and the Jews goes far back in time and is deep-rooted. There is no question that war between the two of us is inevitable. For this reason it is not in the interest of Western governments to expose the interests of their people to all kinds of retaliation for almost nothing. It is hoped that people of those countries will initiate a positive move and force their governments not to act on behalf of other states and other sects. This is what we have to say, and we pray to God to preserve the nation of Islam and to help them drive their enemies out of their land.

American politicians have painted a distorted picture of Islam, of Muslims and of Islamic fighters. We would like you to give us the true picture that clarifies your viewpoint....

The leaders in America and in other countries as well have fallen victim to Jewish Zionist blackmail. They have mobilized their people against Islam and against Muslims. These are portrayed in such a manner as to drive people to rally against them. The truth is that the whole Muslim world is the victim of international terrorism, engineered by America at the United Nations. We are a nation whose sacred symbols have been looted and whose wealth and resources have been plundered. It is normal for us to react against the forces that invade our land and occupy it....

Quite a number of Muslim countries have seen the rise of militant movements whose purpose is to stand up in the face of the pressure exerted on the people by their own governments and other governments. Such as in the case in Egypt and Libya and North Africa and Algiers, and such as was the case in Syria and in Yemen. There are also other militant groups currently engaged in the fight against the unbelievers and the Crusaders as is the case in Kashmir and Chechnya and Bosnia and the African Horn. Is there any message you wish to convey to our brothers who are fighting in various parts of the Islamic world?

...Tell the Muslims everywhere that the vanguards of the warriors who are fighting the enemies of Islam belong to them and the young fighters are their sons. Tell them that the nation is bent on fighting the enemies of Islam. Once again, I have to stress the necessity of focusing on the Americans and the Jews, for they represent the spearhead with which the members of our religion have been slaughtered. Any effort directed against America and the Jews yields positive and direct results—God willing. It is far better for anyone to kill a single American soldier than to squander his efforts on other activities....

John Miller's Interview Begins

You come from a background of wealth and comfort to end up fighting on the front lines. Many Americans find that unusual.

Bin Laden: This is difficult to understand, especially for him who does not understand the religion of Islam. In our religion, we believe that God has created us for the purpose of worshipping him. He is the one who has created us and who has favored us with this religion. God has ordered us to make holy wars and to fight to see to it that His word is the highest and the uppermost and that of the unbelievers the lowermost. We believe that this is the call we have to answer regardless of our financial capabilities. This too answers the claims of the West and of the secular people in the Arab world. They claim that this blessed awakening and the people reverting to Islam are due to economic factors. This is not so. It is rather a grace from God, a desire to embrace the religion of God. And this is not surprising. When the holy war called, thousands of young men from the Arab Peninsula and other countries answered the call, and they came from wealthy backgrounds. Hundreds of them were killed in Afghanistan and in Bosnia and in Chechnya.

You have been described as the world's most wanted man, and there is word that the American government intends to put a price on your head—in the millions—when you are captured. Do you think they will do that? And does it bother you?

Bin Laden: We do not care what the Americans believe. What we care for is to please God. Americans heap accusations on whoever stands for his religion or his rights or his wealth.... It does not scare us that they have put a price on my head. We as Muslims believe that our years on this earth are finite and predetermined. If the whole world gets together to kill us before it is our time to go, they will not succeed. We also believe that livelihoods are preordained. So no matter how much pressure America puts on the regime in Riyadh to freeze our assets and to forbid people from contributing to this great cause, we shall still have God to take care of us; livelihood is sent by God; we shall not want....

Mr. Bin Laden, you have issued a *fatwa* calling on Muslims to kill Americans where they can, when they can. Is that directed at all Americans, just the American military, just the Americans in Saudi Arabia?

Bin Laden: God has ordered us to glorify the truth and to defend Muslim land, especially the Arab peninsula...against the unbelievers. After World War II, the Americans grew more unfair and more oppressive towards people in general and Muslims in particular.... The Americans started it and retaliation and punishment should be carried out following the principle of reciprocity, especially when women and children are involved. Through history, America has not been known to differentiate between the military and the civilians or between men and women or adults and children. Those who threw atomic bombs and used the weapons of mass destruction against Nagasaki and Hiroshima were the Americans. Can the bombs differentiate between military and women and infants and children? America has no religion that can deter her from exterminating whole peoples. Your position against Muslims in Palestine is despicable and disgraceful. America has no shame.... We believe that the worst thieves in the world today and the worst terrorists are the Americans. Nothing could stop you except perhaps retaliation in kind. We do not have to differentiate between military or civilian. As far as we are concerned, they are all targets, and this is what the *fatwa* says.... The *fatwa* is general [comprehensive], and it includes all those who participate in, or help the Jewish occupiers in killing Muslims.

Ramzi Yousef was a follower of yours. Do you remember him and did you know him?

Bin Laden: After the explosion that took place in the World Trade Center [February 1993], Ramzi Yousef became a well-known Muslim figure. Muslims have come to know him. Unfortunately, I did not know him before this incident. I, of course, remember who he is. He is a Muslim who wanted to protect his religion jealously from the oppression practiced by America against Islam. He acted with zeal to make the Americans understand that their government was attacking Muslims in order to safeguard the American-Jewish interests....

Wali Khan Amin Shah was captured in Manila. American authorities believe he was working for you, funded by you, setting up training camps there and part of his plan was to plan out the assassination or attempted assassination of President Clinton during his trip to Manila.

Bin Laden: Wali Khan is a Muslim young man; his nickname in Afghanistan was The Lion. He was among the most courageous Muslim young men. He was a close friend, and we used to fight from the same trenches in Afghanistan. We fought many battles against the Russians until they were defeated and put to shame and had to leave the country in disgrace. As to what you said about him working for me, I have nothing to say. We are all together in this; we all work for God, and our reward comes from Him. As to what you said about the attempt to assassinate President Clinton, it is not surprising. What do you expect from people attacked by Clinton, whose sons and mothers have been killed by Clinton? Do you expect anything but treatment by reciprocity?

The federal government in the U.S. is still investigating their suspicions that you ordered and funded the attacks on the U.S. military in Al-Khobar and Riyadh.

Bin Laden: We have roused the nation and the Muslim people, and we have communicated to them the *fatawa* of our learned scholars who the Saudi government has thrown in jail in order to please the American government for which they are agents.... We have communicated their *fatawa* and stirred the nation to drive out the enemy who has occupied our land and usurped our country and suppressed our people and to rid the Land of the Two Sacred Mosques from their presence. Among the young men who responded to our call are Khalid al-Said, Abdul Azeez al-Me'them, Mahmud al-Hadi and Muslih al-Shamrani. We hope God receives them as holy martyrs. They have raised the nation's head high and washed away a great part of the shame that has enveloped us as a result of the weakness of the Saudi government and its complicity with the American government.... Yes, we have instigated and they have responded. We hope God grants their families solace.

You've been painted in America as a terrorist leader. To your followers, you are a hero. How do you see yourself?

Bin Laden: As I have said, we are not interested in what America says. We do not care. We view ourselves and our brothers like everyone else. God created us to worship Him and to follow in His footsteps and to be guided by His Book [*Qur'an*]. I am one of the servants of God, and I obey His orders. Among those is the order to fight for the word of God...and to fight until the Americans are driven out of all the Islamic countries.

No one expected the *mujahideen* to beat the Russians in Afghanistan. It came as a surprise to everyone. What do you see as the future of American involvement in the Middle East, in taking on groups like this?

Bin Laden: ...God has granted the Muslim people and the Afghani *mujahideen*, and those with them, the opportunity to fight the Russians and the Soviet Union.... They were defeated by God and were wiped out. There is a lesson here. The Soviet Union entered Afghanistan late in December of '79. The flag of the Soviet Union was folded once and for all on the 25th of December just 10 years later. It was thrown in the waste basket. Gone was the Soviet Union forever. We are certain that we shall—with the grace of God—prevail over the Americans and over the Jews, as the Messenger of God [Muhammad] promised us in an authentic prophetic tradition [*Hadith*] when he said: "The hour of resurrection shall not come before Muslims fight Jews and before Jews hide behind trees and behind rocks."

We are certain—with the grace of God—that we shall prevail over the Jews and over those fighting with them. Today, however, our battle against the Americans is far greater than our battle was against the Russians. The Americans have committed unprecedented stupidity. They have attacked Islam and its most significant sacrosanct symbols.... We anticipate a black future for America. Instead of remaining the United States, it shall end up separated states and shall have to carry the bodies of its sons back to America.

What do you see as the future of the Saudi Royal family and their involvement with America and the U.S. military?

Bin Laden: History has the answer to your question. The fate of any government which sells the interests of its own people and betrays the nation and commits offenses which furnish grounds for expulsion from Islam is known. We expect for the ruler of Riyadh the same fate as the Shah of Iran. We anticipate this to happen to him and to the influential people who stand by him and who have sided with the Jews and the Christians giving them free reign over the Land of the Two

Sacred Mosques. These are grave offenses that are grounds for expulsion from the faith. They shall all be wiped out....

Describe the situation when your men took down the American forces in Somalia.

Bin Laden: After our victory in Afghanistan and the defeat of the oppressors who had killed millions of Muslims, the legend about the invincibility of the superpowers vanished. Our boys no longer viewed America as a superpower. So, when they left Afghanistan, they went to Somalia and prepared themselves carefully for a long war. They had thought that the Americans were like the Russians, so they trained and prepared. They were stunned when they discovered how low the morale of the American soldier was. America had entered with 30,000 soldiers in addition to thousands of soldiers from different countries in the world.... As I said, our boys were shocked by the low morale of the American soldier, and they realized that the American soldier was just a paper tiger. He was unable to endure the strikes that were dealt to his army, so he fled, and America had to stop all its bragging and all that noise it was making in the press after the Gulf War in which it destroyed the infrastructure and the milk and dairy industry that was vital for the infants and the children and the civilians, and blew up dams which were necessary for the crops people grew to feed their families. Proud of this destruction, America assumed the titles of world leader and master of the New World Order. After a few blows, it forgot all about those titles and rushed out of Somalia in shame and disgrace, dragging the bodies of its soldiers. America stopped calling itself world leader and master of the New World Order, and its politicians realized that those titles were too big for them and that they were unworthy of them. I was in Sudan when this happened. I was very happy to learn of that great defeat that America suffered, so was every Muslim....

Many Americans believe that fighting army to army, like what happened in Afghanistan, is heroic for either army. But setting off bombs, killing civilians, like in the World Trade Center, is terrorism.

Bin Laden: ...After our victory over the Russians in Afghanistan, the international and the American mass media conducted fierce campaigns against us.... They called us terrorists even before the *mujahideen* had committed any act of terrorism against the real terrorists who are the Americans. On the other hand, we say that American politicians and their religion do not believe in differentiating between civilians and military, between infants and animals, or among any human groups....

Our mothers and daughters and sons are slaughtered every day with the approval of America and its support. And, while America blocks the entry of weapons into Islamic countries, it provides the Israelis with a continuous supply of arms, allowing them thus to kill and massacre more Muslims. Your religion does not forbid you from committing such acts, so you have no right to object to any response or retaliation that reciprocates your own actions. But, and in spite of this, our retaliation is directed primarily against the soldiers only and against those standing by them. Our religion forbids us from killing innocent people such as women and children. This, however, does not apply to women fighters. A woman who puts herself in the same trench with men, gets what they get....

The American people, by and large, do not know the name Osama bin Laden, but they soon likely will. Do you have a message for the American people?

Bin Laden: I say to them that they have put themselves at the mercy of a disloyal government, and this is most evident in Clinton's administration.... We believe that this administration represents Israel inside America. Take the sensitive ministries such as the Ministry of Exterior and the Ministry of Defense and the CIA, you will find that the Jews have the upper hand in them. They make use of America to further their plans for the world, especially the Islamic world. The American presence in the Gulf provides support to the Jews and protects their rear. And while millions of Americans are homeless and destitute and live in abject poverty, their government is busy occupying our land and building new settlements and helping Israel build new settlements in the point of departure for our Prophet's [Muhammad] midnight journey to the seven heavens [from Jerusalem]. America throws her own sons in the Land of the Two Sacred Mosques for the sake of protecting Jewish interests....

The American government is leading the country towards hell.... We say to the Americans as people and to American mothers, if they cherish their lives and if they cherish their sons, they must elect an American patriotic government that caters to their interests, not the interests of the Jews. If the present injustice continues with the wave of national consciousness, it will inevitably move the battle to American soil, just as Ramzi Yousef and others have done [World Trade Center bombing 1993]. This is my message to the American people. I urge them to find a serious administration that acts in their interest and does not attack people and violate their honor and pilfer their wealth....

In America, we have a figure from history from 1897 named Teddy Roosevelt. He was a wealthy man, who grew up in a privileged situation who fought on the front lines. He put together his own men—hand chose them—and went to battle. You are like the Middle East version of Teddy Roosevelt.

Bin Laden: I am one of the servants of God. We do our duty of fighting for the sake of the religion of God. It is also our duty to send a call to all the people of the world to enjoy this great light and to embrace Islam and experience the happiness in Islam. Our primary mission is nothing but the furthering of this religion.... Let not the West be taken in by those who say that Muslims choose nothing but slaughtering. Their brothers in East Europe, in Turkey and in Albania have been guided by God to submit to Islam and to experience the bliss of Islam. Unlike those, the European and the American people and some of the Arabs are under the influence of the Jewish media....

Published with the permission of FRONTLINE, a documentary series on PBS. This material was originally published on FRONTLINE'S web site "Hunting Bin Laden" http://www.pbs.org/wgbh/pages/frontline/

6

An Open Letter to Fellow Muslims in Pakistan

(24 September 2001)

Faxed to *Al Jazeera*, the letter was signed by Osama bin Laden and read on air. It called on Pakistanis to resist an American attack on Afghanistan.

A PROCLAMATION

In the name of God, the most Merciful and most Gracious

Sunday, Rajab 1, 1422 A.H. [24 September 2001]

God has reserved their reward and their light for the martyrs.

To our Muslim brothers in Pakistan,

Peace be upon you.

The news of the death of our brother Muslims in Karachi while expressing their opposition to the Crusade of American forces and their allies in the Muslim lands of Pakistan and Afghanistan has reached us with great sorrow. We ask God to accept them as martyrs and to join them with the prophets, the *caliphs*, the martyrs and those of goodwill, and to provide for their families. Those who left behind children are my children and I will, God willing, take care of them.

It's not a surprise that the Islamic nation in Pakistan will die defending Islam. It is considered on the front line of defending Islam, as Afghanistan was on the front line of defending itself and Pakistan during the Russian invasion more than 20 years ago. We hope that these brothers will be the first martyrs in the battle of Islam in this era against the new

Jewish-Christian Crusader campaign that is led by the Chief Crusader Bush under the banner of the Cross. We tell our Muslim brothers in Pakistan to use all their means to resist the invasion of the American Crusader forces in Pakistan and Afghanistan.

I convey to you good news, my beloved brothers, that we are steadfast in the way of *jihad*, following in the footsteps of the Prophet (PBUH) with the believing heroes, the people of Afghanistan and under the leadership of our *amir*, the warrior Mullah Muhammad Omar.

We ask God to help us defeat the infidels and the oppressors and to crush the new Jewish-Christian Crusader campaign in the lands of Pakistan and Afghanistan.

"*If God supports you, no force will conquer you, if He does not give you His support, who else can help you. The faithful know that He is their only support.*" [Qur'an 3:160]

Your brother in Islam,

Osama bin Muhammad bin Laden

7

Interview in *Ummat* (Karachi, Pakistan)

(28 September 2001)

In an interview in *Ummat*, an Urdu language paper based in Karachi, Pakistan, Bin Laden states that Al Qaeda had nothing to do with the 11 September 2001 attacks in Washington, D.C. and New York City. He suggests that other countries, the Jews or U.S. secret agencies were behind the attacks.

Ummat: You have been accused of involvement in the attacks in New York and Washington. What do you want to say about this? If you are not involved, who might be?

Bin Laden: In the name of God, the most Gracious, the most Merciful, Praise be to God, who is the Creator of the whole universe and who made the Earth as an abode for peace, for the whole humankind. God is the Sustainer, who sent the Prophet Muhammad (PBUH) for our guidance. I am thankful to the *Ummat* Group of Publications, which gave me the opportunity to convey my viewpoint to the people, particularly the valiant and believing people of Pakistan who refused to believe the lies of the demon [Pakistani dictator General Pervez Musharraf].

I have already said that I am not involved in the 11 September attacks in the United States. As a Muslim, I try my best to avoid telling a lie. I had no knowledge of these attacks, nor do I consider the killing of innocent women, children and other humans as an appreciable act. Islam strictly forbids causing harm to innocent women, children and other people. Such a practice is forbidden, even in the course of a battle.

It is the United States which is perpetrating every maltreatment on women, children and common people of other faiths, particularly the followers of Islam. All that has been going on in Palestine for the last 11 months is sufficient to call the wrath of God upon the United States and Israel. There is also a warning for those Muslim countries, which witnessed all these as a silent spectator. What had been done earlier to the innocent people of Iraq, Chechnya and Bosnia? Only one conclusion could be derived from the indifference of the United States and the West to these acts of terror and the patronage of the tyrants by these powers: America is an anti-Islamic power and it is patronizing the anti-Islamic forces. Its friendship with the Muslim countries is just a show, rather deceit. By enticing or intimidating these countries, the United States is forcing them to play a role of its choice. Look around and you will see that the slaves of the United States are either rulers or enemies of Muslims.

The U.S. has no friends, nor does it want to keep any because the prerequisite of friendship is to come to the level of the friend or consider him at par with you. America does not want to see anyone equal to it. It expects slavery from others. Therefore, other countries are either its slaves or subordinates. However, our case is different. We have pledged slavery to Almighty God alone, and after this pledge, there is no possibility to become the slave of someone else. If we do, it will disregard both our Sustainer and His fellow beings. Most of the world's nations upholding their freedom are the religious ones, which are the enemies of the United States, or the U.S. itself considers them as its enemies.

The countries which do not agree to become U.S. slaves are China, Iran, Libya, Cuba, Syria, Afghanistan, Pakistan, Bangladesh, Iraq, Sudan, Indonesia, Malaysia and Russia. Whoever committed the act of 11 September is not the friend of the American people. I have already said that we are against the American system, not against its people, whereas in these attacks, common American people have been killed. According to my information, the death toll is much higher than what the U.S. government has stated. But the Bush Administration does not want the panic to spread. The United States should look within itself to try to find the perpetrators of these attacks, for people who are part of the U.S. system but are dissenting against it, or for those who are working for some other system—persons who want to make the present century a century of conflict between Islam and Christianity so that their own civilization, nation, country, or ideology can survive. They can be anyone, from Russia to Israel and from India to Serbia. Within the U.S. there are dozens of well-organized and well-equipped groups who are capable of causing large-scale destruction. Then you cannot forget the American Jews, who have been annoyed with President Bush ever since the elections in Florida and want revenge against him.

Then there are the intelligence agencies in the U.S., which require billions of dollars worth of funds from Congress and the government every year. This [funding issue] was not a big problem during the existence of the former Soviet Union, but after its demise the budget of these agencies has been in danger. They needed an enemy. So, they first started propaganda against Osama and the Taliban, and then this incident happened. You see, the Bush Administration approved a budget of $40 billion. Where will this huge amount go? It will be provided to the same agencies, which need huge funds and want to exert their importance. Now they will spend the money for their expansion and for increasing their importance.

I will give you an example. Drug smugglers from all over the world are in contact with the U.S. secret agencies. These agencies do not want to eradicate narcotics cultivation and trafficking because their importance will be diminished. The people in the U.S. Drug Enforcement Department are encouraging the drug trade so that they can show performance and get multi-million dollar budgets. General Noriega was made a drug baron by the CIA, and, in need, he was made a scapegoat.

In the same way, whether it is President Bush or any other U.S. president, they cannot bring Israel to justice for its human rights abuses or to hold it accountable for such crimes. What is this? Is it not that there exists a government within the government in the United States? That secret government must be asked who carried out the attacks.

Ummat: A number of world countries have joined the call of the United States for launching attacks on Afghanistan. These also include a number of Muslim countries. Will Al Qaeda declare a *jihad* against these Islamic countries as well?

Bin Laden: I must say that my duty is only to awaken the Muslims, to tell them what is good for them and what is not, what Islam says, and what the enemies of Islam want. Al Qaeda was set up to wage *jihad* against infidelity, particularly to counter the onslaught of the infidel countries against the Islamic states. *Jihad* is the sixth undeclared pillar of Islam.[1] Every anti-Islamic person is afraid of *jihad*. Al Qaeda wants to keep *jihad* alive and active and make it a part of the daily life of the Muslims. It wants to give it the status of worship. We are not against any Islamic country, and we do not consider a war against an Islamic country as *jihad*. We are in favor of armed *jihad* only against those infidel governments which are killing innocent Muslim men, women and children just because they are Muslims.

Supporting U.S. policy is the need of some Muslim countries and the compulsion of others. However, they should think as to what will remain of their religious and moral position if they support the attack of the Christians and the Jews on a Muslim country like Afghanistan. The orders of Islamic religious law for such individuals, organizations and countries are clear, and all the scholars of the Muslim brotherhood are unanimous on them. We will do the same, which is being ordered by the Commander of the Faithful Muhammad Omar [leader of the Taliban] and the Islamic scholars. The hearts of the people of Muslim countries are beating with the call of *jihad*. We are grateful to them.

Ummat: The losses caused in the attacks in New York and Washington have proved that giving an economic blow to the U.S. is not too difficult. U.S. experts admit that a few more such attacks can bring down the American economy. Why isn't Al Qaeda targeting America's economic pillars?

---

(1) The first five are the testimony of faith "*There is no god except God and Muhammad is the Messenger of God*," prayers, fasting in Ramadan, pilgrimage to Mecca and giving alms [*zakat*].

Bin Laden: I have already said that we are not hostile to the United States. We are against the [U.S. government] system, which makes other nations slaves of the United States, or forces them to mortgage their political and economic freedom. This system is totally in the control of American Jews, whose first priority is Israel, not the United States. It is clear that the American people are themselves the slaves of the Jews and are forced to live according to the principles and laws laid down by them. So the punishment should reach Israel. In fact, it is Israel, which is giving a blood bath to innocent Muslims, and the U.S. is not uttering a single word.

***Ummat*:** Why aren't the enemies of Islam being harmed through other means, apart from the armed struggle? For instance, urging Muslims to boycott Western products, banks, shipping lines and TV channels.

Bin Laden: The first thing is that Western products can only be boycotted when the Muslim nation is fully awakened and organized. Secondly, Muslim companies should become self-sufficient in producing goods equal to the products of Western companies. An economic boycott of the West is not possible unless economic self-sufficiency is attained and substitute products are produced.

You see wealth scattered all across the Muslim World, but not a single TV channel has been acquired which can preach Islamic injunctions according to modern requirements and attain international influence. Muslim traders and philanthropists should make it a point that, if the weapon of public opinion is to be used, it is to be kept in the hand. Today's world is a world of public opinion, and the fates of nations are determined through its pressure. Once the tools for building public opinion are obtained, everything that you asked for can be done.

***Ummat*:** The entire propaganda about your struggle has so far been made by the Western media. But no information is being received from your sources about the network of Al Qaeda and its *jihad* successes. Would you comment?

Bin Laden: In fact, the Western media is left with nothing else. It has no other theme to survive for a long time. Then we have many other things to do. The struggle for *jihad* and the successes are for the sake of God and not to annoy His bondsmen. Our silence is our real propaganda. Rejections, explanations, or corrigendum only waste your time, and through them the enemy wants you to engage in things which are not of use to you. These things are pulling you away from your cause.

The Western media is unleashing such baseless propaganda, which surprises us, but it reflects on what is in their hearts, and gradually they themselves become captive of this propaganda. They become afraid of it and begin to harm themselves. Terror is the most dreaded weapon in the modern age, and the Western media is mercilessly using it against its own people. It can add fear and helplessness to the psyche of the people of Europe and the United States. It means that what the enemies of the United States cannot do, its media is doing. You can understand how a nation which suffers from fear and helplessness will perform in war.

Ummat: What will be the impact of the freeze of Al Qaeda accounts by the U.S.?

Bin Laden: God opens up ways for those who work for Him. The freezing of accounts will not make any difference for Al Qaeda or other *jihad* groups. With the grace of God, Al Qaeda has more than three alternative financial systems, which are all separate and totally independent of each other. This system is operating under the patronage of those who love *jihad*. What to say of the United States, even the combined world cannot budge these people from their path. These people are not in hundreds but in thousands and millions. Al Qaeda is comprised of modern educated youth who are as aware of the cracks inside the Western financial system as they are aware of the lines in their hands. The very flaws of the Western fiscal system are becoming its own noose, and this system cannot recuperate in spite of the passage of so many days.

Ummat: Are there safe areas other than Afghanistan, where you can continue *jihad*?

Bin Laden: There are areas in all parts of the world where strong *jihad* forces are present, from Indonesia to Algeria, from

Kabul to Chechnya, from Bosnia to Sudan, and from Burma to Kashmir. Then it is not the problem of my person. I am a helpless servant of God, constantly in fear of my accountability before God. It is not a question of Osama but of Islam and, in Islam too, of *jihad*. Thanks to God, those waging *jihad* can walk today with their heads raised. *Jihad* was present when there was no Osama, and it will remain as such even when Osama is no longer here. God opens up ways and creates affinity in the hearts of people for those who walk on the path of God with their lives, property and children. Believe it! Through *jihad* a man gets everything he desires, and the biggest desire of a Muslim is life after death. Martyrdom is the shortest way of attaining an eternal life.

Ummat: What do you say about the Pakistani government's policy with respect to an attack on Afghanistan?

Bin Laden: We are thankful to the faithful and the valiant people of Pakistan who erected a blockade in front of the evil forces and stood in the first file of battle. Pakistan is a great hope for the Islamic brotherhood. Its people are awakened, organized and rich in the spirit of faith. They backed Afghanistan in its war against the Soviet Union and extended every help to the *mujahideen* and the Afghan people. The very same Pakistanis are standing shoulder to shoulder with the Taliban. If such people emerge in just two countries, the domination of the West will diminish in a matter of days. Our hearts beat with Pakistan and, God forbid, if a difficult time comes, we will protect it with our blood. Pakistan is sacred for us like a place of worship. We are the people of *jihad*, and fighting for the defense of Pakistan is the best of all *jihad*s to us. It does not matter to us who reforms Pakistan. The important thing is that the spirit of *jihad* is alive and stronger in the hearts of the Pakistani people.

8

A Warning to the United States

(7 October 2001)

Two hours after U.S. forces began air strikes against the Taliban regime and Al Qaeda in Afghanistan, *Al Jazeera* broadcast this statement by Bin Laden that was recorded in late September or early October 2001.

Praise be to God, and we beseech Him for help and forgiveness. We seek refuge with the Lord from our bad and evildoing. He whom God guides is rightly guided, but he whom God leaves to stray, for him you will find no protector to lead him to the right way. I witness that "*There is no god except God and Muhammad is the Messenger of God.*"

There is the United States hit by Almighty God at its most vulnerable spot, destroying, praise be to God, its most prestigious buildings. There is the United States, filled with terror from its north to its south and from its east to its west, praise be to God. What the United States is suffering today is insignificant compared to what we have suffered for decades. Our Islamic nation has undergone humiliation and contempt for more than 80 years. Its sons are being killed, its blood is being shed, its sacred places are being attacked, and it is not being ruled according to what God has decreed. Despite this, no one hears and no one heeds.

When Almighty God blessed a group of Muslims, the vanguards of Islam, He allowed them to destroy the United States. I ask Almighty God to elevate their status and grant them Paradise. He is the one who is capable of doing so. When they responded to the call their oppressed sons, brothers, and sisters in Palestine, and in many other Islamic countries, the world at large shouted. The infidels shouted, followed by the hypocrites.

Although they did not do anything wrong, one million Iraqi children have thus far died in Iraq. Despite this, we have heard no condemnation by anyone in the world or a *fatwa* by the rulers' scholars. Israeli tanks and tracked vehicles have entered to wreak havoc in Palestine—in Jenin, Ramallah, Rafah, Beit Jala, and in other places in the land of Islam—but no voices have been raised nor a limb moved.

But when the sword fell on the United States after 80 years, hypocrisy raised its ugly head lamenting the deaths of these killers who have abused the blood, honor, and sanctuaries of the Muslims. The least one can say about these people is that they are morally depraved. They have championed falsehood, supported the butcher against the victim, the oppressor against the innocent child. May God show them His wrath and give them the punishment they deserve.

I say that the situation is clear and obvious. After this event senior U.S. officials, starting with Bush, the head of the world's infidels, spoke out. They came out in arrogance and force with their men and have turned even the countries that belong to Islam to this treachery. They came out to fight this group of people who declared their faith in God and refused to abandon their religion. They came out to fight Islam in the name of terrorism. Every Muslim should rush to defend his religion.

When hundreds of thousands of people, young and old, were killed in the farthest point on earth in Japan, this was not a war crime [for them] but rather a debatable issue. When they bombed Iraq and killed a million children, it was a debatable issue. But when a dozen of their people were killed in Nairobi and Dar es Salaam(1), Afghanistan and Iraq were bombed. Hypocrisy stood in force behind the head of the world's infidelity, behind the *Hubal* of the age—namely, America and its supporters.

---

(1) The bombings of the U.S. Embassies in Nairobi, Kenya and Dar es Salaam, Tanzania on 7 August 1998 resulted in the deaths of 224 people and injured over 4,000.

These events have divided the whole world into two sides—one of faith, where there is no hypocrisy; and another of infidelity, from which we hope God will protect us. The winds of faith and change have blown to remove falsehood from the [Arabian] Peninsula of the Prophet Muhammad (PBUH).

To the United States, I have only these few words: I swear by Almighty God, who has raised the heavens without pillars, that neither the United States nor he who lives in the United States will enjoy security before we can see it as a reality in Palestine and before all the infidel armies leave the land of Muhammad (PBUH).

God is great and glory to Islam. May God's peace, mercy, and blessings be upon you.

9

Interview with Tayseer Allouni

(21 October 2001)

On 21 October, Bin Laden was interviewed for approximately one hour by Tayseer Allouni, *Al Jazeera* correspondent in Kabul, Afghanistan, in a tent in Afghanistan. The interview was not broadcast until *CNN* quoted excerpts and published the transcript of the interview on 5 February 2002.

Osama bin Laden: May God greet you.

Tayseer Allouni: A question that is repeated on the tongues of a lot of people all-around the world: The U.S. claims that it has convincing proof of your involvement in the events of New York and Washington. What is your answer to that?

OBL: Praise be to God, the Lord of the worlds. May God's Peace and Blessings be upon Muhammad, his pure family and his noble Companions.

To proceed: As to its description that these acts were terroristic, then that description is wrong. These young men, whom God has cleared the way for, they have shifted the battle to the heart of the United States, and they have destroyed its most outstanding landmarks, their economic landmarks and their military landmarks, with the grace of God. And they have done this from what we understand, and we have incited and roused for this before, and it is in self-defense, in defense of our brothers and sons in Palestine and for freeing our holy sites. And if inciting for this is terrorism, and if killing the ones that kill our sons is terrorism, then let history witness that we are terrorists.

TA: Alright, but Sheikh, those who monitor your speeches and documents have connected the oath you have given recently, and you have said word for word: "I swear by God Almighty, Who lifted the sky without effort, that America will never enjoy safety, until safety becomes a reality for us living in Palestine." So, it is easy for any follower of these events to connect between the terrorist events that happened in New York and Washington and that previous statement. So, what is your opinion of these statements?

OBL: Making connections is easy. If it implies that we have incited for this, then yes, we've been inciting for years, and we released *fatawa* and documents concerning this issue and other incitements which were published and broadcasted in the media. So if they mean, or if you mean, that there is connection due to the incitement, then that is true. So we incite, and incitement is obligatory today, and God has asked this from the best of humans, the Prophet (PBUH).

God (SWT) said: "*Then fight O Muhammad* (PBUH) *in the cause of God. You are not tasked* (held responsible) *except for yourself, and incite the believers* (to fight along with you), *it may be that God will restrain the evil might of the disbelievers. And God is stronger in might and stronger in punishing*" [Qur'an 4:84]. And what He meant as the goal for the disbelievers is fighting and combat. So that connection is right; we have incited and roused for the killing of Americans and Jews. That is true.

TA: Alright, Sheikh Osama bin Laden, the Al Qaeda Organization is facing today a state that dominates the world militarily, politically and technologically. So, with what reason does the Al Qaeda Organization, whose material capabilities don't precisely come close to the capabilities of the U.S., so with what logic can an organization, like Al Qaeda, defeat the U.S.A. militarily, for example?

OBL: Praise be to God...I say that the battle isn't between the Al Qaeda Organization and the world Crusaders. The battle is between Muslims—the people of Islam—and the world Crusaders. And that organization, with the grace of God, used to be with our Afghan *mujahideen* brothers, and the people used to say words like this and even stronger: "How could you defeat the Soviet Empire?" And at that time, the Soviet Empire was a force that was very, very strong, which scared the whole world, and NATO used to shake in fear in front of the Soviet Empire. So, where is that strong force that God (SWT) sent toward us and our *mujahideen* brothers?

The Soviet Empire has become—with God's grace—a figment of the imagination. Today, there is no more Soviet Empire. It split into smaller states, and Russia is left. So the One [God], who prolonged us with one of His helping hands and stabilized us to defeat the Soviet Empire, is capable of prolonging us again and allowing us to defeat America on the same land and with the same sayings, and that is the grace of God (SWT). So we believe that the defeat of America is something achievable—with the permission of God (SWT)—and it is easier on us—with the permission of God (SWT)—than the previous defeat of the Soviet Empire.

TA: How do you think it's easy? Why do you think it's easier?

OBL: We have tried…like our brothers who have engaged in battle with the Americans, similar to the example in Somalia. We have not found before a force that can be mentioned. There is a very huge awe about America, which it uses to scare people before it engages in battle. So our brothers who were here in Afghanistan tried, and God has cleared the path for them with some of the *mujahideen* in Somalia. So America left, dragging behind the tails of humiliation, defeat and loss, without turning back for anything. It retreated before expected, and it forgot all that great media hype about the New World Order, and how it was the master of that order, and that it can do whatever it pleases. It forgot all those facts, and it picked up its armies and it retreated in defeat with God's grace (SWT). So we fought against the Russians, from '79 until '89, 10 years—with the grace of God (SWT)—then we continued against the Communists in Afghanistan. Today we are at the end of the second week, and what a difference, like night and day, between both battles. We implore God (SWT) to prolong us with one of His helping hands and to break America, for He is capable of that.

TA: Alright Sheikh, in connection to the land, you have said that you will defeat America on this land. Don't you think that the existence of the Al Qaeda Organization on the land of Afghanistan is making the Afghan people pay a high price?

OBL: Well, that view is partial and incomplete, and only from one angle. When we first came to Afghanistan to give victory to the *mujahideen* when the Russians entered in 1399 A.H. (1979 A.D.), the Saudi government officially asked us not to enter Afghanistan. Due to my entry into Afghanistan, and due to my family's closeness to the Saudi governmental system, a letter arrived, commanding Osama not to enter Afghanistan and to stay with the immigrants in Peshawar. Because in case the Russians were to imprison or capture Osama, then that would be proof showing Saudi backing of the *mujahideen* against the Soviet Empire. During that time the whole world shook in fear of the Soviet Empire, and I am not exaggerating about this prohibition [to enter Afghanistan], so from their point of view, this seemed damaging to them. They were forced because of their opinions.

When we came to the Afghans the first time, we endured what we had to endure in a desire to resurrect the Islamic self, and to protect the Muslim children and offspring here, and for victory for the religion. That is a duty on all the Muslims, not just the Afghans. So if I went, or some of my brothers that came for *jihad*, acted upon this duty, [which is] to bring victory to our brothers in Palestine, then that does not mean that Osama alone has to endure this. It is a duty for all the Islamic nation to endure this, because it is in the way of God and *jihad* is designated [obligated] today on all of us, on the Afghans and others. It is true that they endure, but this is an Islamic duty, and it is a duty for them and others to support this....[Interrupted]

TA: Let us go back to what happened....

OBL: ...in addition to the matters related to the bombing of the Afghans that say it is only due to us [the *mujahideen*], the reason is not personal. America didn't start by taking my money and didn't hurt me at all, but due to our incitement against the Jews and the Americans in protection of the Islamic nation, those words came from them. It is a known fact that America is against the establishment of any Islamic state, and the Prince of Believers [Mullah Muhammad Omar of Kandahar] has declared that on more than one occasion, and so have a lot of the big students [Taliban], indicating that they are targeted because of their religion, not just because of the presence of Osama bin Laden. Like he [Mullah Omar] said, the British came, and they were defeated in Afghanistan before Osama was to be found here, and the Russians came, before we did, and now the Americans have come. We implore God to defeat them like He defeated their previous allies.

TA: Let us go back to the transgressions that happened in New York and Washington. What is your analysis about what happened—its effect on America, and its effect on the Islamic world? The question in two parts, if you please.

OBL: I say the events that happened on Tuesday 11th September in New York and Washington is truly a great event in all measures, and its claims until this moment are not over and are still continuing. If the fall of the towers, with the twins on their head, was a huge event, then consider the events that followed it...let us talk about the economic consequences which are still continuing.

According to their own admission, the share of losses on the Wall Street Market reached 16%. They said that this number is a record, which has never happened since the opening of the market more than 230 years ago. This large collapse has never happened. The gross amount that is traded in that market reaches $4 trillion. So if we multiply 16% with $4 trillion to find out the loss that affected the stocks, it reaches $640 billion of losses from stocks, with God's grace (SWT). So this amount, for example, is the budget of Sudan for 640 years. They have lost this due to an attack, with the success of God, that lasted only one hour. The daily income of the American nation is $20 billion. The first week they didn't work at all due to the psychological shock of the attack, and even until today some don't work due to the attack. So if you multiply $20 billion by one week, it comes out to

$140 billion, and it is even bigger than this. If you add it to the $640 billion, we've reached how much? Approximately $800 billion. The cost of the building and construction losses? Let us say more than $30 billion. Then they have fired or liquidated until today, or a couple of days ago, from the airline companies more than 170,000 employees, including cargo plane companies, and commercial airlines. American studies and analysis have mentioned that 70% of the American people, even until today, still suffer from depression and psychological trauma after the incident of the two towers, and the attack on the Defense Ministry, the Pentagon—thanks to God's grace (SWT). One of the well-known American hotel companies, Intercontinental, has fired 20,000 employees—thanks to God's grace (SWT). Those claims cannot be calculated by anyone due to their very large scale, multitude and complexity—and it is increasing thanks to God's grace (SWT)—so watch as the amount reaches no less than $1 trillion by the lowest estimate—thanks to God's grace (SWT)—due to these successful and blessed attacks. We implore God to accept those brothers within the ranks of the martyrs and to admit them to the highest levels of Paradise.

But I mention that there are also other events that took place, bigger, greater and more dangerous than the collapse of the towers. It is that this Western civilization, which is backed by America, has lost its values and appeal. The immense materialistic towers were destroyed, which preach Freedom, Human Rights and Equality. It became a total mockery and that clearly appeared when the U.S. government interfered and banned the media outlets from airing our words which don't exceed a few minutes, because they felt that the truth had started to appear to the American people, and that we truly aren't terrorists by the definition they want, but because we are being violated in Palestine, in Iraq, in Lebanon, in Sudan, in Somalia, in Kashmir, in the Philippines and in every place. This is a reaction from the young men of this Islamic nation against the violations by the American government. Therefore, they declared what they declared, and they ordered what they ordered, and they forgot everything they mentioned about Free Speech, and Unbiased Opinion and all those matters. So I say that Freedom and Rights in America, and Human Rights, have been sent forward to the guillotine with no return unless they are quickly reinstated.

The government will take the American people and the West in general will enter into a choking life, into an unsupportable hell, because of the fact that those governments have very strong ties and are under the payroll of the Zionist lobby, which serves the needs of Israel, who kills our sons and our children without right so that they can keep on ruling with total control.

TA: As for the effects of these actions on the Islamic world, there has been a clash of opinions. There are some who say things that have been believed in the Islamic world, and you hear all the official statements, and the statements of the people who can make statements, always saying that those attacks are terrorist actions and that these are innocent civilians, and that we won't accept those attacks, and that those things don't concord with the modern Islamic religion, and along those lines. So, what is your opinion concerning what you have been able to follow of news concerning what is happening in the Islamic world with the network that you have or run all around the world?

OBL: I say that events have proved in a very clear manner the magnitude of the terrorism America inflicts in the world. So Bush admitted that there can only be two kinds of people: One being Bush and his followers, and any nation that doesn't follow the Bush government, or the World Crusade, then they are guaranteed to be with the terrorists. So, what kind of terrorism is more terrifying and clearer than that?

So a lot of countries that can't speak for themselves followed that strong world terrorism, and were also forced to say at the beginning that they were with him [Bush], and they all know without any doubt that we fight to protect our brothers and our holy sites. So the declarations of the leaders, either in the East or the West, were that the causes and roots of terrorism have to be removed. After asking what they are, they said it is the Palestine issue. We are part of a fair issue, but fearing America, they could not say that our issue is fair, so they call us terrorists and then ask us to fix the Palestine issue. Based on those recent events and what they ensued, Bush and Blair quickly moved and said that now is the time to create an independent nation for Palestine. God be glorified!! [Amazing]. During the last 10 years the time was not ready, only until the attacks happened??

So they won't wise up without the language of beatings and killings. As they kill us, without a doubt we have to kill them until we obtain a balance in fear. This is the first time that the scale of terror got closer between both sides, between the Muslims and the Americans in recent times. Those Americans did to us whatever they pleased, and the victim isn't even allowed to cry. Then Clinton comes out and tells us that Israel has the right to defend itself after the slaughter of Qana [in Lebanon]. They didn't even give the Israelis a warning! And when the new President Bush came with Minister Colin Powell, within the first months of their rule, they said that they would move the U.S. embassy from Tel Aviv to Jerusalem, and Jerusalem will be the eternal capital of Israel, and the Congress and the Senate clapped for them. That is hypocrisy beyond any hypocrisy, and this is a clear mistreatment.

They will not wise up unless the attacks fall on their heads, and with the grace of God (SWT), the battle has moved inside America. We will strive to keep it going—with God's permission—until victory is attained or until we meet God (SWT) [through martyrdom].

TA: But Sheikh, from what I see from your answers, you always speak about Palestine and about the Palestinian issue. So let me ask you the question, your latest statements, or precisely a statement that appeared a few years ago that preached killing Jews and Crusaders, and we remember that the title had between quotes a famous saying of the Prophet, "Expel the polytheists from the Arabian Peninsula" [Narrated by al-Bukhari 2932 and Muslim ibn al-Hajjaj 3089], you concentrated on the expulsion of the Americans from the Arabian Peninsula. So in your latest speeches we see a decrease in that. You have put forth the Palestinian issue, or like you call it the Al-Aqsa Mosque issue, to the forefront, and you moved the issue of the Land of the Two Sacred Mosques to a secondary spot, so to speak. So what is your opinion or argument on this matter?

OBL: I say that with no doubt *jihad* is mandatory on all Muslims to free the Al-Aqsa Mosque, or to save the weak in Palestine and in Lebanon and in Iraq and in all Islamic lands, and there is no doubt that freeing the Arabian peninsula from the polytheists is also mandatory on all Muslims.

Concerning the talk that Osama has put the Palestinian issue to the forefront, that is not true. "Al-Abd al-Faqir" has a speech from the year 1407 A.H. [1986] that incites Muslims to boycott American products, and I used to say that the Americans take our money and give it to the Jews so they can kill our children with it in Palestine. That is mandatory on all Muslims and this is mandatory on all Muslims, and there are a lot of mandatory things in *jihad*, like Kashmir among others, and from the battle front that was created a few years ago, the title of which was called: "The World Islamic Front for Jihad against the Jews and the Crusaders."(1) So our mention of those two issues or two topics is of utmost importance. Some of the events of recent times might push one issue over the other, so we move towards that direction without ignoring the other.

TA: What are the events that have pushed you to the Palestinian issue?

OBL: In recent times, the new rise of the blessed Uprising [*Intifada* of the Palestinians], the Uprising of Rajab, helped push towards that direction, and that was the biggest reason that helped this issue. Concerning our pushing, we only strive to do our duty without feeling religiously ashamed. All the above issues affect each other. The attack on the Americans concerning the Palestine issue helps in regards to the Land of the Two Sacred Mosques' issue, and *vice versa*, and attacking the Americans because they are considered to be a protective shield for the Jews in the areas of Tabook [a northern Saudi

---

(1) The World Islamic Front for Jihad against the Jews and the Crusaders was announced on 23 February 1998 by Bin Laden.

province close to Jordan, home of the King Faisal Air Base and the eastern regions of Saudi Arabia].

TA: Alright Sheikh, now concerning the Jews and the Crusaders, like you say, you have written *fatawa* concerning the presence of *jihad* against the Jews and Crusaders. From what we have seen from other *fatawa* written by scholars, there are some that support you, but there are also some who have argued and some who have protested your *fatawa*. They ask, under which basis can we kill a Jew just because of his religion? Or the Crusader or the Nazarene [Christian] because of his religion only? So your *fatawa* have differed and don't have any relation with the *fatawa* of the other scholars.

OBL: Praise be to God. I will say that these issues have raised a lot of *fatawa* from the Muslims. In Pakistan there are a lot of *fatawa* that appeared from scholars, one of the biggest being *Mufti* Nizamudeen Shaamzi [Head legal advisor of the Taliban], and in the land of the Arabs, precisely the Land of the Two Sacred Mosques, a lot of approved and repeated *fatawa* appeared. One of the best of them being that of Sheikh Hammood bin Abdullah bin Uqla ash-Shu'aybee, may God bless his life, who is one of the biggest scholars in the home of the Land of the Two Sacred Mosques, who incites the duty of fighting the Americans and fighting the Israelis in Palestine, making their blood and wealth permissible. There also appeared a *fatwa* from Sheikh Sulaymaan al-Ulwaan, and there also appeared a book written by one of the students of knowledge, *The Truth about the Modern Crusader Wars*, and he denounced those who say that this fighting is invalid, and whoever disagrees with true Islamic law, and spoke against other wrongdoings. Yes, so he wrote well, we implore God to bless him.

TA: What about the killing of innocent civilians?

OBL: Killing innocent civilians, like Americans and other educated people say, is something very strange to say. I mean, who is the one that said that our children and our civilians are not innocents and that their blood is permissible? In the case we kill their civilians, the whole world yells at us from east to west, and America starts pushing its allies and puppets. Who is the one that said that our blood isn't blood and their blood is blood? Who is the one that declared this? What about the people that have been killed in our lands for decades? More than 1,000,000 children died in Iraq and are still dying, so why don't we hear people cry or protest or anyone who reassures or anyone who gives condolences?

And it is said in truth of our Prophet (PBUH) in the accurately reported *Hadith*: "A woman has entered hell because of a cat she tied without giving it food or without letting it eat from the blessings of the earth" [Narrated by al-Bukhari (2236) and Muslim ibn al-Hajjaj (2242)]. And that is just because of a cat, so what about the millions of Muslims who are getting killed? Where are the educated? Where are the writers? Where are the scholars? Where are the free? Where are the ones who have one atom of faith in their hearts? How do these people move when civilians die in America, when we are killed everyday? Children are killed everyday in Palestine. There is a great dysfunction in people today which needs to be stopped right away by all means, and to recalculate the numbers [of the dead]. There is a strong instinct in humans in which they lean towards the strong without feeling it, so when they talk about us, they know we will not answer them. And if they stand behind the lines of the governments and the Americans, they will think that they will feel something we don't.

A long time ago, one of the kings that came on the ancient Arabs killed a man from the Arabs(2), so the people became tamed to the fact that kings kill humans. So the brother of the deceased stood in the front of the king and killed him, and when the victim who lost his brother was victorious, the people criticized him, saying: "You kill a king just because of your brother?" So who permitted that king? They are both equal souls, and the blood of the Muslims is equal, and in those times their blood was equal. That gentle man replied: "My brother is my king." And today all our brothers in Palestine are our kings, so we kill the kings of disbelief and the kings of the Crusaders, and the civilians among the disbelievers,

---

(2) The story is mentioned in the 85th Surah (al-Burooj), and narrated by Muslim (4/7148).

as opposed to the number of our sons they kill. This is correct both religiously and logically.

TA: So you say that this is treatment with the same action? They kill our innocent, so we kill theirs?

OBL: Yes, so we kill their innocents, and that is valid both religiously and logically. Because some of the people who talk about this issue, some talk about it from a religious point of view....

TA: What is their proof?

OBL: They say that this is wrong and impermissible, and for proof, they say that the Prophet (PBUH) forbade the killing of children and women, and that is true. It is valid and has been said by the Prophet (PBUH) [in authentic narration]....

TA: This is what we are asking about exactly! This is what we are exactly questioning ourselves about!

OBL: ...But this forbidding the killing of children and innocents...is not absolute and there are other writings that uphold it. God's (SWT) saying: "*And if you punish* [your enemy, O you believers in the Oneness of God], *then punish them with the like of that with which you were afflicted...*" [Qur'an 16:126].

The scholars and people of the knowledge, among them the author of *al-Ikhtiyarat*, and Ibn al-Qayyim, may God have mercy on him, and Shawkaani, and a lot of others, and Qurtubi, may God have mercy on him in his *Explanation of the Qur'an*, say that if the disbelievers were to kill our children and women, then we should not feel ashamed to do the same to them, mainly to deter them from trying to kill our children and women again. And that is from a religious standpoint, and those who speak without any knowledge in Islamic law, saying that killing such a child is not valid and what not, and having full knowledge that those young men, that God cleared the way for, didn't intend to kill children, but instead, they attacked the biggest center of military power in the world, the Pentagon, which contains more than 64,000 workers, a military base which has a big concentration of army and intelligence.... [Interrupted]

TA: What about the World Trade Center...?

OBL: As for the World Trade Center, the ones who were attacked and who died in it were a financial power. It wasn't a children's school! And it wasn't a residence. And the general consensus is that most of the people who were in there were men that backed the biggest financial force in the world that spreads worldwide corruption. Those individuals should stand for God, and to re-think and re-do their calculations. We treat others like they treat us. Those who kill our women and our innocent, we kill their women and innocent until they stop from doing so.

TA: But now, Sheikh Osama, the media outlets, and the security services also, say that you lead a network with a very big reach, which spreads over 40 or 50 countries as some say, and that Al Qaeda has very big capabilities, and you use those capabilities a lot to order missions. That you support many Islamic Organizations or movements which are called in some places "terrorist." The question that we ask you is: What is the magnitude of the involvement of Al Qaeda, or what is the type of involvement that exists between Al Qaeda and with the personality of Osama bin Laden?

OBL: Praise be to God. I say in response to what you said, and which I have stated before, that this matter doesn't only concern His humbled servant [Osama bin Laden], and that it is not about Al Qaeda. We are the children of an Islamic nation, with Prophet Muhammad (PBUH) as its leader, our Lord is one (SWT), our Prophet is one (PBUH), our *qibla* is one, we are one Islamic nation, and our Book [the *Qur'an*] is one. And this blessed Book, with the traditions of our generous Prophet (PBUH), has religiously commanded us with the brotherhood of faith, and all the true believers are brothers.

So the situation isn't like the West portrays it, that there is an "organization" with a specific name [such as Al Qaeda] and so on. That particular name is very old. It was born without any intention from us. Brother Abu Ubaida al-Banshiri, may God have mercy on him, created a military base to train the young men to fight against the vicious, arrogant, brutal, terrorizing Soviet empire, which was a truth to all observers.

So this place was called "The Base" ["Al Qaeda"], as in a training base, so this name grew and became. We aren't separated from this Islamic nation. We are the children of the Islamic nation, and we are an inseparable part of it, and from those public demonstrations which spread from the Far East, from the Philippines, to Indonesia, to Malaysia, to India, to Pakistan, reaching Mauritania...and so we discuss the conscience of this Islamic nation.

These young men who sacrificed themselves—may God accept them—in New York and Washington, they are the ones who speak the truth about the conscience of this Islamic nation, and they are its vibrant conscience that sees that it is imperative to take revenge against the evildoers and transgressors and criminals and terrorists that terrorize the true believers. Not all terrorism is restrained or ill-advised. There is terrorism that is ill-advised, and there is terrorism that is a good deed. If we follow their words, the criminal and the thief feel that they are terrorized by the police. So, do we tell the police that they are terrorists and that they terrorized the thief? No, the terrorism of the police towards the criminals is a good deed, and the terrorism that is being exercised by the criminals on the true believers is wrong and ill-advised. America and Israel practice ill-advised terrorism, and we practice terrorism that is a good deed which deters those from killing our children in Palestine and other places....

TA: Alright, Sheikh Osama, what is your strategy concerning the Arab states? What is being seen is that some Arab states have discussed what happened in New York and Washington, and they have backed the American claims against you and by standing behind what happened in New York and Washington. Some Arab states were most strong in their criticism, like for example the latest speech of the Saudi Interior Minister, who warned against you personally, and warned against the following of your curriculum and what you say. So, do you have a specific strategy for the Arab nations? And what is your answer to the latest declaration by the Saudi Interior Minister?

OBL: I assure that we are a part of this Islamic nation, that our goal is the victory of our Islamic nation, and the struggle to lift the humiliation, transgression, helplessness and the submissive attitude, and the removal of the man-made laws that America has forced on its agents in the area so that this Islamic nation could be ruled by the Book that has been sent down by its Creator, God (SWT).

I listened to some of the words of the Interior Minister, and he blamed us directly, also saying that "those people call Muslims disbelievers"—we seek God's refuge from this! We think that the Muslims are Muslims, and we don't call any Muslims disbelievers unless they specifically commit one of the well-known acts of annulment of Islam, while having full knowledge that this is one of the actions of annulment in religion.

I say that, in general, our concern is that this Islamic nation unites either under the words of the Book of God (SWT) or His Prophet (PBUH), and the movement of this Islamic nation to the establishment of the righteous ruler [*Caliph*] of the Islamic nation, which has been prophesized by our Prophet (PBUH) in his *Hadith* [Narrated by at-Tirmidhi], that the righteous *Caliph* will return with the permission of God (PBUH), and the Islamic nation is asked to unite itself under this Crusaders' campaign, the strongest, most powerful, and most ferocious Crusaders' campaign to fall on the Islamic nation since the dawn of Islamic history. There have been past Crusader wars, but there has never been a campaign like this one before.

Bush has declared with his own tongue [words]: "Crusade attack" [Bin Laden pronounced the words in English]. So, the oddity in this is that they have said what we didn't have to say [That this war is a Crusade]. Some people also believe, as it is said about us, like the Minister's words, that we label Muslims as disbelievers—we seek God's refuge from this! But, when Bush speaks, people make apologies for him, and they say that he didn't mean that this war is a Crusade, even though he himself said that it was a Crusade!

The image of the world today is split in two parts, like Bush said, either you are with us, or you are with terrorism. Either you are with the Crusade, or you are with Islam. Bush's image today is of him being in front of the line, carrying his big Cross while yelling. And I swear by God Almighty, whoever walks behind Bush or his plan, has rejected the teachings [faith] of Muhammad (PBUH), and this ruling is one of the clearest of rulings in the Book of God and the tradition of the Prophet (PBUH), and I advise, like I have advised before and like a lot of scholars have advised before, that the proof for this is the Almighty's words while speaking to the true believers:

> "*O you who believe! Take not the Jews and the Christians for your friends and protectors; they are but friends and protectors to each other. And if any among you takes them as friends and protectors, then surely he is one of them...*"; and this is the ruling: "*And if any among you takes them as friends and protectors, then surely he is one of them. Verily, God guides not a people unjust.*" [Qur'an 5:51]

The scholars of knowledge have said whoever takes the disbelievers as friends, protectors, and leaders has become a disbeliever, and the biggest signs of alliance are favoring their victory, in speaking, discussing and writing. So, whoever walks behind Bush and his campaign against the Muslims, then he has disbelieved in God (SWT) and His Prophet (PBUH), and God also says in the verse that follows the previous one:

> "*And you see those in whose heart there is a disease* [of hypocrisy], *they hurry for their friendship* [protection], *saying: 'We fear lest some misfortune or disaster may befall us.' May God bring a victory or a decision according to His Will. Then they will become regretful for what they have been keeping as a secret in themselves. And those who believe will say: 'Are these the men* [hypocrites] *who swore their strongest oaths by God that they were with you* [Muslims]?' *All that they did has been in vain* [because of their hypocrisy], *and they have become the losers.*" [Qur'an 5:52-53]

Ibn Katheer, may God have mercy on him, has said in his *Explanation of the Qur'an*: There were a lot of Companions who didn't know that the spearhead of the hypocrites was the disbeliever and the hypocrite, Abdullah ibn Ubayy ibn Salul.

So, when the arguments happened between the Muslims and the Jews, and when the Prophet (PBUH) decided to punish the Jews, the spearhead of hypocrisy [Abdullah ibn Ubayy] moved and stood with the Jews, and he stood in the way of the Prophet (PBUH) with the Jews, so these verses came down for this reason, and its likes. So, the ones who take the disbelievers as leaders, friends and protectors, then they have disbelieved in God (SWT) and His Prophet, so I add the following verse, to stress what I previously stated; because the one who has taken the disbelievers as leaders and protectors has become an apostate, so this verse came down:

> "*O you who believe! Whoever from among you turns back on his religion* [Islam], *God will bring people whom He will love and they will love Him; humble towards the believers, stern towards the disbelievers, fighting in the Way of God, and never afraid of the blame of the blamers. That is the Grace of God which He bestows on whom He wills. And God is All-Sufficient for His creatures' needs, All-Knower.*" [Qur'an 5:54]

So, I tell the Muslims to be very weary and careful of befriending Jews and Christians, and whoever helps them with one word, let him be devout to God, and to renew his faith so he can repent about what he did....

TA: Even the word?

OBL: Even the word, whoever upholds [supports] them with one word....

TA: Falls into this apostasy?

OBL: Falls into apostasy, a terrible apostasy, and "*There is neither power nor strength except from God.*"

TA: But Sheikh, a big part of the Islamic nation falls into this....

OBL: No...No, it is not a big part. This is the rule of God (SWT), and a clear statement in His generous Book, and it is one of the clearest of rulings!

TA: And the Arab and Islamic governments...?

OBL: Anyone that...it is no use for you to say Amr or Zayd [Meaning 'so and so']. If you know the truth, you will know its followers. You will not know the truth by looking at men. This is the Book of God (SWT) which is a constant for us. If the world became full of people who want to change things in it, that won't affect us, and it won't change our convictions at all. It is either truth or it is mischief. Either it is Islam or disbelief. So these verses...[Interrupted]

TA: Just to make things clear, if you please. Isn't it possible to forgive those states that are considered to be impotent and weak? [Literally, whose command has been defeated]. Let us take the state of Qatar, for example. The state of Qatar is a small state, whose Foreign Minister once said that he is surrounded by a supreme force that can easily wipe out his existence. Therefore, he is forced to become an ally of America and others. Isn't it possible to forgive such states? Like Kuwait, for example? Or Bahrain?

OBL: Concerning these matters, the matters that concern Islam, the matters concerning the killing of true believers and Muslims...so what the previously mentioned people do, who use compulsion [being forced] as an excuse, that is not the same compulsion that is allowed by Islamic law. That compulsion is not religiously allowed.

Now let's say, if the Emir of Qatar came and he ordered one of his men to kill your son, then we came to that soldier asking him why he killed the son of brother Tayseer, so he says: "Well brother, I am forced to do it! And you know brother Tayseer that you mean a great deal to me, but I am obligated [to kill your son]!" So the blood of the Muslims will be lost with these kinds of excuses, with this compulsion that isn't backed by the Islamic law. The soul of that soldier isn't better than the soul of your son. If he is killed, he will be killed by violation and oppression, but he [the soldier] isn't allowed to obey the Tyrant by killing your son. So this compulsion isn't religiously permitted.

TA: What is your opinion about what is being said concerning your examples and the "Clash of Civilizations"? Your constant use and repetition of the word "Crusade" and

"Crusader" shows that you...uphold that saying, the "Clash of Civilizations"....

OBL: I say that there is no doubt in this. This is a very clear matter, proven in the Book [*Qur'an*] and the tradition of the Prophet, and any true believer who claims to be faithful shouldn't discredit these truths, no matter what 'so and so' says about it. What goes for us is whatever is found in the Book of God and the tradition of the Prophet (PBUH). But, the Jews and America have come up with a fairy tale [fiction] that they tell the Muslims, and they've been unfortunately followed by the local rulers [of the Muslims] and a lot of people who are close to them, by using "world peace" as an excuse. That is a fairy tale [fiction] which has no basis whatsoever!

TA: ...Peace?

OBL: The peace that they push on Muslims is to ready and prepare them to get slaughtered, and the slaughter still goes on. So, if we try to defend ourselves, they call us "terrorists," and the slaughter still goes on. So it is said [accurately narrated] that the Prophet (PBUH) said in truth: "The Hour [Day of Judgment] will not come until the Muslims fight the Jews and kill them. When a Jew hides behind a rock or a tree, it [each rock or tree] will say: 'O Muslim, O servant of God! There is a Jew behind me, come and kill him!' All the trees will do this except the box-thorn [*al-Gharqad*, a type of thorny bush], because it is the tree of the Jews" [Narrated by al-Bukhari (3593), Ahmad, at-Tirmidhi, Ibn Maajah].

And whoever claims that there is permanent peace between us and the Jews, then he has disbelieved from what has been sent down to Muhammad (PBUH), and the battle is between us and the enemies of Islam, and that will go on until the Hour [Day of Judgment], and the so-called "Peace" or "Peace Award" [Nobel Peace Prize], that is a fairy tale that is given to the biggest blood-shedders. That man [Ronald] Reagan, the perpetrator of the Der Yassin massacre, was awarded the Peace Prize. That traitor Anwar al-Sadat, the one who sold the land and the [Palestinian] issue and the blood of the martyrs, was awarded the Peace Prize.

We are in a time, like is said in truth by our Prophet in this *Hadith*: "There will come upon the people years of deceit in which the liar will be believed, the truthful disbelieved, the treacherous will be trusted and the trustworthy held to be treacherous, and the despicable will speak out. It was said: 'Who are the despicable ones?' He said: 'The lowly, ignoble man who speaks out about the public affairs'."[(3)]

And unfortunately, that is ruling on the Islamic world today, with its big leaders, and its famous rulers. So it is a trick. They trick people and lie to them, but, with the permission of God, the liberation and grace of God is close, and the promised victory is close—God willing.

TA: So we can deduce from the words of Sheikh Osama bin Laden that he refers to the ordeal that Afghanistan is going through right now, and the war that America is waging with its allies, that it falls in the circle of a battle between the Crusaders, or whom you call Crusaders, and Islam. Alright, so how do you see an exit from this ordeal?

OBL: We are in a strong and brutal battle, like I have mentioned today, between us and the Jews, with Israel being the spearhead, and whoever backs it from Zionists and Crusaders. So we have not hesitated in the killing of the Jews who conquered the sanctuary of our Prophet (PBUH). And the ones who kill our children, women and brothers night and day, and whoever stands in their trench, he only has himself to blame.

So, if you meant how the exit from this ordeal is, then this is in the hands of the others. Like we have been violated [transgressed against], so our first duty is to remove this violation. Whoever violated us, let him remove the violation. The Jews, it appears to us and appears from the writing of the Prophet (PBUH) that we will have to fight them under that name and on this land, in this blessed land which has the sanctuary of our Prophet (PBUH).

---

(3) Narrated by Ahmad (7899), Ibn Maajah (4036), and others; this chain of narration is weak; however, it has another chain of narration reported by Ahmad (8440), and it has a witnessing narration reported by Ahmad also (3/220).

And the United States has engaged its people and it engaged itself over and over for more than 53 years. It was the one which recognized Israel, and it was the one which supported it, and it was the one that dispatched a general air bridge in 1393 A.H. (1973) during the days of Nixon, from America to Tel Aviv, with weapons and aid and men, which effected the events of the battle. So how could we not fight it [America]? It is a duty on every Muslim to fight it [America]. So if it [America] wants to survive, we have said some simple words, but America [in return] has terrorized and it has erased its values.

They have made laughable claims. They said that there is ciphering [hidden messages] in Osama's letters intended for terrorists. It is like we are living in the times of pigeon carriers, without the existence of telephones, without travelers, without the Internet, without regular mail, without faxes, without e-mail. These are laughable matters. They belittle people's intellects and are just words.

We swore that America will never dream of safety until safety becomes a reality for us in Palestine. That has exposed the American government, and that it lives as an agent of Israel, and it puts Israel's needs on top of the needs of its own people. So the case is easy, America won't be able to leave this ordeal unless it leaves the Arabian Peninsula, and it stops its involvement in Palestine, and in all the Islamic world. If we gave this equation [problem] to any child in any American school, he would easily solve it within a second. But, according to Bush's actions, the equation won't be solved unless the swords fall on their heads, with the permission of God.

TA: Alright, Sheikh Osama, do you have any message you want to address to the viewers?

OBL: I say: Concerning this ordeal and this battle between Islam and Crusaders, I want to reiterate that we will continue—with the permission of God—this *jihad* and the incitement of the Islamic nation for it, until we meet Him while He is pleased with us, and the war, like we have been promised, that is going on between us and the Jews.

So any nation that joins the Jewish trenches has only itself to blame, and as Sheikh Sulaiman Abu Ghaith has declared in some of his previous statements concerning America and Britain, so that should not be etched [meaning, those sayings shouldn't be taken literally], but indeed he gave some of the other nations a chance to review their calculations.

What is Japan's concern? What is making Japan join this hard, strong and ferocious war? It is a blatant violation of our children in Palestine, and Japan didn't predict it would be at war with us, so it should review where it stands. What is the concern of Australia in the farthest south with the case of those weak Afghans? And those weak in Palestine? What is Germany's concern with this war?

Besides disbelief and Crusade, it is a war which is repeating [bringing back] the Crusades, similarly to the previous wars. Richard the Lion Heart, and Barbarossa from Germany, and Louis from France...similar is the case today, when they all immediately went forward the day Bush lifted the Cross. The Crusader nations went forward. What is the concern of the Arab nations in this Crusaders' War? They entered it openly, without disguise, in broad daylight. They have accepted to be ruled by the Cross.

Everyone, who supports Bush with one word even without offering facilitations and aid, and whatever is so-called facilitations, is only a great traitor. They change its names by not calling it military aid. They join them in killing our sons, and they tell us that it is not facilitation and help? How can we believe that this system [the Arab governments] is collecting aid to help the weak Afghans, while being the main reason in openly giving the Land of the Two Sacred Mosques to the Americans and their allies? How can we believe them while they are one of main reasons for the death of more than one million children? I say to those people, who walk behind those rulers, don't they have hearts? Don't they have faith? How can they declare faith while they are helping those fornicating disbelievers against the children of Islam? They help them against our children in Iraq and Palestine.

I say to the ones who talk about the innocents in America, they haven't tasted yet the hurt of the loss of children, and they haven't tasted the look on the faces of their children as Palestinians and others have. With what right do our families in Palestine get denied safety? The helicopters hunt them while they are in their homes, while they are among their women and children; they remove the bodies and wounded everyday. So those fools cry about the deaths of Americans, and they don't cry about the deaths of our sons? Don't they fear receiving a similar punishment? And our Prophet (PBUH) said in truth: "He who does not join the warlike expedition [*jihad*], or equip, or looks well after a warrior's family when he is away, will be smitten by God with a sudden calamity" [Narrated by Abu Dawood (2/2497)].

So let them fear God, and repent, and let them remove the siege from those innocent children. So the Westerners are free. Europe wants to enter the war, that is their prerogative, but our duty is to fight whoever is in the trench of the Jews. America and the American people are free; they have entered the trench, and they will get what is coming to them.

And concerning us, we are in worship and in *jihad*, it is said in truth about our Prophet (PBUH): "Verily a man's standing firm in the ranks for one hour [in *jihad*] in the way of God, the Mighty and Majestic, is more virtuous than 60 years of worship."[4] So what matter is better than that? Under the pride of God (SWT), we ask the Almighty to accept from us and from you, and concerning the Muslims, I tell them to trust in the victory of God (SWT), and to answer the call of God (SWT), and the order of His Prophet (PBUH), with *jihad* against world disbelief. And I swear by God, happy are the ones who are martyred today, happy are the ones who are honored to stand under the banner of Muhammad (PBUH), under the banner of Islam, to fight the world Crusade. So let every person among them come forward to fight those Jews and Americans, and their killing is from the most important duties and most pressing things. Let them remember the teaching

---

[4] Collected by al-Bayhaqee; Al-Albaanee called it *saheeh* in *Saheeh Jaami As-Sagheer* (5151).

of the Prophet (PBUH), when he said to the boy Ibn Abbas, may God be pleased with both of them: "Young man, I shall teach you some words [of advice]: Be mindful of [preserve] God, and God will protect you. Be mindful of [preserve] God, and you will find Him in front of you. If you ask [for something], ask God. If you seek help, seek help of God. Know that if the world were to gather together to help you with anything, it would help you only with something that God had already preordained for you, and that if they gather together to harm you with anything, they would harm you only with something that God had already preordained for you. The pens have been lifted and the pages have dried" [Narrated by Ahmad, at-Tirmidhi, and others]. So don't discuss the killing of Americans with anyone, trust in the divine favor of God, and remember your appointment with God (SWT) with the presence of the Best of Prophets (PBUH).

And in conclusion, I would like to dedicate a call to the brothers in Pakistan, to the position of the Pakistani government, with a lot of sorrow. Pakistan is one of the biggest pillars of this unlucky alliance, this Crusaders' Alliance. So the movement of our brothers in Pakistan will lead to—with the permission of God (SWT)—a big attack on this unlucky [wretched] Crusader Alliance. Whoever has stood with America, by aiding them with material or immaterial things; that is disbelief and the biggest rejection of the creed and teachings of Islam. It is a duty on the brothers in Pakistan to make a strong serious move, for the victory of the religion of God (SWT) and the victory of the Prophet Muhammad (PBUH). Islam of today is calling them, O Islam! O Islam! O Islam!

Have I not delivered the message? God bear witness!

Have I not delivered the message? God bear witness!

Have I not delivered the message? God bear witness!

[Crying]

Have I not delivered the message? God bear witness!

And may the peace and mercy of God be upon all the Muslims.

Source: http://islamicawakening.com

10

Speech Against the Crusaders and the U.N.

(3 November 2001)

Shot in late October/early November 2001, the following video speech was broadcast by *Al Jazeera* on 3 November 2001. Bin Laden was dressed in camouflage and armed with an AK-47.

We praise God, seek His help, and ask for His forgiveness. We seek refuge in God from the evils of our souls and our bad deeds. A person who is guided by God will never be misguided by anyone, and a person who is left by God to go astray can never be guided by anyone. I bear witness that there is no god except God alone, Who has no partner.

Amid the huge developments and in the wake of the great strikes that hit the United States in its most important locations in New York and Washington, an unprecedented and huge media clamor was raised. It conveyed the opinions of people on these events, and people divided into two parties. The first party supported these strikes against U.S. tyranny, while the second denounced them. Afterward, when the United States launched its unjust campaign against the Islamic Emirate in Afghanistan, people also split into two parties. The first supported these campaigns, while the second denounced and rejected them.

These tremendous incidents, which have split people into two parties, are of great interest to Muslims, since many of the rulings pertain to them. These rulings are closely related to Islam and the acts that corrupt a person's Islam. Therefore, the Muslims must understand the nature and truth of this conflict so that it will be easy for them to determine where they stand.

While talking about the truth of the conflict, opinion polls in the world have shown that a little more than 80 per cent of Westerners, of Christians in the United States and elsewhere, have been saddened by the strikes that hit the United States. The polls have shown that the vast majority of the sons of the Islamic world were happy about these strikes because they believe that the strikes were in reaction to the huge criminality practiced by Israel and the United States in Palestine and other Muslim countries.

After the strikes on Afghanistan began, these groups changed positions. Those who were happy about striking the United States felt sad when Afghanistan was hit, and those who felt sad when the United States was hit were happy when Afghanistan was hit. These groups comprise millions of people.

The people of Afghanistan had nothing to do with the attacks on America, and, although there is no evidence of the involvement of the Afghani people in what happened, the entire West, with the exception of a few countries, supports this unfair, barbaric campaign. The campaign, however, continues to unjustly annihilate the villagers and civilians, children, women and innocent people. The positions of the two sides are very clear. Mass demonstrations have spread from the farthest point in the eastern part of the Islamic world to the farthest point in the western part of the Islamic world, and from Indonesia, the Philippines, Bangladesh, India and Pakistan to the Arab world and Nigeria and Mauritania.

This clearly indicates the nature of this war. This war is fundamentally religious. The people of the East are Muslims. They sympathize with Muslims against the people of the West, who are the Crusaders. Those who try to cover this crystal clear fact, which the entire world has admitted, are deceiving the Islamic nation. They are trying to deflect the attention of the Islamic nation from the truth of this conflict. This fact is proven in the Book of Almighty God [the *Qur'an*] and in the teachings of our Messenger [Muhammad], (PBUH).

Under no circumstances should we forget this enmity between us and the infidels; for, the enmity is based on creed. We must be loyal to the believers and those who believe that there is no god except God. We should also renounce the atheists and infidels. It suffices me to seek God's help against them. God says: "*Never will the Jews or the Christians be satisfied with thee unless thou follow their form of religion*" [Qur'an 2:120].

It is a question of faith, not a war against terrorism, as Bush and Blair try to depict it. Many thieves belonging to this nation were captured in the past. But, nobody moved. The masses which moved in the East and West have not done so for the sake of Osama. Rather, they moved for the sake of their religion. This is because they know that they are right and that they resist the most ferocious, serious, and violent Crusader campaign against Islam ever since the message was revealed to Muhammad, (PBUH). After this has become clear, the Muslim must know and learn where he stands *vis-à-vis* this war.

After the U.S. politicians spoke and after the U.S. newspapers and television channels became full of a clear crusading hatred in this campaign that aims at mobilizing the West against Islam and Muslims, Bush left no room for doubts or the opinions of journalists. He openly and clearly said that this war is a Crusader war. He said this before the whole world to emphasize this fact.

What can those who allege that this is a war against terrorism say? What terrorism are they speaking about at a time when the Islamic nation has been slaughtered for tens of years without hearing their voices and without seeing any action by them? But when the victim starts to take revenge for those innocent children in Palestine, Iraq, southern Sudan, Somalia, Kashmir and the Philippines, the rulers' scholars and the hypocrites come to defend the clear blasphemy. It suffices me to seek God's help against them.

The common people have understood the issue, but there are those who continue to flatter those who colluded with the unbelievers to anesthetize the Islamic nation to prevent it from carrying out the duty of *jihad* so that the word of God will be above all words. The unequivocal truth is that Bush has carried the Cross and raised its banner high and stood at the front of the queue. Anyone who lines up behind Bush in this campaign has committed one of the 10 actions that disavow one's Islam. Muslim scholars are unanimous that allegiance to the infidels and support for them against the believers is one of the major acts that disavow Islam.

"*There is neither strength nor power except from God.*" Let us investigate whether this war against Afghanistan that broke out a few days ago is a single and unique one, or if it is a link in a long series of Crusader wars against the Islamic world. Following World War I, which ended more than 83 years ago, the whole Islamic world fell under the Crusader banner—under the British, French and Italian governments. They divided the whole world, and Palestine was occupied by the British. Since then, and for more than 83 years, our brothers, sons and sisters in Palestine have been badly tortured. Hundreds of thousands of them have been killed, and hundreds of thousands of them have been imprisoned or maimed.

Let us examine recent developments. Take for example the Chechens. They are a Muslim people who have been attacked by the Russian bear which embraces the Christian Orthodox faith. The Russians have annihilated the Chechen people in their entirety and forced them to flee to the mountains where they were assaulted by snow, poverty and diseases. Nonetheless, nobody moved to support them. "*There is neither strength nor power except from God.*"

This was followed by a war of genocide in Bosnia, in the heart of Europe, in sight and hearing of the entire world. For several years our brothers have been killed, our women have been raped, and our children have been massacred in the safe havens of the United Nations and with its knowledge and cooperation. Those who refer our tragedies today to the United Nations so that they can be resolved are hypocrites who deceive God, His Prophet and the believers. Are not our tragedies but caused by the United Nations? Who issued the Partition Resolution on Palestine in 1947 and surrendered the land of Muslims to the Jews? It was the United Nations in its resolution in 1947.

Those who claim to be Arab leaders and continue to appeal to the United Nations have disavowed what was revealed to Prophet Muhammad, (PBUH). Those who refer things to international law have disavowed the legitimacy of the *Qur'an* and the tradition of Prophet Muhammad, (PBUH). This is the United Nations from which we have suffered greatly. Under no circumstances should any Muslim or sane person resort to the United Nations. The United Nations is nothing but a tool of crime. We are being massacred everyday, while the United Nations continues to sit idly by.

Our brethren in Kashmir have been subjected to the worst forms of torture for over 50 years. They have been massacred, killed and raped. Their blood has been shed, and their houses have been trespassed upon. Still, the United Nations continues to sit idly by. Today, and without any evidence, the United Nations passes resolutions supporting unjust and tyrannical America, which oppresses these helpless people who have emerged from a merciless war at the hands of the Soviet Union.

Let us look at the second war in Chechnya, which is still underway. The entire Chechen people are being embattled once again by this Russian bear. The humanitarian agencies, even the U.S. ones, demanded that President Clinton should stop supporting Russia. However, Clinton said that stopping support for Russia did not serve U.S. interests. A year ago, [Russian President] Putin demanded that the Cross and the Jews should stand by him. He told them: You must support us and thank us because we are waging a war against Muslim fundamentalism. The enemies are speaking very clearly. While this is taking place, the leaders of the region hide and are ashamed to support their brothers.

Let us examine the stand of the West and the United Nations in the developments in Indonesia when they moved to divide the largest country in the Islamic world in terms of population. This criminal, Kofi Annan, was speaking publicly and putting pressure on the Indonesian government, telling it: You have 24 hours to divide and separate East Timor from Indonesia. Otherwise, we will be forced to send in military forces to separate it by force. The Crusader Australian forces were on Indonesian shores, and in fact they landed to separate East Timor, which is part of the Islamic world.

Therefore, we should view events not as separate links, but as links in a long series of conspiracies, a war of annihilation in the true sense of the word. In Somalia, with the excuse of restoring hope, 13,000 of our brothers were killed. In southern Sudan, hundreds of thousands were killed. But when we move to Palestine and Iraq, there are no limits as to what can be said. Over one million children have been killed in Iraq, and the killing is continuing. As for what is taking place in Palestine these days, I can only say we have no one but God to complain to.

What is taking place cannot be tolerated by any nation. I do not say from the nations of the human race, but from other creatures, from the animals. They would not tolerate what is taking place. A confidant of mine told me that he saw a butcher slaughtering a camel in front of another camel. The other camel got agitated while seeing the blood coming out of the other camel. Thus, it burst out with rage and bit the hand of the man and broke it.

How can the weak mothers in Palestine endure the killing of their children in front of their eyes by the unjust Jewish executioners with U.S. support and with U.S. aircraft and tanks? Those who distinguish between America and Israel are the real enemies of the Islamic nation. They are traitors who betray God and His Prophet, and who betrayed their Islamic nation and the trust placed in them. They anesthetize the Islamic nation.

These battles cannot be viewed in any case whatsoever as isolated battles, but rather, as part of a chain in the long, fierce, and ugly Crusader war. Every Muslim must stand under the banner of "*There is no god except God and Muhammad is the Messenger of God.*"

I remind you of what our Prophet (PBUH) told Ibn Abbas, may God be pleased with him. He told him: "Boy, I am going to teach you a few words. Obey [preserve] God, He will protect you. Obey [preserve] Him, you will find Him on your side. If you ask for something, ask God. If you seek help, seek the help of God. You should know that if all people come together to help you, they will only help you with something that God has preordained for you. And if they assemble to harm you, they will only harm you with something that God has preordained for you. God wrote man's fate and it will never change."

I tell the Muslims who did their utmost during these weeks: You must continue along the same march. Your support for us will make us stronger and will further support your brethren in Afghanistan. Exert more effort in combating this unprecedented war crime. Fear God, O Muslims and rise to support your religion. Islam is calling you: O Muslims, O Muslims, O Muslims.

God bear witness that I have conveyed the message. God bear witness that I have conveyed the message. God bear witness that I have conveyed the message. God's peace and blessings be upon you.

11

Interview with Hamid Mir

(7 November 2001)

Hamid Mir, of *Dawn* and the editor of *Ausaf* (Pakistan), interviewed Bin Laden at an undisclosed location near Kabul. The interview was published in *Dawn* on 10 November 2001. In the interview Bin Laden says Al Qaeda has chemical and nuclear weapons as a deterrent.

Hamid Mir: After the American bombing of Afghanistan on October 7, you told *Al Jazeera* that the September 11 attacks had been carried out by some Muslims. How did you know they were Muslims?

Osama Bin Laden: The Americans themselves released a list of the suspects of the September 11 attacks, saying that the persons named were involved in the attacks. They were all Muslims, of whom 15 belonged to Saudi Arabia—two were from the United Arab Emirates and one from Egypt. According to the information I have, they were all passengers. *Fateha* [Chapter one of the *Qur'an*] was read on their souls [held for them] in their homes. But America said they were hijackers.

HM: In your statement of October 7, you expressed satisfaction over the September 11 attacks, although a large number of innocent people perished in them, hundreds among them were Muslims. Can you justify the killing of innocent men in the light of Islamic teachings?

OBL: This is a major point in jurisprudence. In my view, if an enemy occupies a Muslim territory and uses common people as human shields, then it is permitted to attack that enemy. For instance, if bandits barge into a home and hold a child hostage, then the child's father can attack the bandits and in that attack even the child may get hurt.

America and its allies are massacring us in Palestine, Chechnya, Kashmir and Iraq. The Muslims have the right to attack America in reprisal. Islamic religious law says Muslims should not live in the land of the infidel for long. The September 11 attacks were not targeted at women and children. The real targets were America's icons of military and economic power.

The Prophet (PBUH) was against killing women and children. When he saw a dead woman during a war, he asked why she was killed. If a child is above 13 and wields a weapon against Muslims, then it is permitted to kill him.

The American people should remember that they pay taxes to their government, they elect their president, their government manufactures arms and gives them to Israel, and Israel uses them to massacre Palestinians. The American Congress endorses all government measures, and this proves all of America is responsible for the atrocities perpetrated against Muslims—all of America, because they elect the Congress.

I ask the American people to force their government to give up anti-Muslim policies. The American people rose against their government's war in Vietnam. They must do the same today. The American people should stop the massacre of Muslims by their government.

HM: Can it be said that you are against the American government, not the American people?

OBL: Yes! We are carrying on the mission of our Prophet Muhammad (PBUH). The mission is to spread the word of God, not to indulge in massacring people. We ourselves are the target of killings, destruction and atrocities. We are only defending ourselves. This is a defensive *jihad*. We want to defend our people and our land. That is why I say that if we don't get security, the Americans, too, will not get security. This is a simple formula that even an American child can understand. This is the formula of live and let live.

HM: The head of Egypt's Al-Azhar has issued a *fatwa* against you, saying that the views and beliefs of Osama bin Laden have nothing to do with Islam. What do you have to say about that?

OBL: The *fatwa* of any official scholar has no value to me. History is full of such scholars who justify usury, who justify the occupation of Palestine by the Jews, who justify the presence of American troops around the Two Sacred Mosques. These people support the infidels for their personal gain. The true scholars support the *jihad* against America. Tell me, if Indian forces invaded Pakistan, what would you do? The Israeli forces occupy our land, and the American troops are on our territory. We have no other option but to launch *jihad*.

HM: Some Western media claim that you are trying to acquire chemical and nuclear weapons. How much truth is there in such reports?

OBL: I heard the speech of American President Bush yesterday. He was scaring the European countries that Osama wanted to attack with weapons of mass destruction. I wish to declare that if America uses chemical or nuclear weapons against us, then we may reply with chemical and nuclear weapons. We have the weapons as a deterrent.

HM: Where did you get these weapons from?

OBL: Go to the next question.

HM: Demonstrations are being held in many European countries against the American attacks on Afghanistan. Thousands of protestors were non-Muslims. What is your opinion about those non-Muslim protestors?

OBL: There are many innocent and good-hearted people in the West. The American media instigates them against Muslims. However, some good-hearted people are protesting against American attacks because human nature abhors injustice.

The Muslims were massacred under U.N. patronage in Bosnia. I am aware that some officers of the State Department resigned in protest. Many years ago the U.S. ambassador in Egypt resigned in protest against the policies of President Jimmy Carter. Nice and civilized individuals are everywhere. The Jewish lobby has taken America and the West hostage.

HM: Some people say that war is no solution to any issue. Do you think that some political formula could be found to stop the present war?

OBL: You should put this question to those who started this war. We are only defending ourselves.

HM: If America got out of Saudi Arabia and the Al-Aqsa Mosque [in Jerusalem] was liberated, would you then present yourself for trial in some Muslim country?

OBL: Only Afghanistan is an Islamic country. Pakistan follows English law. I don't consider Saudi Arabia an Islamic country. If the Americans have charges against me, we too have a charge sheet against them.

HM: Pakistan's government decided to cooperate with America after September 11, which you don't consider right. What do you think Pakistan should have done but to cooperate with America?

OBL: The government of Pakistan should have the wishes of the people in view. It should not have surrendered to the unjustified demands of America. America does not have solid proof against us. It just has some surmises. It is unjust to start bombing on the basis of those surmises.

HM: Had America decided to attack Pakistan with the help of India and Israel, what would have Pakistan done?

OBL: What has America achieved by attacking Afghanistan? We will not leave the Pakistani people and the Pakistani territory at anybody's mercy. We will defend Pakistan. But we have been disappointed by Gen. Pervez Musharraf. He says that the majority is with him. I say the majority is against him.

Bush has used the word Crusade. This is a Crusade declared by Bush. It is not wisdom to barter off the blood of Afghan brethren to improve Pakistan's economy. He will be punished by the Pakistani people and God. Right now a great war in Islamic history is being fought in Afghanistan. All the big powers are united against the Muslims. It is a grace from God to us to participate in this war.

HM: A French newspaper has claimed that you had kidney problems and had secretly gone to Dubai for treatment last year. Is that correct?

OBL: My kidneys are all right. I did not go to Dubai last year. One British newspaper has published an imaginary interview with an Islamabad dateline with one of my sons who lives in Saudi Arabia. All this is false.

HM: Is it correct that a daughter of Mullah Omar is your wife, or your daughter is Mullah Omar's wife?

OBL: [Laughs] All my wives are Arabs and all my daughters are married to Arab *mujahideen*. I have a spiritual relationship with Mullah Omar. He is a great and brave Muslim of this age. He does not fear anyone but God. He is not under any personal relationship or obligation to me. He is only discharging his religious duty. I, too, have not chosen this life out of any personal consideration.

12

Message to the Youth of the Muslim Nation

(9 December 2001)

Posted on-line at *azzam.com*, Bin Laden's message is addressed to young Muslims, calling them to rally to the cause of Islam. Some experts have doubted its authenticity.

My beloved brothers in Islam,

Peace be upon you, and may God's mercy and blessings be upon you.

We have been struggling right from our youth, sacrificing our homes, families and all the luxuries of this worldly life in the path of God. We ask God to accept our efforts. In our youth, we fought with and defeated the former U.S.S.R., with the help of God, a world superpower at the time, and now we are fighting the U.S.A. We have never let the Muslim nation down. We should realize that this life is temporary, and eventually we have to return to God (SWT), the Lord of the Heavens and the Earth.

"Truly to God we belong and truly to God we shall return."

Muslims are being humiliated, tortured and ruthlessly killed all over the world, and it is time to fight these Satanic forces with the utmost strength and power. Today, the whole of the Muslim nation is depending, after God, upon the Muslim youth, hoping that they will never let them down.

Jihad has become obligatory upon each and every Muslim. We advise the Muslim youth not to fall victim to the words of some scholars who are misleading the Muslim nation by stating that *jihad* is still voluntary. The time has come when all Muslims in the world, especially the youth, should unite and soar against disbelievers and continue *jihad* till these forces are crushed to naught, all the anti-Islamic forces are wiped off the face of this Earth, and Islam takes over the whole world and all the false religions.

> "*And fight them until there is no more oppression, and there prevail justice and faith in God altogether and everywhere; but if they cease, verily God does see all that they do.*" [Qur'an 8:39]

We ask God (SWT) to rank us amongst His truthful servants.

And peace be upon you, and may God's mercy and blessings be upon you.

Your brother,

Osama bin Laden

13

Bin Laden's Supplication

(14 December 2001)

Published in *Al-Majallah* (London), October 27-November 2, 2002, this document's authenticity has not been confirmed.

In the name of God, the Merciful, the Compassionate.

The will of one seeking the support of Almighty God, Osama bin Muhammad bin Laden.

Praise be to God and peace be upon the Master of the Messengers, his family, and his Companions. We ask for God's forgiveness, seek His guidance, and seek refuge in Him for our sins and evil actions. And such as God guides there can be none to lead astray; to such as God rejects from His guidance, there can be no guide. I witness that "*There is no god except God and Muhammad is the Messenger of God.*" We pray to God (SWT) to accept us with the martyrs and the virtuous ones among His worshippers and to make us die Muslims.

God commanded that when death approaches any of us that we make a bequest to parents and next of kin and to Muslims as a whole who are in the ill-omened age like parents and next of kin. What grieves them grieves me and saddens me; and God (SWT) is a witness to what I say. God bears witness that the love of *jihad* and death in the cause of God have dominated my life, and 'The Verse of the Sword' permeated every cell in my heart: "*And fight the pagans all together as they fight you all together*" [Qur'an 9:36]. How many times did I wake up to find myself reciting this glorious verse!

If every Muslim asks himself why our Islamic nation has reached this state of humiliation and defeat, then his obvious answer is because it rushed madly for the comforts of life and discarded the Book of God behind its back, though it is the only one that has its cure and deliverance in the fleeting and afterlife. The Jews and Christians have tempted us with the comforts of life and its cheap pleasures, and invaded us with their materialistic values before invading us with their armies, while we stood like women doing nothing because the love of death in the cause of God has deserted our hearts.

My *mujahideen* brothers and I were grieved when we saw our Islamic nation in the East and West watching the United States, the head of unbelief, inflicting the worst of torments on oppressed men, women, and children, while the Islamic nation watched the painful scene as if it were watching an entertainment movie. The principal cause of our Islamic nation's ordeal is its fear of dying in the cause of God. The situation was overturned as we saw the cowardly Crusaders and the humiliated Jews remain steadfast in the fighting while the soldiers of our Islamic nation lifted a white flag and surrendered to the enemies like women—may God give us strength. Only very few of the students of religion [Taliban] remained steadfast. The rest surrendered or fled before they encountered the enemy. Today, the Islamic nation has failed to support us and to support the loyal ones from the Taliban who established the first Islamic state in Afghanistan that applied God's law. The evidence of this is America's hatred for the Taliban and their fundamental laws.

It, in collusion with its agents in the Northern Alliance and other governments who mobilized their intelligence services to serve the United States, Britain, and the infidel West, repealed the fundamental laws that the Taliban's government had enacted. It repealed the laws on veils and growing beards, and restored the practices of imitating the infidels.

The Islamic nation is guided to the straight path by its clerics. Our disease today is that the Islamic nation's clerics have turned away from their mission of guiding the Islamic nation. Their aberrance and misguidance have reached a level that the Muslim cannot believe. They came to Afghanistan to deter its clerics from destroying the Buddhist statues, but the virtuous Taliban's clerics sent them back empty handed.

The argument of Sheikh (...) and his companions was the need to satisfy the Jews, Christians, and their public opinion. They forgot Almighty God's words: "*Never will the Jews or the Christians be satisfied with you unless you follow their form of religion*" [Qur'an 2:120].

These clerics betrayed their mission of serving the Islamic nation and its causes, championed its enemies, and became hostile to its *mujahid* vanguards who inflicted on the United States the first defeat in its history, and which, God willing, will be like the Mutah conquest that was commanded by the Messenger of God and led to the disappearance of their state.

The New York and Washington actions represented the third of the increasing blows dealt to the United States. The first was the bombing of the Marines in Lebanon, and the second was the bombing of the U.S. Embassy in Nairobi from where the U.S. invasion of Somalia was launched, during which 31,000 of our brothers were killed under the U.N. flag. Despite the setback that God (SWT) has tried us with, this battle will lead to the disappearance of the United States and the infidel West, even if after dozens of years.

O youth of the Islamic nation. Crave death and life will be given to you. Listen to the few of the Islamic nation's clerics who are adhering to the rule, guiltlessness, and loyalty, and who are hostile to those loyal to the Islamic nation's enemies who have adopted the temporal ideas and the customs and corruptions of the pagan nations, such as borrowing from usurious banks, the criminal penal codes, and the secular dealings and insurances, and allowed the establishment of parties, labor associations, women's societies, all of which are unacceptable fads, as the ancestral clerics and their successors had unanimously ruled.

O clerics of Islam. You are today a small minority, and I know you by name and read your statements and your truthful *fatawa*. But I do not want to mention you by name so as not to give the enemies of God the excuse they are looking for to persecute you in these days that are critical for us.

O women kinfolk. Do not ever use cosmetics or imitate the whores and mannish women of the West. Be a school that graduates men and *mujahideen* in the cause of God, protect your honor, and be a good example for the mothers of the faithful.

O wives. May God bless you. You were, after God (SWT), the best support and the best help from the first day you knew that the road was full of thorns and mines. You left the comforts of your relatives and chose to share the hardships next to me. You renounced worldly pleasures with me. Renounce them more after me. Do not think of remarrying, and you need only to look after our children, make sacrifices and pray for them.

As to you my children, forgive me because I have given you only a little of my time since I answered the call of *jihad*. I have shouldered the Muslims' concerns and the concerns of their causes. I have chosen a road fraught with dangers and for this sake suffered from hardships, embitterment, betrayal and treachery. If it were not for treachery, the situation would not be what it is now, and the outcome would not be what it is now. I advise you to fear God, for it is the most precious provision in life. I advise you not to work with Al Qaeda and the Front [Islamic Front for Fighting the Jews and Christians], as Umar Bin-al-Khattab advised his son Abd Allah, may God be pleased with them. He forbade him from becoming *Caliph* and said: "If it is good, then we have had our share; if it is bad, then it is enough for all the family of al-Khattab what Umar had had from it."

My last advice to all the *mujahideen*, wherever they are: Recover your breath and forget for the time being the fight against the Jews and Crusaders. Devote yourselves to purging your ranks of the agents and the weak, and the bad clerics who are refraining from *jihad* and who have let the Islamic nation down.

Your brother Abu-Abd Allah Osama bin Muhammad bin Laden

Friday, 28 Ramadan 1422 A.H. (14 December 2001)

14

The Gaunt Tape

(26 December 2001)

Looking haggard, Bin Laden made this tape in late November 2001. *Al Jazeera* aired a five-minute segment on 26 December and broadcast the full 33-minute video on 27 December 2001.

We praise God, seek His help, and ask for His forgiveness. We seek refuge in God from the evils of our souls and our bad deeds. A person who is guided by God will never be misguided by anyone, and a person who is not guided by God can never be guided by anyone. I bear witness that "*There is no god except God and Muhammad is the Messenger of God.*"

Three months after the blessed strikes against world infidelity and its leader, America, and almost two months after the fierce Crusade against Islam, it gives us pleasure to speak about some of the ramifications of these events. These events have revealed extremely important truths to Muslims. It has become clear that the West in general and America in particular bear an unspeakable Crusader hatred against Islam.

Those who have lived under the continuous U.S. bombardment the past months by the various kinds of aircraft are well aware of this. Many innocent villages have been destroyed and millions of people made homeless during freezing cold weather. Although they were innocent, these oppressed men, women, and children now live in tents in Pakistan. On mere suspicion, America launched this fierce campaign. Had America had enough evidence that made it certain that those who carried out this action belonged to Europe—such as the IRA—it would have had a lot of means to address this problem. Because the matter was mere suspicion pointing to the Islamic world, the Crusader hatred against the Islamic world appeared very clearly.

While saying this, I would like to emphasize the truth of the conflict between us and the United States. This truth is very important and serious, not only for the Muslims but also for the entire world. The United States leveled accusations against this group of *mujahideen* who left their countries to undertake *jihad* for the sake of God. These accusations are not based on any evidence. It is only a case of tyranny, injustice and aggression. Praise be to Almighty God, the history of the Arab *mujahideen* is clear and clean. Those *mujahideen* left 20 years ago when the true, detestable terrorism appeared at the hands of the Soviet Union against those heroes and the innocent people in Afghanistan. The Arab *mujahideen* left their work, universities, families, and kinfolk to please God and champion the religion of God and the oppressed Muslims. It is unreasonable as some people allege that those who left their countries to champion the oppressed should go today to kill innocent people.

At that time America supported all those who took part in *jihad* against and fought the Russians. When God granted His grace to the Arab *mujahideen* to support the oppressed in Palestine and innocent children, America became angry and hostile to all those who fought in Afghanistan.

What is going on in Palestine is extremely clear. All of humanity since the time of Adam, may peace be upon him, have agreed on this [what is going on in Palestine]. Although the natural instincts of people may become corrupt, and people may differ on many things, there are natural instincts which God preserves and thus never become corrupt, except in the case of those who go astray and go too far in injustice and aggression. One of the agreed-upon facts is that people cannot kill children, even if some injustice and aggression is committed against them. What happened in Palestine and what is happening there today in terms of the deliberate murder of children is very ugly. This highest degree of injustice and aggression threatens all of humanity. Except in rare cases, history has never known anyone who killed children. This was the method of the Pharaoh. God granted grace to and saved the Israelites from the Pharaoh. "*And remember, we delivered you from the people of the Pharaoh, they set you hard tasks and punishments, slaughtered your sons and let your womenfolk live*" [Qur'an 14:6].

The head of injustice, infidelity, and aggression, namely, the Pharaoh, was known for slaying children. However, the Israelites have used the same method against our Palestinian children. The whole world saw the Israeli soldiers killing Muhammad al-Durrah and many others. The whole world—both in the East and the West and regardless of their sects—condemned that action. However, America is pressing ahead with its injustice by supporting the unjust ones and aggressors against our people in Palestine. Almighty God explained that if a soul commits aggression and reaches the level of killing a soul without guilt, then this is extremely ugly. What is uglier than this is the killing of innocent children. God says: On that account, "*We ordained for the children of Israel that if anyone slew a person—unless it be for murder or spreading mischief in the land—it would be as if he slew the whole people; and if anyone saved a life, it would be as if he saved the life of the whole people*" [Qur'an 5:32].

It is as if they—Israel, backed by America—have killed all the children in the world. What will prevent Israel from killing our children tomorrow in Tabuk, al-Jawf, and other areas? What will the rulers do if Israel expands its territories, according to their unjust and false books, and announces that its borders reach Medina? What will the rulers do while they are subservient to this Zionist-American lobby?

Therefore, fair-minded people must wake up. What befell Muhammad al-Durrah and his brothers will befall their [the rulers'] children and women in the future. "*There is neither power nor strength except from God.*" So, this issue is of utmost gravity. The United States is practicing a detestable terrorism in its ugliest forms in Palestine and Iraq. Bush the father—the ill-famed man—was the reason behind the killing of over one million children in Iraq, in addition to men and women.

What happened on September 11th is nothing but a reaction to the continuing injustice being done to our children in Palestine, Iraq, Somalia, southern Sudan, and elsewhere, as well as Kashmir and Asia. This truth concerns the Islamic nation in its entirety. This is something that requires people to rise from their slumber and rush to find a solution to this disaster which threatens mankind. Those who condemned these operations looked at the [September 11th] event as an isolated event. They did not connect it to previous events and the reasons behind it. Therefore, their view is parochial and is neither grounded in Islamic religious law nor in reason. They simply saw the people, the United States, and the media criticizing these operations. Therefore, they criticized them.

In doing so, they act just like the wolf, which upon seeing a lamb, said: "You are the one who muddied my water last year." The Lamb replied: "It was not me who did it." The wolf replied: "No, it was you." The Lamb then said: "I was born only this year." The wolf replied: "So, it was your mother who muddied my water." The wolf then ate the lamb. Upon seeing her child being torn under the fangs of this wolf, the poor mother, motivated by the sentiment of motherhood, butted the wolf without causing him any injury. The wolf cried, saying: "Look at this terrorist." So, the parrots repeated what the wolf said. They said: "Yes, we denounce the butting of the wolf by the female sheep." Where were you when the wolf ate the female sheep's lamb?

These blessed and successful strikes were reactions to what has happened in our land—in Palestine, Iraq, and elsewhere. By continuing this policy, America [changes his thought] with the assumption of power by George Bush the son, who started his term in office by launching violent air strikes on Iraq to affirm a policy of injustice and aggression and that the blood of Muslims has no value. This led to this blessed reply, thanks to Almighty God. These blessed attacks have great meaning, for they have clearly shown that this arrogant and supercilious power, the *Hubal* of the age, America, is fragile, and America, thanks to Almighty God, despite having great economic power, collapsed very quickly.

Those who carried out the attacks [September 11th] were not 19 Arab countries, and those who moved were not the armies and ministries of Arab countries, which have become used to the submission and injustice afflicting us in Palestine and elsewhere. Rather, they were 19 youths; I hope God will accept them. They shook America's throne and struck the U.S. economy in the heart. They struck the largest military power deep in the heart, thanks to Almighty God. This is clear proof that this international usurious, damnable economy, which America uses along with its military power to impose infidelity and humiliation on weak people, can easily collapse. Thanks to Almighty God, those blessed attacks, as the Americans themselves have admitted, inflicted on the New York and other markets more than a trillion dollars in losses. With small capabilities, they studied in the enemy's schools and used the enemy's planes. So they did not need training camps. Rather, God helped them, and they taught those arrogant people, who see freedom as meaningless if not belonging to the white race, a tough lesson. Americans believe that other people must be humiliated and enslaved. They do not react, but rather applaud their leaders when they strike us, as was the case before in Iraq.

Despite America's recent show of its military power in Afghanistan, and despite its pouring of anger on the weak people of Afghanistan, we learned, thanks to Almighty God, great and important lessons on how to confront this arrogant power. For example, if the front-line with the enemy is 100 kilometers long, the line should be wide. This means we should not be satisfied with a defensive line that is 100, 200, or 300 meters wide. Rather, the line should be a few kilometers wide. Wide and long trenches should be dug, thereby reducing the intensity of the U.S. bombing before the destruction of these lines. There should be light and fast forces to move from one line to another and from one defensive unit to another. We learned this following the intensive U.S. bombardment of the northern lines and the Kabul lines. In this way, years will pass and America—God willing—will not be able to break the lines of the *mujahideen*.

On the other hand, fighting has two elements: The fighters and the money to buy weapons. This truth is asserted in many verses in God's Book [the *Qur'an*]. "*God has purchased of the Believers their persons and their goods for theirs in return is the Garden of Paradise*" [Qur'an 9:111]. So the two elements of fighting are money and souls.

Although U.S. military power is far from us and our weapons cannot reach their aircraft, it is possible to absorb these attacks through wide defensive lines. There is another way by hitting the economic structure, which is basic for the military power. If their economy is destroyed, they will be occupied with their own affairs rather than enslaving weak peoples. It is very important to concentrate on hitting the U.S. economy by all possible means.

We have witnessed the true crimes of those who call themselves humanists and claim to be defenders of freedom. Only seven grams of explosives is needed to kill a human being, yet the United States has used bombs weighing seven million grams, proving their hatred of the Taliban and Muslims.

When the youth, may God receive them as martyrs, blew up the U.S. embassy in Nairobi [7 August 1998], less than two tons of explosives were used. The United States said it was a terrorist act with a weapon of mass destruction. However, the U.S. did not refrain from dropping two shells, each weighing seven million grams. After they [the Americans] bombed entire villages, without any justification, to terrorize people and make them scared of hosting the Arabs or coming close to them, the [U.S.] Secretary of Defense said it was their right to annihilate people as long as they are Muslims and not Americans. This is a blatant crime. It is clear and conspicuous, and all the statements you hear them say that it was carried out by mistake are pure and clear lies.

A few days ago, they claimed they bombed Al Qaeda positions in Khost and dropped—in what they said was a mistake—a guided missile on a mosque while Muslims were praying. An investigation confirmed that scholars were performing their Ramadan night prayers in the mosque. They had a meeting after these prayers with the hero *Mujahid* Sheikh Jalal-al-Din Haqqani, one of the most prominent former leaders of the *jihad* against the Soviet Union, who rejected this U.S. occupation of Afghanistan. The Americans killed 150 Muslim worshippers. This was their fate, but Sheikh Jalal was not hurt, may God grant him long life. This is the Crusader hatred.

Those who repeat words, without realizing their meaning, should be careful when they say that they condemn terrorism. Terrorism against the United States is commendable because it is a response to injustice, aimed at forcing the United States to stop its support of Israel, which kills our people.

The issue is very clear, cannot you be reasonable? America and the Western leaders have repeatedly said that Hamas and Islamic Jihad in Palestine and other warring organizations are terrorist organizations. If self-defense is terrorism, what is then legitimate? Our defense and our fighting are not different from the fighting of our brothers, such as Hamas, in Palestine. We fight for the sake of Almighty God and to make the word of God the higher word and the word of the unbelievers the lower one, and to end the oppression inflicted on the weak in Palestine and elsewhere.

This matter is very clear. No wise Muslim should stand in that trench under any pretext. This is the most dangerous, fiercest, and most savage Crusader war launched against Islam. God willing, the end of America is imminent, and its end does not depend on whether this servant of God, Osama, is alive or dead, for the awakening of the Islamic nation has begun. This has been the fruit of these operations.

I beseech Almighty God to accept these young men as martyrs and to group them together with the prophets, the pious believers, the martyrs, and the virtuous people, and those are the best of companions. These young men have done a great deed, a glorious deed. May God reward them well. We beseech God to make them good assets for their mothers and fathers. They have raised the heads of Muslims, and they gave the United States a lesson which it will not forget, God willing. In a previous interview with *ABC* television, I warned that if it enters into a conflict with the sons of the Land of the Two Sacred Mosques, the United States will forget the horrors of Vietnam. This, indeed, is the case; praised be God. What is to come is even greater, God willing.

Fifteen young men came from the Land of the Two Sacred Mosques; we beseech God to accept them as martyrs. They came from the land of faith, which houses the Muslims' largest treasure. A saying by the Prophet (PBUH) says: "Faith sticks to the sacred Medina as a snake sticks to its hole." Also, two young men came from the eastern part of the Arabian Peninsula, from the United Arab Emirates. Another, Ziyad al-Jarrah, came from Al-Sham [Greater Syria], and we beseech God to accept him as a martyr. Another, Muhammad Atta, came from Egypt. We beseech God to accept them all as martyrs. With their action, these young men gave great examples. They showed that the faith in their hearts dictates many requirements. It dictates that souls must be given for the sake of God. These men opened a great door to virtue and goodness.

Those we hear in the media saying that martyrdom-seeking operations are unacceptable are only repeating the whims of tyrants, the whims of America and its agents. An Islamic nation of 1,200 million Muslims is being butchered from east to west every day—in Palestine, in Iraq, in Somalia, in southern Sudan, in Kashmir, in the Philippines, in Bosnia, in Chechnya, and in Assam—and we do not hear anything from them. But if the victim and oppressed rise to sacrifice their souls for their religion, then we hear their voices. No one hears the voice of the 1,200 million Muslims who are being butchered. But if one man rises to defend the victims, they rise to repeat the whims of the tyrants, with no mind and no reason.

In the story of the boy, the king, the magician, and the monk, there is clear proof that one can sacrifice one's self for the sake of God. There is another meaning here; namely, that victory, as people tend to believe, is not recognized only through ostensible gains. Rather, victory is adherence to principles.

God mentioned the people of the rift, eternalized their story, and praised them for holding on to their faith. They were threatened with fire if they refused to give up their faith; however, they refused to announce unbelief in Almighty God and were placed into the fire. When toward the end of the story of the boy, the unjust king ordered they be thrown into the rift, a weak woman came carrying her son. When she saw the fire she became desperate and worried about her son. As the Prophet said, the son told his mother to be patient because she was right.

No Muslim would, in any case, wonder what was gained by the perpetrators of the September 11th attacks or say that they wasted their lives, and whoever says so is a complete ignoramus. They won the satisfaction of Almighty God and the heaven God promised them. For victory is not only material gain but also adherence to principle.

In a tradition of the Prophet (PBUH), an ignorant boy shuttled between a magician and a monk. Once, when an animal blocked a road to people, the boy said he would now know who was better, the monk or the magician. Given his ignorance, the boy was unable to decide who was better, which would have given him peace of mind. He asked God to show him who was better. If the monk was dearer to God, then he would kill this animal. The boy then took a stone and killed the animal. The monk came to the boy and told him: "My son, you are today better than me." Despite the monk's knowledge and the boy's ignorance, God filled the heart of this boy with the light of faith. The boy then started to sacrifice for the sake of God.

The youth of Islam expect their scholars to say such words. They expect them to tell those who carried their heads on their shoulders for the sake of God the words that the scholar told that boy. They expect them to say: You are now better than us. This is the truth.

In a tradition of the Prophet (PBUH), people differ from one another based on the extent of their faith in God. It is not only the acquisition of knowledge, but also the use of it. As the Prophet (PBUH) said: "He who struggled against them with his hand is a believer, he who struggled against them with his tongue is a believer, and he who struggled against them with his heart is a believer." And whoever fails to do any of these has no grain of faith.

They struggled against the biggest infidelity with their hands and hearts. We hope God will accept them as martyrs. Those, as was reported in *Sahih Al-Jami* [a book containing the Prophet's traditions], are Hamzah bin Abd al-Muttalib, the best of all martyrs, an unknown man whose heart God filled with faith, and a man who stood up to rebuke an unjust *imam*, and the *imam* scolded him and then killed him.

This person won a great deal. He did not live in the time of the followers [who lived after the time of the Prophet Muhammad and followed his traditions] and even did not live in the time of the esteemed Companions. God elevated this person to the status of the best of all martyrs. Our Prophet (PBUH) urged us to do this. So how could a sane Muslims say: How did this person benefit? This is manifest misguidance. We ask God to spare us such misguidance.

God enabled those young people to say to the head of world infidelity—America and its allies: You are in the wrong, and you are misguided. They sacrificed themselves for the sake of "*There is no god except God.*"

There is much to say about these grave events. However, I will talk briefly and concentrate on the need to continue the *jihad*, militarily and economically, against the United States. Praise be to God, the United States has declined. The economic bleeding continues, but it requires further attacks. Young people should make an effort to look for the key pillars of the U.S. economy and attack them, God willing.

Before I conclude, I would like to mention those heroes, those men, those great giants, who removed the disgrace that befell our nation. I would like to recite some poetry in praise of them and all those who follow the path of the Prophet Muhammad (PBUH). Before that, I would like to emphasize a point, which is that the battles that are taking place around the clock today in Afghanistan, especially against the Arab *mujahideen* and the Taliban, have clearly revealed the extent of powerlessness of the U.S. government, the extent of U.S. weakness, and the fragility of the U.S. soldier. Despite a huge development in military technology, they could not do anything, except by relying on the renegades and the hypocrites. What is the difference today between Babrak Karmal, who brought in the Russians to occupy his country and the deposed President Burhannuddin? Religion is innocent of Burhannuddin. Is there any difference between the two? The former brought in the Russians to occupy the land of Islam, and the latter brought in the Americans to occupy the land of Islam. This shows, as I have clearly mentioned, the weakness of the American soldier, praise be to Almighty God. Therefore, the opportunity should be taken, and young people should continue *jihad* and attacks against the Americans.

I conclude by reciting some poetry about those heroes who came from the land of the Hejaz, from the land of faith—from Ghamid, Zahran, Bani-Shihr, Harb, and Najd. We pray to God to accept them all [as martyrs]. There are also those who came from sacred Mecca: Salim and Nawwaf al-Hazimi and Khalid al-Mihdar. There are those who left from sacred Medina. Those people forsook life and its pleasures for the sake of "*There is no god except God.*"

I bear witness that they are sharper than any sword,
How often have they encountered hardship,
Staged assaults and showed fortitude.
How different are those who sold their souls to God,
Who smile in the face of death while the sword frowns on them,
Who use their chests as shields to protect their call.
When darkness spreads and gluttonous fangs bite us,
When our land is overfilled with blood,
When the tyrant moves freely in it,
And from the battlefield shining swords and horses disappear,
And the sound of music and drums becomes louder than moans,
Their storms blew to destroy his buildings and tell him,
We shall not stop the raids unless you depart our land.
God's peace, mercy, and blessings be upon you.

15

On Palestine

(28 March 2002)

The following communiqué appeared in the *Al-Quds Al-Arabi* newspaper (London). In it Bin Laden speaks on the current state of affairs in Palestine.

Praise be to God who says: "*O Prophet, strive against the infidels and the hypocrites,*" [Qur'an 9:73] and peace and prayers be upon the head of the *mujahideen* and the leader of those who on the Day of Judgment are identified by the shining emblems on their foreheads and their arms. Peace and prayers be upon the Prophet's kin and upon his Companions who carried the banner and defended the Islamic faith and the Muslim's sanctuary.

The Almighty says: "*Those who conceal what we have revealed of the clear signs and the guidance after we have made them clear in the Scripture, such are whom God curses and such are those who are cursed by those who curse*" [Qur'an 2:159].

The Islamic nation, who numbers one billion, to the Islamic nation of *jihad*, the Islamic nation of martyrdom and self-martyrdom, to the Islamic nation that became the best community ever raised for mankind, to our Islamic nation we say: How identical is tonight with yesterday. How numerous are the lessons, but how little is the learning. For how long have we been made to drink from the cups of humiliation and forced to part with the fathers since our affairs have been presided over by the lowly ones.

He who sees things with clarity and discernment, he who comprehends things through the logic of reason, and he who probes the depth of events will know very well that the Islamic nation has awakened from its slumber and has come to know its route, whose features have manifested themselves and whose milestones have appeared. The Islamic nation by now knows that when clemency is damaging, forgiveness is a sign of incapacity, that patience is usually good except over what may bring harm to religion, that perseverance is usually praiseworthy except when the moment for action is opportune.

The Islamic nation has risen in the form of the Al-Aqsa uprising [Palestinian *Intifada*] and the stone has spoken in the hands of the noble *mujahideen*, whether man or woman, young or old. As a result, the Jews have tried to escape but to no avail. They have found no refuge and have been totally exposed, even as they hide behind walls, facing exploding human bodies that make them taste death, that chase them with terror and inflict a tremor on them so much so that they have become like frightened asses fleeing from a lion.

Then came the New York military expedition to set afire the homes of today's *Hubal*, crushing its towers, disgracing its arrogance, undoing its magic, stripping all the banners that marched behind it, and proclaiming the beginning of its downfall, God willing.

These enormous events are the blessed *jihad* that pursues its march toward the aspired goal and the promised eventuality, and that has come in order to expose the feeble excuse and refutable pretext which says: "What may we do, nothing is within our means, it is just not up to us."

Such an excuse has no place any more. No heart will accommodate it, and no conscience will accept it. In view of the bloody events to which our Islamic nation is being subjected, everyone today has to strive and work seriously. People's leadership, at all levels, must move in order to stop the surging bloodletting and to scandalize these overt treacheries. Any such leadership that cannot move because of the pressure or terror exercised against them by these regimes, the least they can do is to allow initiative taking by others who are more resourceful, more daring and more capable of effecting change, reinstating matters in their appropriate places, so as to warn against inaction and detraction and to avoid the process of ill-advised waiting and forbidden monopoly. It is *jihad* which motivated those you men who responded to the Almighty who says: "*When the forbidden months are past, then fight and slay the pagans wherever you find them, and seize them, beleaguer them, and lie in wait for them in every stratagem...*" [Qur'an 9:5].

It is this *jihad* which is capable of instigating and mobilizing others from among the children of the Islamic nation. Whereas *jihad* will continue until the Day of Resurrection, our days as individuals are numbered, and we shall later stand before Almighty God who says: "*Then shall anyone who has done an atom's weight of good, see it, and anyone who has done an atom's weight of evil, shall see it*" [Qur'an 99:7-8].

Abu Rughal has continued for a century to reincarnate in the Islamic nation, reappearing time after time in his person and treacherous personality, seeking to bring about defeat, to bring down the banner, to bury *jihad* alive, to provide infidelity with success and to reinforce its foundations.

The initiative of Prince Abdullah ibn Abd al-Aziz is none but another trick of the tricks of Abu Rughal, and a conspiracy and another form of the repeated forms of treason perpetrated by the rulers of the region against our causes in general and against the cause of Al-Aqsa in particular.

As he proclaims such a thing, he follows the way of his father who aborted the uprising of the year 1354 A.H. [1936] by virtue of a false promise made by him and by the English government. He deceived the Palestinians who ended the uprising, permitting the English occupation to continue until 1366 A.H. [1948] when Palestine was handed over to the Jews. As such, he also follows the way of his likes of the traitorous rulers who mobilized the English-commanded seven armies under the leadership of the English government's man [Glubb Pasha]. In doing so, they brought to an end the serious popular move in the direction of liberating Palestine, and thus complemented the conspiracy by signing a truce that brought about a cease-fire in the year 1367 A.H. [1949]. Their greatest treason aimed at ending the first Al-Aqsa uprising, however, was hatched at Oslo in 1412 A.H. [1992].

And the fact that he has now initiated the betrayal of the first of the two *qiblas* and the third sacred mosque and that he strived to choke the matter of the whole Islamic nation because of his lust for power is not surprising [amazing] at all; for he betrayed the Two Sacred Mosques earlier when he let the Americans enter the Land of the Two Sacred Mosques under the pretext of the necessity to get help from them for three months. Now we can see this occupation by disbelievers has been going on to this day for 13 years. No doubt that this proposal is a clear rescue of the occupying Jewish state and an evident support for it while the American forces are establishing military bases in the Land of the Two Sacred Mosques to threaten the entire region and to attack the Muslim people in Iraq. Regarding the statements that the Saudi regime would not allow its land to be used to attack Iraq, it is obvious that these statements are not credible because, if he had really said that, he would have expelled the American forces out the Land of the Two Sacred Mosques.

The fate of the tyrants and traitors is so clear that it doesn't need to be explained further, and their fate is a proof for belief and sense of honor in the sons of the Islamic nation. King Abdullah ibn al-Sharif Hussain, for instance, was killed by one of the Palestinian heroes...and Anwar al-Sadat—who was accused of betrayal by the Arab rulers who followed him on the same path afterwards—was killed by one of the Islamic Egyptian heroes, Khaled al-Islambouli...and as you see the small and big traitors are experiencing the same fate every traitor should meet!

What the "Pharaohnian" media [U.S. media] calls the "Saudi proposal" is nothing but an insolent conspiracy and evident plot that is known in the political dictionary as "Seats of betrayal". However, according to the dictionary of Islamic religious law it is "Al-Ridda" [Breaking away from Islam] because the support and assistance to the disbelievers against the Muslims, which is considered to be one of the ten nullifiers of Islam that drive out from the Islamic creed and from which every single Muslim, regardless of his position and situation, has to distance oneself and has to dissociate oneself from those who do it, for it is a deed of the tyrants, and you will have no belief until you disbelieve in the tyrant. "*Whoever rejects evil and believes in God has grasped the most trustworthy hand-hold that will never break*" [Qur'an 2:256].

The one who sells a handbreadth [of land] is willing to sell a country...and the one who abandons one drop of blood doesn't care about rivers of blood...and the one who chokes a people is willing to choke the Islamic nation...and the one who plugs his ears is going to close his eyes tomorrow.

O Islamic nation! Stand up against oppression and tyranny, repression and aggression, humiliation and abasement. Bread is not dearer to us than our religion, and our property is not worthier than our honor, and death is not more difficult for us than life in humiliation and abasement! So the means are possible and accessible for every individual of this Islamic nation, and they are as follows:

1. Refusal of the [Saudi] capitulation proposal and strive for mobilization of the Islamic nation in order to take to the streets for demonstrations and civil disobedience till the fall of the treacherous regimes.
2. Strive for rebelling against the heads of disbelief and hypocrisy who have broken away from their religion and betrayed their Islamic nation and to kill them.
3. Attack the American institutions that are spread throughout the world in general and on the land of our Arab and Islamic nation in particular.
4. Boycott American and Jewish products.
5. Kill the Americans and Jews with a bullet or a knife or stones, etc.
6. Support the *mujahideen* and stand behind them, strengthen them and pray for them.

Heroism is a work, and you are its pioneers; and sacrifice is the price you are paying for it...dignity and honor is a fruit. You are worthy of harvesting it. You are still proving to the whole Islamic nation day after day that the religion is precious and the holy places are above blood and souls! So continue under the blessings of God and go on under His guidance, hoping for success from God, and we remain on the path of *jihad*, sticking to the pact. So your blood is our blood and your honor is our honor, and your children are our children, and the blood of [Muhammad] Dura and his brothers will not become lost. By God—except Whom there is no other god—we will support you and not abandon you till the victory and Palestine returns to the Islamic nation or we shall taste what Hamza ibn Abdul Mutalib tasted [martyrdom]: "*And those who do wrong will come to know by what overturning they will be overturned*" [Qur'an 26:227].

O God! Remove the power from the Arab and non-Arab tyrants and make the best of us our rulers. Take away from us the worst of us and lead this Islamic nation to a good state in which those who obey You become mighty and those who disobey You become humiliated, and in which the Islamic nation is ruled with the good and the evil is prohibited.

"*Verily, God will help those who help His* [cause]." [Qur'an 22:40]

Osama bin Muhammad bin Laden

16

The Nineteen Martyrs' Video

(9 September 2002)

In a one-hour video commemorating the 9/11 attacks in Washington, D.C. and New York City, Bin Laden praised the 9/11 hijackers in the following excerpts. It was broadcast by *Al Jazeera* on 9 September 2002.

When you talk about the New York and Washington raids, you talk about those men who changed the course of history and cleansed the chapters of the Islamic nation from the filth of the treasonous rulers and their followers, regardless of their names and titles.

Those great men entrenched faith in the hearts of the believers, demonstrated loyalty [to God] and dissociation [from infidels] and torpedoed decades of scheming by the Crusaders and their agent rulers in the region.

Time does not allow us to mention all these men for what they are worth. The pen cannot numerate their good qualities and the effects of their blessed raids.

Muhammad Atta was the leader of the group, from Egypt, the destroyer of the first tower. He was a serious, diligent and faithful person. He carried the Islamic nation's concerns. We beseech God to accept him as a martyr.

Ziad Jarrah, purity and clarity, from Lebanon, Bilad al-Sham [Greater Syria], a descendant of Abi-Ubaydah Bin-al-Jarrah [a leader in early Islam], may God be pleased with him.

Marwan al-Shehhi, from the United Arab Emirates, the destroyer of the second tower. Life in this world wanted him, but he ran away from it because he wanted to meet God.

Hani Hanjour, from Al-Ta'if, the destroyer of the center of U.S. defense, the Pentagon. Clear purity and a splendid sacrifice. We beseech God to accept him as a martyr.

17

Letter to the American People

(September/October 2002)

This nine-page letter first appeared on the Internet in Arabic and was then translated and circulated by Islamists in Great Britain. Some experts have doubted the authenticity of the letter, arguing there are several *Qur'an*ic references in it that are erroneous, mistakes that Osama bin Laden would be unlikely to make.

In the Name of God, the Most Gracious, the Most Merciful,

"*Permission to fight* [against disbelievers] *is given to those* [believers] *who are fought against, because they have been wronged and surely, God is able to give them* [believers] *victory*" [Qur'an 22:39].

"*Those who believe, fight in the cause of God, and those who disbelieve, fight in the cause of Taghut* [anything worshipped other than God, e.g. Satan]. *So fight you against the friends of Satan; ever feeble is indeed the plot of Satan*" [Qur'an 4:76].

Some American writers have published articles under the title 'On What Basis Are We Fighting?' These articles have generated a number of responses, some of which adhered to the truth and were based on Islamic law, and others which have not. Here we want to outline the truth—as an explanation and a warning—hoping for God's reward, seeking success and support from Him. While seeking God's help, we form our reply based on two questions directed at the Americans:

(Q 1) Why are we fighting and opposing you?

(Q 2) What are we calling you to do, and what do we want from you?

As to the first question: Why are we fighting and opposing you? The answer is very simple:

1. Because you attacked us and continue to attack us:

(a) You attacked us in Palestine:

(i) Palestine has been under military occupation for more than 80 years. The British handed over Palestine, with your help and your support, to the Jews, who have occupied it for more than 50 years; years overflowing with oppression, tyranny, crimes, killing, expulsion, destruction and devastation. The creation and continuation of Israel is one of the greatest crimes, and you are the leaders of its criminals. Of course, there is no need to explain and prove the degree of American support for Israel. The creation of Israel is a crime which must be erased. Each and every person whose hands have become polluted in the contribution towards this crime must pay its price, and pay heavily for it.

(ii) It brings us both laughter and tears to see that you have not yet tired of repeating your fabricated lies that the Jews have a historical right to Palestine, as it was promised to them in the *Torah*. Anyone who disputes this alleged fact with them is accused of anti-Semitism. This is one of the most fallacious, widely-circulated fabrications in history. The people of Palestine are pure Arabs and original Semites. It is the Muslims who are the inheritors of Moses and the inheritors of the real *Torah* that has not been changed. Muslims believe in all of the prophets, including Abraham, Moses, Jesus and Muhammad, peace and blessings of God be upon them all. If the followers of Moses have been promised a right to Palestine in the *Torah*, then the Muslims are the most worthy nation of this. When the Muslims conquered Palestine and drove out the Romans, Palestine and Jerusalem returned to Islam, the religion of all the prophets, peace be upon them.

Therefore, the call to a historical right to Palestine cannot be raised against the Islamic nation that believes in all the prophets of God (peace and blessings be upon them)—and we make no distinction among them.

(iii) The blood pouring out of Palestine must be equally avenged. You must know that the Palestinians do not cry alone; their women are not widowed alone; their sons are not orphaned alone.

(b) You attacked us in Somalia; you supported the Russian atrocities against us in Chechnya, the Indian oppression against us in Kashmir, and the Jewish aggression against us in Lebanon.

(c) Under your supervision, consent and orders, the governments of our countries which act as your agents, attack us on a daily basis.

(i) These governments prevent our people from establishing Islamic religious law, using violence and lies to do so.

(ii) These governments give us a taste of humiliation and place us in a large prison of fear and subdual.

(iii) These governments steal our Islamic nation's wealth and sell it to you at a paltry price.

(iv) These governments have surrendered to the Jews, and handed them most of Palestine, acknowledging the existence of their state over the dismembered limbs of their own people.

(v) The removal of these governments is an obligation upon us, and a necessary step to free the Islamic nation, to make Islamic religious law the supreme law and to regain Palestine. Our fight against these governments is not separate from our fight against you.

(d) You steal our wealth and oil at paltry prices because of your international influence and military threats. This theft is indeed the biggest theft ever witnessed by mankind in the history of the world.

(e) Your forces occupy our countries; you spread your military bases throughout them; you corrupt our lands, and you besiege our sanctities, to protect the security of the Jews and to ensure the continuity of your pillage of our treasures.

(f) You have starved the Muslims of Iraq, where children die every day. It is a wonder that more than 1.5 million Iraqi children have died as a result of your sanctions, and you did not show concern. Yet when 3,000 of your people died, the entire world rises and has not yet sat down.

(g) You have supported the Jews in their idea that Jerusalem is their eternal capital and agreed to move your embassy there. With your help and under your protection, the Israelis are planning to destroy the Al-Aqsa Mosque. Under the protection of your weapons, Sharon [Prime Minister of Israel] entered the Al-Aqsa Mosque, to pollute it as a preparation to capture and destroy it.

2. These tragedies and calamities are only a few examples of your oppression and aggression against us. It is commanded by our religion and intellect that the oppressed have a right to return the aggression. Do not await anything from us but *jihad*, resistance and revenge. Is it in any way rational to expect that after America has attacked us for more than half a century that we will then leave her to live in security and peace?

3. You may then dispute that all the above does not justify aggression against civilians for crimes they did not commit and offenses in which they did not partake.

(a) This argument contradicts your continuous repetition that America is the land of freedom and it leads this world. Therefore, the American people are the ones who choose their government by way of their own free will, a choice which stems from their agreement to its policies. Thus, the American people have chosen, consented to, and affirmed their support for the Israeli oppression of the Palestinians, the occupation and usurpation of their land, and its continuous killing, torture, punishment and expulsion of the Palestinians. The American people have the ability and choice to refuse the policies of their government and even to change it if they want.

(b) The American people are the ones who pay the taxes which fund the planes that bomb us in Afghanistan, the tanks that strike and destroy our homes in Palestine, the armies which occupy our lands in the Arabian Gulf, and the fleets which ensure the blockade of Iraq. These tax dollars are given to Israel for it to continue to attack us and penetrate our lands. So, the American people are the ones who fund the attacks against us, and they are the ones who oversee the expenditure of these monies in the way they wish, through their elected candidates.

(c) Also, the American army is part of the American people. It is this very same people who are shamelessly helping the Jews fight against us.

(d) The American people are the ones who employ both their men and their women in the American forces which attack us.

(e) This is why the American people cannot be innocent of all the crimes committed by the Americans and Jews against us.

(f) Almighty God legislated the permission and the option to defend oneself. Thus, if we are attacked, then we have the right to attack back. Whoever has destroyed our villages and towns, then we have the right to destroy their villages and towns. Whoever has stolen our wealth, then we have the right to destroy their economy. And whoever has killed our civilians, then we have the right to kill theirs.

The American government and press still refuse to answer the question: Why did they attack us in New York and Washington?

If Sharon [Prime Minister of Israel] is a man of peace in the eyes of Bush, then we are also men of peace! America does not understand the language of manners and principles, so we are addressing it using the language it understands.

As for the second question that we want to answer: What are we calling you to, and what do we want from you?

1. The first thing that we are calling you to is Islam.

(a) The religion of monotheism; of freedom from associating partners with Him, and rejection of this; complete love of Him, the Exalted; of complete submission to His laws; and of the discarding of all the opinions, orders, theories and religions which contradict Islam. He sent down to His Prophet Muhammad (PBUH). Islam is the religion of all the prophets and makes no distinction among them—peace be upon them all. It is to this religion that we call you—the seal of all previous religions. It is the religion of monotheism, sincerity, the best of manners, righteousness, mercy, honor, purity and piety. It is the religion of showing kindness to others, establishing justice between them, granting them their rights, and defending the oppressed and the persecuted. It is the religion of enjoining the good and forbidding the evil with the hand, tongue and heart. It is the religion of *jihad* in the way of God so that God's word and religion reign supreme. And it is the religion of unity and agreement on obedience to God and total equality between all people, without regarding their color, gender or language.

(b) It is the religion whose book—the *Qur'an*—will remain unchanged after the other divine books and messages have been changed. The *Qur'an* is the miracle until the Day of Judgment. God has challenged anyone to bring a book like the *Qur'an,* or even ten verses like it.

2. The second thing we call you to is to stop your oppression, lies, immorality and debauchery that has spread among you.

(a) We call you to be a people of manners, principles, honor, and purity, to reject the immoral acts of fornication, homosexuality, intoxicants, gambling and trading with interest. We call you to all of this that you may be freed from that which you have become caught up in; that you may be freed from the deceptive lies that you are a great nation, that your leaders spread among you to conceal from you the despicable state to which you have reached.

(b) It is saddening to tell you that you are the worst civilization witnessed by the history of mankind:

(i) You are the nation who, rather than ruling by the religious law of God in its constitution and laws, chooses to invent your own laws as you will and desire. You separate religion from your policies, contradicting the pure nature which affirms the absolute authority to God, your Creator. You flee from the embarrassing question posed to you: How is it possible for Almighty God to create His creation, grant them power over all the creatures and land, grant them all the amenities of life, and then deny them that which they are most in need of: knowledge of the laws which govern their lives?

(ii) You are the nation that permits usury, which has been forbidden by all religions. Yet you build your economy and investments on usury. As a result of this, in all its different forms and guises, the Jews have taken control of your economy, through which they have then taken control of your media, and now control all aspects of your life making you their servants and achieving their aims at your expense; precisely what Benjamin Franklin warned you against.

(iii) You are a nation that permits the production, trading and usage of intoxicants. You also permit drugs, and only forbid the trade of them, even though your nation is the largest consumer of them.

(iv) You are a nation that permits acts of immorality, and you consider them to be pillars of personal freedom. You have continued to sink down this abyss from level to level until incest has spread among you, in the face of which neither your sense of honor nor your laws object. Who can forget your President Clinton's immoral acts committed in the official Oval Office? After that you did not even bring him to account, other than that he 'made a mistake', after which everything passed with no punishment. Is there a worse kind of event for which your name will go down in history and be remembered by nations?

(v) You are a nation that permits gambling in all its forms. The companies practice this as well, resulting in the investments becoming active and the criminals becoming rich.

(vi) You are a nation that exploits women like consumer products or advertising tools, calling upon customers to purchase them. You use women to serve passengers, visitors, and strangers to increase your profit margins. You then rant that you support the liberation of women.

(vii) You are a nation that practices the trade of sex in all its forms, directly and indirectly. Giant corporations and establishments are established on this, under the name of art, entertainment, tourism and freedom, and other deceptive names you attribute to it.

(viii) And because of all this, you have been described in history as a nation that spreads diseases that were unknown to man in the past. Go ahead and boast to the nations of man that you brought them AIDS as a Satanic American Invention.

(ix) You have destroyed nature with your industrial waste and gases more than any other nation in history. Despite this, you refuse to sign the Kyoto agreement so that you can secure the profit of your greedy companies and industries.

(x) Your law is the law of the rich and wealthy people, who hold sway in their political parties, and fund their election campaigns with their gifts. Behind them stand the Jews, who control your policies, media and economy.

(xi) That which you are singled out for in the history of mankind is that you have used your force to destroy mankind more than any other nation in history; not to defend principles and values, but to hasten to secure your interests and profits. You dropped a nuclear bomb on Japan, even though Japan was ready to negotiate an end to the war. How many acts of oppression, tyranny and injustice have you carried out, O callers to freedom?

(xii) Let us not forget one of your major characteristics: your duality in both manners and values; your hypocrisy in manners and principles. All manners, principles and values have two scales: one for you and one for others.

(a) The freedom and democracy that you call to is for yourselves and for the white race only. As for the rest of the world, you impose upon them your monstrous, destructive policies and governments, which you call 'American friends'. Yet you prevent them from establishing democracies. When the Islamic party in Algeria wanted to practice democracy and they won the election, you unleashed your agents in the Algerian army onto them to attack them with tanks and guns, to imprison and torture them—a new lesson from the 'American book of democracy'!

(b) Your policy on prohibiting and forcibly removing weapons of mass destruction to ensure world peace only applies to those countries which you do not permit to possess such weapons. As for the countries you consent to, such as Israel, they are allowed to keep and use such weapons to defend their security. Anyone else who you suspect might be manufacturing or keeping these kinds of weapons, you call them criminals and you take military action against them.

(c) You are the last ones to respect the resolutions and policies of international law, yet you claim to want to selectively punish anyone else who does the same. For more than 50 years Israel has been pushing U.N. resolutions and rules against the wall with the full support of America.

(d) As for the war criminals which you censure and form criminal courts for—you shamelessly ask that your own are granted immunity! However, history will not forget the war crimes you committed against the Muslims and the rest of the world. Those you have killed in Japan, Afghanistan, Somalia, Lebanon and Iraq will remain a shame that you will never be able to escape. It will suffice to remind you of your latest war crimes in Afghanistan, in which densely populated innocent civilian villages were destroyed, bombs were dropped on mosques causing the roof of a mosque to come crashing down on the heads of the Muslims praying inside. You are the ones who broke the agreement with the *mujahideen* when they left Qunduz, bombing them in Jangi fort, and killing more than 1,000 of your prisoners through suffocation and thirst. God alone knows how many people have died by torture at the hands of you and your agents. Your planes remain in the Afghan skies, looking for anyone remotely suspicious.

(e) You have claimed to be the vanguards of Human Rights, and your Ministry of Foreign Affairs issues annual reports containing statistics of those countries that violate any Human Rights. However, all these things vanished when the *mujahideen* hit you, and you then implemented the methods of the same documented governments that you used to curse. In America you captured thousands of Muslims and Arabs and took them into custody, without reason, court trial, or even disclosing their names. You issued newer, harsher laws. What is happening at Guantanamo is a historical embarrassment to America and its values, and it screams into your faces—you hypocrites, "What is the value of your signature on any agreement or treaty?"

3. Third, what we call you to is to take an honest stance with yourselves—and I doubt you will do so—to discover that you are a nation without principles or manners, and that values and principles to you are something which you merely demand from others, not that which you yourself must adhere to.

4. We also advise you to stop supporting Israel, and to end your support of the Indians in Kashmir, the Russians against the Chechens, and to also cease supporting the Manila government against the Muslims in the southern Philippines.

5. We also advise you to pack your luggage and get out of our lands. We desire for you goodness, guidance, and righteousness, so do not force us to send you back as cargo in coffins.

6. Sixth, we call upon you to end your support of the corrupt leaders in our countries. Do not interfere in our politics and method of education. Leave us alone, or else expect us in New York and Washington.

7. We also call you to deal with us and interact with us on the basis of mutual interests and benefits, rather than the policies of sub dual, theft and occupation, not to continue your policy of supporting the Jews because this will result in more disasters for you.

If you fail to respond to these conditions, then prepare to fight the Islamic nation. The nation of monotheism puts complete trust in God and fears none other than Him. The nation which is addressed by its *Qur'an* with the words: "*Do you fear them? God has more right that you should fear Him if you are believers. Fight against them so that God will punish them by your hands and disgrace them and give you victory over them and heal the breasts of a believing people. And remove the anger of their* [believers'] *hearts. God accepts the repentance of whom He wills. God is All-Knowing, All-Wise*" [Qur'an 9:13-1].

The nation of honor and respect: "*But honor, power and glory belong to God, and to His Messenger and to the believers*" [Qur'an 63:8]. "*So do not become weak* [against your enemy], *nor be sad, and you will be superior* [in victory] *if you are indeed* [true] *believers*" [Qur'an 3:139].

The nation of martyrdom; the nation that desires death more than you desire life: "*Think not of those who are killed in the way of God as dead. Nay, they are alive with their Lord, and they are being provided for. They rejoice in what God has bestowed upon them from His bounty and rejoice for the sake of those who have not yet joined them, but are left behind* [not yet martyred] *that on them no fear shall come, nor shall they grieve. They rejoice in a grace and a bounty from God and that God will not waste the reward of the believers*" [Qur'an 3:169-171].

The nation of victory and success that God has promised: "*It is He Who has sent His Messenger with guidance and the religion of truth* [Islam], *to make it victorious over all other religions even though the polytheists hate it*" [Qur'an 61:9]. "*God has decreed that 'Verily it is I and My Messengers who shall be victorious.' Verily God is All-Powerful, All-Mighty*" [Qur'an 58:21].

The Islamic nation was able to dismiss and destroy previous evil empires like yours. The Islamic nation rejects your attacks, wishes to remove your evils, and is prepared to fight you. You are well aware that the Islamic nation, from the very core of its soul, despises your haughtiness and arrogance.

If the Americans refuse to listen to our advice and the goodness, guidance and righteousness that we call them to, then be aware that you will lose this Crusade Bush began, just like the other previous Crusades in which you were humiliated by the hands of the *mujahideen*, fleeing to your home in great silence and disgrace. If the Americans do not respond, then their fate will be that of the Soviets who fled from Afghanistan to deal with their military defeat, political break up, ideological downfall and economic bankruptcy.

This is our message to the Americans, as an answer to theirs. Do they now know why we fight them and over which form of ignorance, by the permission of God, we shall be victorious?

18

Message to U.S. Allies

(12 November 2002)

In an audiotape released by *Al Jazeera* on 12 November 2002, Bin Laden refers to recent attacks in Bali, Yemen and Moscow, and calls President Bush the "pharaoh of this age."

In the name of God, the Merciful, the Compassionate, from the servant of God, Osama bin Laden, to the peoples of the countries allied with the tyrannical U.S. government: May God's peace be upon those who follow the right guidance. The road to safety begins by ending the aggression. Reciprocal treatment is part of justice.

The incidents that have taken place since the raids on New York and Washington up until now—like the killing of the Germans in Tunisia and the French in Karachi, the bombing of the giant French tanker in Yemen, the killing of the Marines in Failaka [in Kuwait] and the British and Australians in the Bali explosions, the recent operation in Moscow and some sporadic operations here and there—are only reactions and reciprocal actions. These actions were carried out by the zealous sons of Islam in defense of their religion and in response to the order of their God and their Prophet (PBUH).

What [U.S. President George] Bush, the pharaoh of this age, was doing in terms of killing our sons in Iraq, and what Israel, the United States' ally, was doing in terms of bombing houses that shelter old people, women and children with U.S.-made aircraft in Palestine were sufficient to prompt the sane among your rulers to distance themselves from this criminal gang.

Our brethren in Palestine have been slain and severely tortured for nearly a century. If we defend our people in Palestine, the world becomes agitated and allies itself against Muslims, unjustly and falsely, under the pretense of fighting terrorism.

What do your governments want by allying themselves with the criminal gang in the White House against Muslims? Do your governments not know that the White House gangsters are the biggest butchers of this age?

[U.S. Secretary of Defense Donald] Rumsfeld, the butcher of Vietnam, killed more than two million people, not to mention those he wounded. [U.S. Vice-President Dick] Cheney and [U.S. Secretary of State Colin] Powell killed and destroyed in Baghdad more than Hulegu of the Mongols.

What do your governments want from their alliance with America in attacking us in Afghanistan? I mention in particular Britain, France, Italy, Canada, Germany and Australia. We warned Australia before not to join in the war in Afghanistan, and against its despicable effort to separate East Timor. It ignored the warning until it woke up to the sounds of explosions in Bali. Its government falsely claimed that they [the Australians] were not targeted.

If you were distressed by the deaths of your men and the men of your allies in Tunisia, Karachi, Failaka, Bali and Amman, remember our children who are killed in Palestine and Iraq every day, remember our deaths in Khost mosques and remember the premeditated killing of our people in weddings in Afghanistan. If you were distressed by the killing of your nationals in Moscow, remember ours in Chechnya.

Why should fear, killing, destruction, displacement, orphaning and widowing continue to be our lot, while security, stability and happiness be your lot? This is unfair. It is time we get even. You will be killed just as you kill, and will be bombed just as you bomb. And expect more that will further distress you. The Islamic nation, thanks to God, has started to attack you at the hands of its beloved sons, who pledged to God to continue *jihad*, as long as they are alive, through words and weapons to establish right and expose falsehood.

In conclusion, I ask God to help us champion His religion and continue *jihad* for His sake until we meet Him while He is satisfied with us. And He can do so. Praise be to Almighty God.

19

Message to Iraqis

(11 February 2003)

On 11 February 2003, *Al Jazeera* broadcast an audio tape in which Bin Laden criticizes Bush and Blair for planning their war on Iraq and calls on Iraqi to carry out martyrdom attacks against U.S. forces.

In the name of God, the Merciful, the Compassionate. A message to our Muslim brothers in Iraq, may God's peace, mercy, and blessings be upon you. O you who believe fear God, by doing all that He has ordered and by abstaining from all that He has forbidden as He should be feared. Obey Him, be thankful to Him, and remember Him always, and die not except in a state of Islam [as Muslims] with complete submission to God.

We are following up with great interest and extreme concern the Crusaders' preparations for war to occupy a former capital of Islam, loot Muslims' wealth, and install an agent government, which would be a satellite for its masters in Washington and Tel Aviv, just like all the other treasonous and agent Arab governments. This would be in preparation for establishing the Greater Israel. God is sufficient for us and He is the best disposer of affairs.

Amid this unjust war, the war of infidels and debauchees led by America along with its allies and agents, we would like to stress a number of important values:

First, show good intentions. This means fighting should be for the sake of the one God. It should not be for championing ethnic groups, or for championing the non-Islamic regimes in all Arab countries, including Iraq. God Almighty says: "*Those who believe fight in the cause of God, and those who reject faith fight in the cause of evil*" [Qur'an 4:76]. So fight you against the friends of Satan: feeble indeed is the cunning of Satan.

Second, we remind that victory comes only from God and all we have to do is prepare and motivate for *jihad*. God Almighty says: "*Oh you who believe! If you will help the cause of God, He will help you and plant your feet firmly*" [Qur'an 47:7]. We must rush to seek God Almighty's forgiveness from sins, particularly the grave sins. The Prophet Muhammad (PBUH) said: "Avoid the seven grave sins: polytheism, sorcery, killing, unless permitted by God, usury, taking the money of orphans, fleeing from combat, and slandering innocent faithful women." Also, all grave sins, such as consuming alcohol, committing adultery, disobeying parents, and committing perjury. We must obey God in general, and should in particular mention the name of God more before combat. Abu-al-Darda, may God be pleased with him, said: "Perform a good deed before an attack because you are fighting with your deeds."

Third, we realized from our defense and fighting against the American enemy that, in combat, they mainly depend on psychological warfare. This is in light of the huge media machine they have. They also depend on massive air strikes so as to conceal their most prominent point of weakness, which is the fear, cowardliness, and the absence of combat spirit among U.S. soldiers. Those soldiers are completely convinced of the injustice and lying of their government. They also lack a fair cause to defend. They only fight for capitalists, usury takers, and the merchants of arms and oil, including the gang of crime at the White House. This is in addition to Crusader and personal grudges by Bush the father.

We also realized that one of the most effective and available methods of rendering the air force of the Crusader enemy ineffective is by setting up roofed and disguised trenches in large numbers. I had referred to that in a previous statement during the Tora Bora battle last year. In that great battle, faith triumphed over all the materialistic forces of the people of evil, for principles were adhered to, thanks to God Almighty. I will narrate to you part of that great battle, to show how cowardly they are on the one hand, and how effective trenches are in exhausting them on the other.

We were about 300 *mujahideen*. We dug 100 trenches that were spread in an area that does not exceed one square mile, one trench for every three brothers, so as to avoid the huge human losses resulting from the bombardment. Since the first hour of the U.S. campaign on 20 Rajab 1422, corresponding to 7 October 2001, our centers were exposed to a concentrated bombardment. And this bombardment continued until mid-Ramadan.

On 17 Ramadan, a very fierce bombardment began, particularly after the U.S. command was certain that some of Al Qaeda leaders were still in Tora Bora, including the humble servant of God [referring to himself] and the brother *Mujahid* Dr. Ayman al-Zawahiri. The bombardment was round-the-clock, and the warplanes continued to fly over us day and night. The U.S. Pentagon, together with its allies, worked full time on blowing up and destroying this small spot, as well as on removing it entirely.

Planes poured their lava on us, particularly after accomplishing their main missions in Afghanistan. The U.S. forces attacked us with smart bombs, bombs that weigh thousands of pounds, cluster bombs, and bunker busters. Bombers, like the B-52, used to fly over head for more than two hours and drop between 20 to 30 bombs at a time. The modified C-130 aircraft kept carpet-bombing us at night, using modern types of bombs. The U.S. forces dared not break into our positions, despite the unprecedented massive bombing and terrible propaganda targeting this completely besieged small area.

This is in addition to the forces of hypocrites, whom they prodded to fight us for 15 days non-stop. Every time the latter attacked us, we forced them out of our area carrying their dead and wounded. Is there any clearer evidence of their cowardice, fear, and lies regarding their legends about their alleged power.

To sum it up, the battle resulted in the complete failure of the international alliance of evil, with all its forces, [to overcome] a small number of *mujahideen*—300 *mujahideen* hunkered down in trenches spread over an area of one square mile under a temperature of—10 degree Celsius. The battle resulted in the injury of 6% of personnel—we hope God will accept them as martyrs—and the damage of 2% of the trenches, praise be to God. If all the world forces of evil could not achieve their goals on a one square mile of area against a small number of *mujahideen* with very limited capabilities, how can these evil forces triumph over the Muslim world? This is impossible, God willing, if people adhere to their religion and insist on *jihad* for its sake.

O *mujahideen* brothers in Iraq, do not be afraid of what the United States is propagating in terms of their lies about their power and their smart, laser-guided missiles. The smart bombs will have no effect worth mentioning in the hills and in the trenches, on plains, and in forests. They must have apparent targets. The well-camouflaged trenches and targets will not be reached by either the smart or the stupid missiles. There will only be haphazard strikes that dissipate the enemy ammunition and waste its money. Dig many trenches. The [early Muslim *Caliph*] Umar, may God be pleased with him, stated: "Take the ground as a shield because this will ensure the exhaustion of all the stored enemy missiles within months." Their daily production is too little and can be dealt with, God willing.

We also recommend luring the enemy forces into a protracted, close, and exhausting fight, using the camouflaged defensive positions in plains, farms, mountains, and cities. The enemy fears city and street wars most, a war in which the enemy expects grave human losses.

We stress the importance of the martyrdom operations against the enemy—operations that inflicted harm on the United States and Israel that have been unprecedented in their history, thanks to Almighty God.

We also point out that whoever supported the United States, including the hypocrites of Iraq or the rulers of Arab countries, those who approved their actions and followed them in this Crusader war by fighting with them or providing bases and administrative support, or any form of support, even by words, to kill the Muslims in Iraq, should know that they are apostates and outside the community of Muslims. It is permissible to spill their blood and take their property.

God says: "*O you who believe! Take not the Jews and the Christians for your friends and protectors: they are but friends and protectors to each other*" [Qur'an 5:51]. And he among you that turns to them [for friendship] is of them. Verily, God guides not a people unjust.

We also stress to honest Muslims that they should move, incite, and mobilize the Islamic nation, amid such grave events and hot atmosphere so as to liberate themselves from those unjust and renegade ruling regimes, which are enslaved by the United States. They should also do so to establish the rule of God on earth. The most qualified regions for liberation are Jordan, Morocco, Nigeria, Pakistan, the Land of the Two Sacred Mosques, and Yemen.

Needless to say, this Crusader war is primarily targeted against the people of Islam. Regardless of the removal or the survival of the Socialist Party or Saddam, Muslims in general and the Iraqis in particular must brace themselves for *jihad* against this unjust campaign and acquire ammunition and weapons. This is a prescribed duty. God says: "[And let them pray with you] *taking all precautions and bearing arms: the unbelievers wish if you were negligent of your arms and your baggage, to assault you in a single rush*" [Qur'an 4:102]. Fighting is support of the non-Islamic banners is forbidden. The Muslims' doctrine and banner should be clear in fighting for the sake of God. He who fights to raise the word of God will fight for God's sake.

Under these circumstances, there will be no harm if the interests of Muslims converge with the interests of the Socialists in the fight against the Crusaders, despite our belief in the infidelity of Socialists. The jurisdiction of the Socialists and those rulers has fallen a long time ago. Socialists are infidels wherever they are, whether they are in Baghdad or Aden. The fighting, which is waging and which will be waged these days, is very much like the fighting of Muslims against the Byzantine in the past. And the convergence of interests is not detrimental. The Muslims' fighting against the Byzantine converged with the interests of the Persians. And this was not detrimental to the Companions of the Prophet.

Before concluding, we reiterate the importance of high morale and caution against false rumors, defeatism, uncertainty, and discouragement. The Prophet said: "Bring good omens and do not discourage people." He also said: "The voice of Abu-Talhah [one of the Prophet's Companions] in the army is better than 100 men."

During the Al-Yarmuk Battle, a man told Khalid bin al-Walid [a Muslim commander]: "The Byzantine soldiers are too many and the Muslims are few." So, Khalid told him: "Shame on you. Armies do not triumph with large numbers but are defeated if the spirit of defeatism prevails." Keep this verse before your eyes: "*It is not fitting for a Prophet that he should have prisoners of war until he hath thoroughly subdued the land*" [Qur'an 8:67]. "*Therefore, when you meet the unbelievers* [in fight], *smite at their necks*" [Qur'an 47:4]. Your wish to the Crusaders should be as came in this verse of poetry: "The only language between you and us is the sword that will strike your necks."

In the end, I advise myself and you to fear God covertly and openly and to be patient in the *jihad*. Victory will be achieved with patience. I also advise myself and you to say more prayers. "*O you who believe! When you meet a force, be firm, and call God in remembrance much* [and often]; *That you may prosper* [Qur'an 8:45]. God, who sent the book [*Qur'an*] unto the Prophet [Muhammad], who drives the clouds, and who defeated the enemy parties, defeat them and make us victorious over them. "*Our Lord! Give us good in this world and good in the Hereafter and save us from the torment of the Fire!*" [Qur'an 2:201]. May God's peace and blessings be upon the Prophet Muhammad and his household.

Source: "Text of Bin Ladin's message broadcast by *Al-Jazeera*, 11 February." *Al-Jazeera* TV, Doha, in Arabic 2001 gmt 11 Feb 03/BBC Monitoring/©BBC

20

Sermon for the Feast of the Sacrifice

(16 February 2003)

Published on Islamist websites and broadcast on *Al Jazeera*, Bin Laden's sermon was issued for a major Muslim holiday, the *Eid al-Adha*, the Feast of Sacrifice, the most important holiday in the Muslim year.

Praise be to God who revealed to his servant and Messenger [the Prophet Muhammad] the verse of the sword to establish truth and abolish falsehood. Praise be to God who said: "*Once the Sacred Months are past,* [and they refuse to make peace] *you may kill the idol worshippers when you encounter them, punish them, and resist every move they make. If they repent and observe the Contact Prayers* [*salat*] *and give the obligatory charity* [*zakat*], *you shall let them go. God is forgiver, most merciful*" [Qur'an 9:5].

And praise be to God who said: "*You shall fight them, for God will punish them by your hands, humiliate them, grant you victory over them, and heal the hearts of the believers*" [Qur'an 9:14]. And blessings and peace be upon our Prophet Muhammad, who said: "I was sent before the hour [Day of Judgment] with the sword so that God alone, with no partner, would be worshipped. He assigned me a livelihood under the shadow of my spear, and assigned humiliation and lowliness to those who disobeyed my commands. Whoever will imitate certain people will be from them" [Ahmad ibn Hanbal, *Musnad*, no. 4868]. He also said, "Drive out the idol worshippers from the Arabian peninsula" [al-Bukhari, *Sahih*, no. 2932].

In a time in which the blood of Muslims is spilled and wasted in Palestine, Chechnya, the Philippines, Kashmir and the Sudan, and our children are dying because of the American siege of Iraq, and in a time in which our wounds have not yet healed from the Crusaders' wars on the Islamic world during the past century, and as a result of the Sykes-Picot agreement[1] between Britain and France, which lead to the division of the Islamic world into pieces and ruins, and where the agents of the Crusaders still rule up until today, the shadows of Sykes-Picot approaches us again. It is the Bush-Blair agreement. But under the same banner and for the same purpose, it is the banner of the Cross, and its ultimate goal is the destruction and looting of the Islamic nation of God's beloved [Muhammad], God's prayers and PBUH.

The Bush-Blair agreement claims that its goal is to destroy terrorism. However, it is no longer a secret, even from the common public, that its goal is to destroy Islam. Nonetheless, the rulers of the region [the Middle East] emphasize in their speeches and ceremonies their support for Bush in the war against terrorism, which is in fact a war against Islam and Muslims, in a clear betrayal to the faith and the Islamic nation, for which they depend on the blessings of the scholars and the palace ministers who serve them.

It is not hidden that the current preparations to attack Iraq are but one link in the chain of already prepared transgressions against the countries of the region, including Syria, Iran, Egypt and Sudan. Yet, the focus to divide the Land of the Two Sacred Mosques takes the lion's share of their plan. This has been a long-standing strategic objective ever since Saudi Arabia transferred its loyalty from Great Britain to the United States six decades ago.

Three decades ago, the United States tried to achieve this objective after the Tenth of Ramadan War [Arab-Israeli War of 1973], on the day when its President Nixon publicly threatened to invade the Land of the Two Sacred Mosques, and was unable to do so at the time due to the grace of God.

---

(1) The Sykes-Picot agreement: a secret exchange of notes in 1916 between Britain, France and Russia relating to the partition of the Ottoman Empire after its defeat. Named after the chief British and French negotiators, Sir Mark Sykes and Charles François Georges-Picot.

With the start of the Second Gulf War, America has established important and dangerous military bases, spread all over the Land of the Two Sacred Mosques, especially near the capital. What remains for them is to divide the land, and today it seems that the suitable time for the division in their eyes has come. So, we suffice with God as our guardian, and He is the ultimate advocate.

In conclusion, America's targeting of the region in general, and the division of the Land of the Two Sacred Mosques in particular, is not a passing summer cloud, but a strategic goal that the cunning American policy has not lost sight of. So, what have the ruling governments in the region prepared to resist this aggressive goal? Nothing worthy of mention, except an even more increased loyalty to the Crusaders. Add to this, the meeting of the Arab Ministers for Internal Affairs [in Tunis, on 13 January 2003] which was convened for the purpose of combating the *mujahideen* and to squeeze the truthful clerics and scholars who are trying to warn the Islamic nation and awaken it to defend itself.

One of the most important objectives of the new Crusade is to pave the way and prepare the region after its division for the establishment of what is to be called the state of Greater Israel, which will include inside its borders extensive parts of Iraq, Egypt, through Syria, Lebanon, Jordan, all of Palestine, and large parts of the Land of the Two Sacred Mosques.

What is meant by Greater Israel and what anguish and perdition will be inflicted upon the whole region? What is being inflicted upon our people in Palestine is but only a model which the Zionist-American alliance wants to repeat throughout the rest of the region—the killing of men, women and children, imprisonment, terrorism, the demolition of homes, the razing of farms, and the destruction of factories. People live in continual fear and paralyzing terror, awaiting death at any moment from a missile or a shell that will demolish their homes, kill their sisters, and bury their babies alive. How will we answer to God tomorrow [on the Day of Judgment]?

What is taking place there is unbearable even for those men who possess the most strength. How could it then be for the feeble mothers while they see their children being killed in their arms? "*We belong to God, and unto Him we shall return*" [Qur'an 2:156]. We suffice with God as our guardian and He is the ultimate advocate. Oh God, I hereby disavow from the deeds of those Jews and Christians and the betraying rulers and those who are like them; and I apologize to you on behalf of those who are refraining from supporting the religion [Islam].

What the establishment of Greater Israel means is the submission of the countries of the region to the Jews. What do you know about the Jews? The Jews transgressed against the Creator Himself. What could they do to the created? The Jews are killers of the prophets and violators of agreements; God has said to them: "*Is it ever so that when they make a covenant a party of them set it aside? The truth is, most of them believe not*" [Qur'an 2:100].

These are the Jews, the lords of usury and the leaders of abomination. They will not leave anything for you, neither life nor religion. God has said about them: "*Have they even a share in* [God's] *dominion? If they have, they would not give mankind even the speck of a date-stone*" [Qur'an 4:52]. Such are the Jews who believe in the core of their religion that all people are their slaves, and whoever refuses is punishable by death. God has said about them: "*That is because they say: We have no duty to the Gentiles* [non-Jews]. *They knowingly lie about God*" [Qur'an 3:75]. These are some of the characteristics of the Jews. Beware of them, and these are some of the features of the Crusaders' plan which you must resist.

Now, what are the means to restrain the infidels' might and save the Muslims' land? To answer this question, I say, and success is only from God, as His prophet Shu'eyb, God's blessings be upon him, said: "*I only desire reform to the best of my power; and my success can only come from God. In Him I trust, and unto Him I turn*" [Qur'an 11:88].

Jihad in the cause of God, be Him glorified, is the means to restrain the infidels' might. God said: "*So fight in the cause of God. You are accountable only for yourself, and urge the believers* [to join the *jihad*]. *Peradventure God will restrain the might of those who disbelieve. God is stronger in might and stronger in inflicting punishment*" [Qur'an 4:84].

In the beginning, I bring good news to you, with the grace of God, that the Islamic nation today possesses great capacities to save Palestine and to save the rest of the Islamic nations, but these capacities are shackled, hence, work must be done to release them. The Islamic nation has been promised victory, but if this victory has been delayed, it is because of our sins and our refraining from supporting God. The Exalted God said: "*O you who believe! If you support God, He will support you and will make your foothold firm*" [Qur'an 47:7].

The Islamic nation has also been promised victory over the Jews, as the Prophet Muhammad, God's blessings and (PBUH), has said: "The hour [Day of Judgment] will not come to pass until the Muslims fight the Jews and kill them, to the extent that the Jew hides behind the rock and the tree; and each rock or tree will say: O' Muslim, O' servant of God, here's a Jew behind me, come and kill him, except for the '*al-Gharqad*' [a type of thorny bush], for it is from the Jews' trees."(2) This speech also cautions that the conclusion of the conflict with the enemies is but with fighting, not with the hindering of the Islamic nation's energies for decades through other means such as the artifice of democracy and the like.

And after this good news, I speak to you about some matters that assist us in our *jihad* in the cause of God, among them I will mention some of the wars in which the Muslims have been victorious during the last two decades, which have increased the confidence of the Islamic nation's sons in themselves and its value in mobilizing the Islamic nation to defend itself against the Zionist-Crusader coalition. In fact, the Islamic nation is the greatest human power if it truly institutes the religion of Islam.

This is what has been historically proven during the past centuries. The Islamic nation is capable of fighting and resisting

---

(2) This *Hadith* occurs in many sources, e.g., Muslim's *Sahih*, no. 5203 and Ahmad ibn Hanbal's *Musnad*, no. 9029.

what are called the 'great nations'. I would like to mention an incident related to the subject of fighting the 'great powers'; historians have mentioned that Al-Mothana al-Shibany[3]—may God have mercy on him—came to Medina requesting reinforcements from the *Caliph* for fighting the Persians. So, the *Caliph* Omar—may God be pleased with him—gave the people a three-day grace period for volunteering, but none did. Omar—may God be pleased with him—acutely understood that the people suffered from a complex with regard to fighting the 'great powers'. So, he ordered Al-Mothana to speak to the people with what God had blessed him [his victory over the Persians], in order to dispel fear from their hearts. Al-Mothana stood, spoke, and invigorated the people, saying: "O people, do not be afraid, we have already mocked the Persians. We have overcome them and have captured the better of the two regions [the western agricultural region] of Iraq. We went against them head to head, and we gained from them, and those among us have become emboldened against them, and God willing, there will be more to come." So, the people became enthusiastic, and Abu Ubayd al-Thaqa? [a Muslim military commander] stood, and the *Caliph* granted him the standard and the people followed him—may God be pleased with them.

Like these honorable people, I hereby say: 'O people, do not let them be great in your eyes, do not let America, nor its army be great in your eyes; for I swear to God, we have stricken them many times, and they have been repeatedly defeated. In combat they are the most cowardly people.'

It became clear to us from our defense, as well as fighting the American enemy, that they depend mainly on psychological warfare due to the huge propaganda instrument they possess, and also on concentrated air raids in an attempt to hide their most apparent weak points: Cowardice and the American soldier's lack of fighting spirit. Were it not for the limited time we now have, I would tell you almost unbelievable stories in our battles with them in Tora Bora and Shahi-Khot in

---

(3) Al-Mothana al-Shibany was a Muslim commander in the wars against the Persians, d. 635 A.D.

Afghanistan. May God make it possible to go into this in detail [in the future].

First of all, I would like to remind you of the some of the defeats of the great powers at the hands of the *mujahideen*. I remind you of the defeat of the former Soviet Union that became nothing but a monument after ten years of devastating fighting at the hands of the sons of the Afghans and those who supported them from the sons of Muslims, by the grace of God. Similarly, the Russian defeat in the lands of Chechnya, where the *mujahideen* gave the greatest examples of self-sacrifice, as the Chechen *mujahideen*, together with their Muslim brethren and supporters, destroyed the Russians' pride and caused them loss after loss. Thus, they withdrew in humiliation after the first war. Later the Russians returned with American support, and Russia is still suffering heavy losses until now from a small group of believers, for whom we pray to God for support and victory.

I also remind you of the defeat of the American forces in the year 1402 A.H. [1982], when the children of Israel invaded Lebanon. The Lebanese resistance sent a truck full of explosives to the American Marines' center in Beirut, killing over 240 of them. May they go to hell and to a bitter end.

Then, after the Second Gulf War, America sent its armies to Somalia and killed 13,000 of the sons of Muslims there. "*There is neither power nor strength except from God.*" At that point, the lions of Islam rose from the Afghan Arabs, and they came to the aid of their brethren in that land against them [the Americans]. Together with their brothers in Somalia, they dragged America's pride through the mud. They killed them. They destroyed their tanks and shot down their planes. Hence, America and her allies fled under cover of night, each avoiding looking at the other. Praise and thanks be to God!

At that time, the youth of *jihad* prepared explosive charges against the Americans in Aden, which detonated. Hence, the cowards had no choice but to flee within 24 hours. Later, in the year 1415 A.H. [1994], there was an explosion in Riyadh [Saudi Arabia] in which four Americans were killed. This was a clear message showing that the local people were opposed to the American policy of supporting the Jews and the occupation of the Land of the Two Sacred Mosques.

Later, in the following year, another explosion took place in al-Khobar, in which 19 people were killed and over 400 wounded. As a result, the Americans were forced to move their large bases from the towns to bases in the desert. In the year 1418 A.H. [1997] the *mujahideen* publicly threatened America regarding the necessity to stop supporting the Jews and to depart the Land of the Two Sacred Mosques. Eventually, the enemy rejected the warning and the *mujahideen* managed, with the grace of God, to deliver two tremendous blows [against the enemy] in East Africa. Later America was warned again and did not take heed. Hence, God sent success unto the *mujahideen* through a great martyrdom operation which destroyed the American destroyer *Cole* in Aden [12 October 2000]. This was a resounding slap in the face for the American military establishment. This operation also uncovered the Yemeni government's collaboration [with the U.S.], just like the other countries in the region.

Then, when the *mujahideen* saw that the gang of black-hearted criminals in the White House was misrepresenting the event, and that their leader, who is a fool whom all obey, was claiming that we envy them for their way of life, while the truth—which the Pharaoh of our time conceals—is that we strike them because of their injustice toward us in the Muslim world, especially in Palestine and Iraq, and because of their occupation of the Land of the Two Sacred Mosques. And when the *mujahideen* saw this they decided to bypass this truth-concealing and to bring the battle right into the middle of his [President Bush's] land and in his own territory.

On that blessed Tuesday, the 23rd of *Jumada al-Thani*, 1422 A.H. [September 11th, 2001], the Zionist-American alliance was still using American tanks and planes and Jewish hands to reap [the lives] of our sons and our people in the land of the blessed Al-Aqsa Mosque, while our sons in Iraq were paying with their lives as a result of the unjust siege by America and her agents. While the Muslim world was still living in a state of great distance from genuinely establishing

Islam and matters were in this state of frustration, desperation and procrastination amongst the Muslims—except those upon whom God had bestowed His mercy—and also the injustice, arrogance and aggression from the Zionist-American alliance, the land of Uncle Sam—heedless in its transgression, thunderous with its tyranny, treating the people with arrogance, roaming the earth proudly without regard to anybody, and believing that it could not be harmed—was struck with disaster.

Oh, do you have any idea what is meant by a disaster? This is when the 'unkempt of hair and dusty of foot' [*mujahideen*][4] pounced—those who are hunted down everywhere, young men who believed in their Lord. Consequently, God had increased their guidance, strengthened their convictions and engraved faith in their hearts. Hence, they, acting in the cause of God, did not fear "*the reprimands of those who seek to find fault*" [Qur'an 5:54] because they desire only what God (SWT) has for them. Their spirits refused to sleep while there was injustice; they sacrificed their lives, but they did not sacrifice their honor.

They carried out the raid by means of enemy planes in a courageous and splendid operation, the like of which had never been known before by mankind. They smashed America's idols and hit the Pentagon in the middle of its heart, and they struck the American economy in its very heart, rubbed America's nose in the dirt and dragged its pride through the mud. Hence, the two towers of New York collapsed, and consequently, their collapse caused an even greater collapse: The collapse of the myth of great America and the collapse of the myth of democracy. It appeared to people that America's values were at their lowest abyss, the myth of the land of freedom was destroyed, the myth of American national security was smashed, and the myth of the CIA collapsed. All praise and thanks to God.

One of the most important positive results of the two raids on New York and Washington was the revelation of the truth

---

(4) A Classical Arabic expression used to describe vagabond heroes; here it is applied to the *mujahideen*.

about the conflict between the Crusaders and the Muslims. The raids revealed the strength of the hatred which the Crusaders feel towards us, as the two raids peeled the lamb's skin off the American wolf and revealed the hideous truth. The whole world awoke from its sleep, and the Muslims became alert to the importance of the principle that positions of alliance and hostility may be taken only in the cause of God.

The spirit of religious brotherhood among Muslims has been strengthened, which is considered a great step towards uniting the Muslims under the statement of monotheism for the purpose of establishing the rightly-guided Caliphate, God willing. And it became clear to people that America, this oppressive power, can be struck, and can be humiliated, insulted and defeated. For the first time, the majority of the American people now understand the truth of the Palestinian case and that what hit them in Manhattan was the result of the oppressive policy of their government.

In summary, America is a great country which possesses tremendous military might and a wide-ranging economy, but all this is based on a frail foundation, and it is possible to target this frail foundation, focusing on the most obvious weak spots. If it is hit in one hundredth of those spots, God willing, it will stumble, wither away and relinquish its leadership of the world and its oppression.

A small group of Islamic youth managed, despite the international alliance standing against them, to provide people with solid proof of the ability to resist and fight against what is called a 'great power'. They managed to defend their religion and serve the objectives of their Islamic nation more than what the governments and peoples of some fifty-odd countries in the Muslim world could do. This is because they have taken *jihad* as a means to defend their faith.

As Abu Hilala[(5)] said: 'Victory has its reasons, as does defeat, and any side that inherits immortality is a winner; the

---

(5) Abu Hilala is the poet Sheikh Dr. Yusuf Abu Hilala, Dean of the Faculty of Education at Al-Hussein University in Ma'an, Jordan. He published a poem in praise of Bin Laden and Al Qaeda in the wake of the September 11th attack and the war in Afghanistan.

paths which lead to exalted ends are different, and the shortest of them is that which sheds blood and which has noble people [standing] at both its sides.'

And the likes of those young heroes in the Islamic nation are many—with God's blessing—but they are shackled, hence, we ought to cooperate, all of us, in order to release them from their bonds, so that they can burst forth as *mujahideen* in the cause of God, for *jihad* is the way for this Islamic nation's pride and security. The limitations and the obstacles that are preventing the Islamic nation's young men from rushing into *jihad* are many, but we will address only the most important.

Before anything else, I want to quote a *Hadith* from the two authoritative collections of traditions. Those who will be guided by it will go through, and those who deviate from it will be lost. The Messenger of God [Muhammad] (PBUH), said: "What brought about the destruction of your predecessors was, that when a respected man from among them stole, they took no action; but when a weak man from among them stole, they punished him in accordance with the law." Take note, oh wise ones. This is one of the reasons for our destruction. "*There is neither power nor strength except from God.*"

I would also like to mention the story of Khalid [ibn al-Walid(6)]'s, may God be pleased with him, conversion to Islam, in order to free the minds from blind obedience. He was asked, after his belated conversion: "Where was your wisdom, Oh Khalid, that you did not perceive the light of prophecy which had been among you for twenty years? Khalid replied: We were led by men whose intellect appeared to us like mountains."(7) The Imam Ahmad ibn Hanbal said: "A lack of understanding is when a man imitates [others] in his religious belief."

The first of those shackles and barriers in our current generation are the rulers and false witnesses from among the

---

(6) Khalid ibn al-Walid: the most important and successful Muslim military leader in the early Muslim conquests. Before converting to Islam he commanded the Meccan army which defeated the Muslim army at the battle Uhud.

(7) Khalid ibn al-Walid refers to his admiration for the leaders of the tribe of Quraysh prior to his conversion to Islam.

impious scholars and the palace ministers, and those with the hired pens and their ilk. As for the rulers, the people have agreed on their powerlessness and betrayal. And as for those who demand that the people should put their hands in the hands of those rulers, despite all this, we ask: When have the people ever withdrawn their allegiance to these rulers, so that they can be advised to restore their allegiance to them? This has never happened, and the result is as you see: We are dominated by unbelievers. It has been said: "He who is unable to plan in tranquil times will never plan well when the situation gets out of control."[8]

Our disagreement with the rulers is not a minor disagreement which can be solved, but rather we are addressing the core pillar of Islam—The testimony that "*There is no god except God and Muhammad is the Messenger of God.*" These rulers have demolished its very foundation by allying themselves with the unbelievers, by passing man-made laws, and by approving and applying the laws of the atheist U.N. Their legitimate ruling status has long been void according to religious laws, and there is no justification to remain under their dominion. There is not enough time here to describe the full details of this, but we have mentioned statements of the "People of Knowledge," may God have mercy on them, in manifesto number 17 of the Authority for Counsel and Reform.[9]

After this, we say: Is it possible for a Muslim to say to other Muslims 'put you hands in the hands of [President] Karzai [of Afghanistan] in order to cooperate with him to constitute Islam, alleviate oppression and prevent America from carrying out her schemes'? It is impossible and inconceivable, because Karzai is an agent brought in by America, and supporting him against the Muslims is an act of annulment from the ten acts that annul Islam and throws those who commit them outside the boundaries of the faith. So, here we

---

(8) A verse of poetry Bin Laden quoted in his letter to King Fahd of Saudi Arabia in 1995.

(9) The Authority for Counsel and Reform was established by Bin Laden after the Saudi government revoked his citizenship.

ought to ask ourselves: What is the difference between Karzai of the non-Arabs and 'Karzai' of the Arabs? Who has appointed and established the rulers of the Gulf States? They are the Crusaders. Those who appointed Karzai of Kabul and shaped 'Karzai' of Pakistan are the same ones who appointed 'Karzai' of Kuwait, 'Karzai' of Bahrain, 'Karzai' of Qatar and the other states. And who appointed 'Karzai' of Riyadh one hundred years ago and brought him in, after he had been a refugee in Kuwait, in order to fight alongside them against the Ottoman state and its provincial governor Ibn al-Rashid? They were the Crusaders, and they still protect these families until today. Hence, there is no difference between 'Karzai' of Riyadh and Karzai of Kabul. "*So, take heed, oh wise ones*" [Commonly quoted verse from the *Qur'an*, no specific references as it is repeated in numerous locations throughout the *Qur'an*]: God, be He glorified said: "*Are your unbelievers better than these? Or* [do you believe that] *they have been given acquittal in the holy books?*" [Qur'an 54:43].

Those rulers who want to solve our problems, one of the most important of which is the Palestinian issue, through the U.N. or through the orders of the U.S.A., as was the case with the initiative of Prince Abd Allah ibn Abd al-Aziz in Beirut, on which all the Arabs agreed—and in which he sold out the blood of the martyrs and sold out the Palestinian land for the pleasure and support of the Jews and America against the Muslims—those rulers have betrayed God and his Messenger [Muhammad], and they have expelled themselves from the boundaries of faith and have betrayed the Islamic nation.

I also say: Those who want to solve our problems through these impotent and treacherous rulers have been deluded by their souls and have misled their nation. They have relied on those [rulers] who have acted tyrannically and have profoundly lost their way. The best that could be said of them is that they are impotent and wicked. Therefore, Muslims should advise them, and if they do not heed the advice, then they [the Muslims] should beware of them and warn others against them.

Muslims should also disavow these evil idols [rulers]. It is well-known that disavowing an evil idol is not considered a voluntary act of righteousness, but rather, it is one of the two pillars of monotheism without which faith cannot be firmly established. God, be He glorified, said: "*He who renounces evil idols and believes in God—he surely grasps a firm support, one that never breaks. God is Hearer*" [Qur'an 2:256]. As for the impious scholars, the palace ministers, and those with the hired pens and their ilk—as the saying goes: 'Every generation has its own regime and its own men.' So, these are the regime's men who distort the truth and bear false witness, even in the sacred city [Mecca], in the sacred mosque [the *Ka'ba*] and in the sacred month. "*There is neither power nor strength except from God.*" And they claim that these betraying rulers are our custodians. "*There is neither power nor strength except from God.*" They say this in order to bolster the regime. These scholars have surely strayed from the straight path. They must be forsaken and be warned against.

The regime bases itself upon its own scholars and shows them on religious programs for the purpose of issuing decrees, only for a few minutes every now and then, in which the regime needs them to provide legitimacy for it and its actions, as was the case when the King opened up the Land of the Two Sacred Mosques to the Americans. He commanded his scholars; consequently, they issued that disastrous religious decree that violated Islam, mocked the intelligence of Muslims, and supported his treacherous action in this grave disaster. The Islamic nation today suffers what it suffers from catastrophes, fear and threats as a consequence of that destructive decision and that hypocritical decree.

Those who read the biographies of truthful religious teachers in times of adversity, such as the biography of Ahmad ibn Hanbal and others, God's mercy be upon them, would recognize the difference between those scholars who practice what they teach and those who flatter [the rulers]—as one can read in *Siyar A'lam al-Nubala*[10] and other books. The poet said: "We

---

(10) The *Siyar a'lam al-nubala'* is a biographical dictionary by the 14th century scholar Shams al-Din Muhammad al-Dhahabi.

patch our world by tearing our religion to pieces; neither our religion survives nor that which we are patching."

As for the second barrier [to *jihad*], it is the scholars and preachers who love the truth and hate falsehood, but refrain from participating in *jihad*. They have devised their own interpretations which have turned the young people against *jihad*. "*There is neither power nor strength except from God.*" They have watched the falsehood spread and grow. So, they gathered to fulfil their obligation to come to the aid of truth, to preach good and forbid evil. Many people have been guided and gained religious knowledge from their hands. They did well, and may God reward them for it. But because falsehood cannot tolerate truth and its people, they [the false rulers] began to harass and terrorize them, preventing them from giving sermons and classes. They laid them off from their jobs and then imprisoned those who persisted in continuing to preach good and forbid evil.

These severe pressures gradually resulted in [people] straying from the right path, except for those upon whom God had mercy. This is only natural, because a man cannot make the right decision under incorrect conditions, especially from the standpoint of his own security. The Messenger of God (PBUH) said: "A judge shall not pronounce judgment between two people at a time when he is angry." This is if he is angry, how could it be if he is afraid?

The terror which the Arab states use against their people has destroyed all aspects of life, including the matters of Islam, as Islam is [by definition] giving counsel, and counsel cannot be given without security. Thus, fear has split the people into groups, some of which I shall now describe.

One group has lapsed, joined the regime and supported it. "*There is neither power nor strength except from God.*" Another group thought that they would not possibly be able to continue to preach and teach, and secure their institutes, associations, groups, their own lives, their high status, or their money unless they praised and insincerely flattered the evil idol. Consequently, they came up with their own corrupt interpretations, and thus they fell into glaring error and caused many people to go astray.

Another group has been protected by God from placating and flattering the treacherous rulers. They were careful to remain under the banner of preaching good and forbidding evil, and they made commendable efforts in preaching for God. However, the pressures we mentioned before were very heavy, and they have not prepared themselves to stand them. Of which, two of the most important pressures are the costs of emigration and *jihad*. In the past two decades, the opportunity was available, but they did not make use of it. Thus, they lost the ability to make the right decision in these most difficult days, except for those upon whom God has bestowed His mercy. Therefore, we see that some of them, to this day, have not taken the decision of *jihad* and resistance.

Supporting and establishing Islam has enormous costs, as well as distinct qualities in God's book [*Qur'an*] and in the biography of the Messenger of God [Muhammad] (PBUH), and also in the biographies of his honorable Companions—may God be pleased with them. He who does not have these qualities will not be able to support Islam. God (SWT) mentions these qualities in His honorable book [the *Qur'an*], such as His saying: "*Oh you who believe, whosoever among you lapses from his religion, God shall bring other people whom He loves and who love Him, who will be humble toward the Believers and stern toward the unbelievers. They will struggle in the cause of God [jihad], and will not fear any reproach from anyone. Such is the grace of God. He bestows it upon whomever He will. God is munificent and omniscient*" [Qur'an 5:54].

In the conversation that took place between the Messenger of God [Muhammad] (PBUH) and Waraqa ibn Nawfal[11], Waraqa said: "I wish I were a young man and still be alive when your people expel you." The Messenger then asked: "Are they really going to expel me?" Waraqa said: "Yes. There has

(11) Waraqa ibn Nawfal was a Christian and the paternal uncle of Khadija, the Prophet Muhammad's wife.

never been a man who brought a revelation like yours, who was not treated with enmity. If the day of your expulsion comes while I am still alive, I shall give you my full support."

So, the state of he who truly wants to take upon himself the obligations of Islam is enmity from the people of falsehood, not peaceful coexistence on their part, as we see, and "*There is neither power nor strength except from God.*" Hence, he who wishes to uphold Islam should strive on its behalf, sacrificing life and possessions in this cause, and as Waraqa said: "If your day comes when I am still alive, I shall fully support you." This is how it was at the time of the oath of al-Aqaba.[12]

Aiding Islam is not just giving lectures, and Islam cannot be sustained by the crumbs of our time and money. For God's reward is precious, and there is a great difference between sitting and giving lectures and sacrificing souls and lives in the cause of God. This is why al-Abbas ibn Abd al-Muttalib[13], who at the time still professed the [polytheistic] religion of his people, wanted to be assured that his nephew Muhammad (PBUH) was safe with the *Ansar*. So, he said to the *Ansar*: "If you are people of strength and perseverance, versed in war and able to withstand alone the hostility of all the Arabs, for they will shoot you with one bow."[14]

I, therefore, say: The early believers needed such qualities in order to protect God's Messenger (PBUH), and they are required today, as well, in order to protect the religion of God's Messenger (PBUH). When al-Abbas concluded his speech, al-Barra ibn Marur of the *Ansar* said: "We heard what you said. And by God, had there been in our hearts something other than what we have said, we would have said it. But we

---

(12) The oath of al-Aqaba took place at a place near Mecca where a delegation of the *Ansar* from Medina met the Prophet Muhammad to swear to protect him if he should come to Medina.

(13) Abbas ibn Abd al-Muttalib, the eponymous father of the Abbassid dynasty, was Muhammad's paternal uncle.

(14) The second half of the sentence is implicit: "if you have all these qualities, then I rely on you to protect my nephew, Muhammad."

work to keep our word, to be truthful, and to sacrifice our lives to defend the Messenger of God."

So, I say: Such is Islam, sustained by loyalty, truthfulness and self-sacrifice for the sake of the Way [Islam]. And when the *Ansar* stood up to give their allegiance, As'ad ibn Zurara[15] said: "Act not in haste, Oh people of Yathrib[16]. We spurred our mounts towards him only after we had recognized that he was the Messenger of God. To take him out of Mecca now isolates you from all the Arabs, and eventually will result in the death of your best men and being bitten by the swords. So, if you can endure all of this—then take him and your reward will be upon God; but if you are afraid for yourselves, then leave him, and this will be more excusable in the sight of God." They answered: "O As'ad, give your hand on behalf of all of us to give allegiance; for by God, we shall neither abandon nor forsake this undertaking."

Such were the qualities of those who wanted to protect and maintain the religion of Islam, may God be pleased with them, and the same is true today. The *mujahideen* say to the scholars and preachers who love the truth and do not flatter falsehood: For you have raised the banner of Islam, and you know that it is truly the religion of God's Messenger and that upholding it truly means isolation from all Arab governments and all non-Arab governments on earth, the killing of your best men, and that you will be bitten by the swords. So, either you endure all this and uphold the banner and your reward will be upon God, or you are afraid for yourselves, hence abandon the banner of defense and fighting. But do not stand as a barrier between the youth of the Islamic nation and *jihad* in the cause of God. This will be more excusable for you in the sight of God.

Now, we will talk about what is the duty of Muslims towards this Crusader-Zionist war against the nation of Islam. God (SWT) said: "*Fight in the cause of God, you are accountable only for yourself, and urge the believers, may God*

---

(15) As'ad ibn Zurara was the first of the *Ansar* to convert to Islam.

(16) Yathrib was the old name of Medina.

ward off the might of those who have disbelieved; God is most mighty and most capable of inflicting punishment" [Qur'an 4:84].

Today, the most important duty, after believing, is to ward off and fight the enemy aggressor. Sheikh al-Islam [Ibn Taymiyah], may God have mercy upon him, said: "To drive off the enemy aggressor who destroys both religion and the world—there is no duty more important than this, after believing, and this is an unconditional rule."

Today *jihad* is obligatory for the whole Islamic nation, which is in a state of sin unless it gives of its sons, its possessions and its powers whatever is enough to maintain *jihad*, which will ward off the might of the infidels away from all Muslims in Palestine and elsewhere. Therefore, it is obligatory on the Muslims to engage in *jihad* in order to establish the truth and abrogate falsehood—each according to his ability. The Messenger of God (PBUH) said in Muslim ibn al-Hajjaj's authoritative book: "Whosoever struggles against them with his arm is a believer, whosoever struggles against them with his tongue is a believer, and whosoever struggles against them in his heart is a believer, but there is not even the slightest measure of belief without this [that is, without at least one of the three]" [Muslim, *Sahih*, no. 71]. This great *Hadith* embraces all believers. For since we are believers, we are then *mujahideen* in the cause of God in order to support Islam.

Hence, a Muslim who is unable to engage in *jihad* with his hand or tongue must engage in *jihad* in his heart. This includes continuously hating the enemies of God, imploring God to curse them, while constantly allying with the believers and the *mujahideen*. He should pray for them and feel the brotherhood of faith that binds him with Muslims throughout the world, and he should feel that the people of faith are in one tent and that the people of disbelief are in another, until God bestows on the Islamic nation one regime which will unite all Muslims under its banner, God willing. He [who engages in *jihad* in his heart] should at least urge himself to engage in *jihad* in the cause of God with his hand and his tongue. This [*jihad* of the mind] is the weakest kind of faith. He should boycott American products and those of her allies. The believer should be particularly careful not to support falsehood, as supporting the infidels against the Muslims—even if only verbally—is flagrant disbelief, as has been determined by the people of knowledge. Let him beware of being among those of whom God said: "*God knows those of you who hold the others back, who say to their brethren: Come, join us! And seldom take part in the fighting*" [Qur'an 33:18]. He should not add the grave sin of avoiding *jihad* to the grave sin of discouraging others.

Today, while sacrificing one's own soul is obligatory on the Islamic nation as a whole, it is especially emphasized for young men more than upon the middle-aged and elderly. Likewise, the obligation of the sacrifice of money is especially emphasized for the wealthy more than others. It is a mercy from God upon the Islamic nation today that He has opened the heart of many of our young people to struggle in His cause and to defend His religion and His servants. It is incumbent upon the Islamic nation to support them, encourage them and facilitate their affairs, so that they can defend it and ward off injustice, shame and sin from it. The Islamic nation is also obligated to maintain the current *jihad* and support it with all its might, which is very difficult, as it is in Palestine, Chechnya, Afghanistan, Kashmir, Indonesia, the Philippines and other Muslim lands. The banner of *jihad* would not remain aloft there in the face of the enemies' cruel attack were it not—besides God's grace—for the immense sacrifice of what cannot even be described from suffering, blood and torn bodies. We pray to God to accept them as martyrs.

I bring good news to you that the *jihad* in Afghanistan is going well, thank God, and that things are improving in favor of the *mujahideen*, with the grace of God. We are now in the second year of fighting, and America has not managed to accomplish its objectives. On the contrary, it has become embroiled in the Afghan swamp. As for what America regarded in the first months of the war as a victory, after taking control of the cities which the *mujahideen* evacuated, it became generally well-known to the military experts, as well as those who are experts in the affairs of Afghanistan specifically, that this was but a tactical withdrawal, which suited the nature of the

Taliban state and the nature of the Afghans throughout their long history of guerrilla warfare. The Taliban state had no regular army to defend the cities.

Therefore, the Afghans relied on—after God—their strength which lies in their ability to conduct guerrilla warfare from the depths of their impassable mountains, with the same tactics with which they had—by the grace of God—previously defeated the Soviet Union's army. This became an established fact after the guerrilla operations began, and the number of operations has risen to two operations daily. Thus, the Americans are in real trouble today, for they are neither able to protect their own forces, nor can they establish a state capable of protecting its own president—let along anyone else.

By the grace of God, coordination among all the *mujahideen* has been achieved in the past year, and everybody is enthusiastic for *jihad* and sees it as their duty. If it were not for their limited means, the number of daily operations could have been easily increased to the limit of the earlier *jihad* against the Russians, and that is what the Americans cannot endure. Hence it is incumbent on the Islamic nation today to support *jihad* in general, including Palestine and Afghanistan. These axes are the most important axes which we must focus on in order to exhaust the Jews, the American's allies, and in order to drain the Americans, the Jews' allies. America's defeat in Afghanistan will be, God willing, the beginning of its end.

You shall suffer no harm from us nor from our brethren the Afghan *mujahideen*, God willing. Hence, we hope that we shall suffer no harm from you. Today the Islamic nation is at the gates of a day of God's days, in which there should be neither weakness nor evil-doing. All the forces of the Muslims must gather against the forces of the infidels. On that day, it is also a must to repent of sins and transgressions, and it is incumbent upon the Islamic nation, now that it's facing this crucial matter—which is very serious and not an amusement—to give up the life of fun and playing, extravagance and luxury, and to toughen itself and prepare itself for the real life, the life of killing and fighting, of shooting and confrontation. Here is what Sheikh al-Islam [Ibn Taymiyah]—may God's mercy be upon him—said about a hard time that was similar to the one in which we find ourselves today. He said: "You should know, may God render you successful, that, according to an authentic tradition transmitted from the Prophet by many chains of transmitters, that the Prophet said: There will always be within my nation a group which knows the truth, who are not affected by whosoever abandons them or opposes them until the Day of Judgment."

This internal strife has split the people into three groups:

1. The triumphant (by God's help) group—the *mujahideen* against those people who spread corruption.
2. The disagreeing group—those people [who spread corruption] together with those who joined them among the pathetic so-called Muslims.
3. The laggards—those who refrain from joining the *jihad*, even though they are true Muslims. So, every man should examine whether he is from the 'triumphant group,' the 'laggards' or the 'disagreeing group,' for there is no fourth group.

He, may God have mercy on him, also said: "By God, if the early Muslims from among the *Muhajirun* and the *Ansar*, such as Abu Bakr, Umar, Uthman, Ali [Successors to Muhammad] and others, were alive today, it would have been one of their most virtuous acts to struggle against those criminal people. Only he who miscalculates and disrespects himself will miss such a battle. By refraining, he is deprived of immense reward in this life and in the hereafter.

I also advise the young people to exert every effort in *jihad*, for it is they upon whom this duty primarily devolves, as was indicated by al-Shatibi[17]—may God's mercy be upon him—in his *al-Muwafaqat*.

You should know that targeting the Americans and the Jews throughout the earth is one of the greatest duties, and the good deed most preferred by God, the Exalted.

---

(17) Abu Ishaq al-Shatibi (d. 1378 or 1388) was a legal scholar. The full name of the book is *al-Muwafaqat fi usul al-fiqh*.

I also urge them [the young people] to rally round the truthful scholars and the sincere preachers, that is, those who practice what they teach. I also urge them to manage their affairs in secrecy, especially the military affairs of *jihad*.

I bring you good news—and our brothers in Palestine in particular—that your brethren *mujahideen* are continuing in the way of *jihad*, targeting the Jews and the Americans. The Mombassa operation[18] is just the first drop which heralds the approaching rain, God willing, may He be praised and exalted. We shall never abandon you. So, go on, continue to fight with God's blessing, and we too, with you, will continue to fight, God willing.

Before concluding, I urge myself, as I urge my Muslim brethren to struggle in the cause of God. In the words of the poet [Al-Tirrimah ibn al-Hakim al-Ta'i (660-743 A.D.)]:

> "I am leading my horse and casting him and myself this year into one of the battles
>
> O Lord, when death arrives, let it not be upon a bier covered with green shrouds
>
> Rather, let my grave be in the belly of a vulture, tranquil in the sky, among hovering vultures [the poet is expressing here the wish to be killed in battle; vultures will, then, eat his corpse].
>
> I shall be martyr resting among a group of young men whom death will overtake in a terrible ravine
>
> Horsemen of [the tribe of] Shayban, who piety united, brave warriors alighting from their mounts [to fight face to face] when the two armies advance to meet each other
>
> When they leave this world they will leave behind suffering and attain that which is promised in the *Qur'an*."

Finally, I instruct myself and my Muslim brethren to fear God both privately and publicly, and to increase imploring

---

(18) On 28 November 2002, Al Qaeda attacked the Paradise Hotel near Mombassa, Kenya and failed to shoot down an Israeli-chartered airliner as it took off from the Mombassa airport. Eighteen people were killed and 80 wounded.

God and beseeching Him to accept our repentance and relieve us of our distress. "*O Lord, give us your blessing in this world and in the next, and protect us from the fires of Hell*" [Qur'an 2:201].

We beseech God (SWT) to free our captives from the hands of the Americans and their agents—foremost among them Sheikh Umar ibn Abd al-Rahman and Sheikh Sa'id ibn Zu'eyr and our brethren in Guantanamo—and to strengthen the *mujahideen* in Palestine and other Muslim lands. May they be victorious, and may He help us triumph over our enemy.

I also urge you, as I urge myself, to increase commemorating God, to read the *Qur'an* often, and to ponder it, for it contains counsel and healing for the heart, and guidance and mercy. God (SWT) said: "*O people, enlightenment has come to you herein from your Lord, and healing for anything that troubles your hearts, and guidance, and mercy for the believers*" (Qur'an 10:57]. "*God's command is always done, but most people do not know*" [Qur'an 12:21]. Our last prayer is: "*Praise be to God, Lord of the Universe*" [Qur'an 1:2].

21

On Saudi Clerics and the Meaning of Jihad

(July 2003)

In July 2003 a number of Islamist Internet forums posted this 90-minute audio-taped speech in which Bin Laden disputes Saudi clerics regarding the meaning of *jihad*. The following are excerpts from the speech which cannot be dated much beyond the fall of the Taliban regime in November 2001.

Since the fall of the Islamic Caliphate state, regimes that do not rule according to the *Qur'an* have arisen. If truth be told, these regimes are fighting against the law of God. Despite the proliferation of universities, schools, books, preachers, imams, mosques, and [people who recite the] *Qur'an*, Islam is in retreat, unfortunately, because the people are not walking in the path of Muhammad (PBUH)....

In order to establish the Islamic state and spread the religion, there must be [five conditions]: a group, hearing, obedience, a *hijra* and a *jihad*. Those who wish to elevate Islam without *hijra* and without *jihad* sacrifices for the sake of God have not understood the path of Muhammad (PBUH)....

We are in a situation of no longer having a country to which to make *hijra*. There was an opportunity [to create such a country]—a rare opportunity. Since the fall of the Caliphate, the Crusaders made sure not to enable the true Islam to establish a state. God decreed that there be events in Afghanistan, and the U.S.S.R. attacked [Afghanistan]. The Crusaders relinquished their resolve [to prevent the establishment of an Islamic state] because of their fear of the U.S.S.R. [They] had no choice but to repel the U.S.S.R. by any and all means, even by means of the *mujahideen*, the fundamentalists, and the young *jihad* warriors of Islam.

Thus the gate opened. But unfortunately, a decade later, the Islamic nation—particularly the clerics, preachers, and sermonizers, and Islamic universities—did not meet the obligation. Those who came to the land of *jihad* in order to support the Muslims and the *mujahideen* were a small handful of the youth of the Islamic nation, in addition to the funds donated by some merchants; these were not sufficient to establish a strong country detached from geographical and tribal loyalties. Our Afghan brothers found themselves in a unique situation; an Islamic state could easily have been established according to Islamic, not national or geographic, standards. But unfortunately...this opportunity was lost, and the people did not take advantage of it. I mention this in order to tell you that it is not an easy thing, and that now conditions have become [even] harder.

Then, God made it possible to establish the Taliban state. The Taliban established [the state] and removed the conflict among the Afghans. They remained [in power] for six years, more or less. But the people remained captive to their fixed ideas and captive to the world media, which launched a mad attack on the Taliban and harmed their reputation....

Afghanistan is [but] a few hours away from the Arabian Peninsula, or from any of the countries of the Islamic world... but the Taliban state disappeared, and they did not lift a finger. I say that I am convinced that thanks to God, this Islamic nation has sufficient forces to establish the Islamic state and the Islamic Caliphate, but we must tell these forces that this is their obligation. Similarly, we need to tell the other forces, those who [are] restricting these forces, that they are sinning by restricting these forces....

There are people who say, and it is no secret, that the *jihad* does not require the [participation] of the entire Islamic nation; these words are true, but their intent is not. It is true that *jihad* cannot include the entire Islamic nation today, and that repelling the aggressive enemy is done by means of a very small part of this Islamic nation; but *jihad* continues to be a commandment incumbent personally upon every Muslim. But they [the clerics identified with the regimes] disagree with us [on] this ruling and say: "If we sent you a few thousand, you would not manage to take them in. It is not logical that we abandon all the breaches [on other fronts] and go, all of us, to wage *jihad*...."

If *jihad* becomes a commandment incumbent personally upon every Muslim, it [*jihad*] rises to the top of the priorities, and there is no doubt of this, as Sheikh al-Islam [Ibn Taymiyah] said: "Nothing is a greater obligation than repelling the aggressive enemy who corrupts the religion and this world—except faith itself."

There is no place to claim that if everyone went to *jihad* it could not take them all in. This [claim] is the product of an abnormal flaw in Islamic religious law, and of the abnormal submission to the [concepts of] this world. When the number of [*mujahideen*] will be sufficient to repel the aggressive enemy, *jihad* will automatically be transformed from a commandment incumbent personally upon every Muslim to a commandment incumbent upon all Muslims as a collective.... He who claims that *jihad* is a tremendous ritual but that there are other [important] rituals does not understand the path of Muhammad (PBUH)....

Most unfortunately, the young people who have the ability to sacrifice [themselves] for the religion [Islam] are suffering by listening to and obeying Islamic clerics who refrain [from fulfilling the commandment of *jihad*], even though such people must not be listened to or obeyed. Therefore, these forces [who obey these clerics] remain paralyzed; they [the clerics] incite them away from carrying out the commandment that is incumbent upon them personally and towards commandments incumbent upon the collective, such as study. [Even] if everyone became a cleric, there would be no religious revival that does not include [the five conditions of] a group, hearing, obedience, a *hijra* and a *jihad*....

Great evil is spreading throughout the Islamic world. The *imams* calling people to hell are those who appear more than others at the side of rulers in the region, the rulers of the Arab and Islamic world. Through the media and their own apparatuses, through their ruin of the country by their adoption of destructive ideas, and laws created by man...from morning to evening, they call the people to the gates of hell....

The heresy against God and His Prophet is being carried out before the eyes and ears of all in newspapers, television, radio, and symposiums, and none oppose it.... In this situation, only one thing takes precedence over all other commandments, apart from faith itself.... This immense obligation [*jihad*]...has no place among the clerics today who do not speak of it. They all, except for those upon whom God had mercy, are busy handing out praise and words of glory to the despotic Arab rulers who disbelieved God and His Prophet. They send telegrams praising those rulers who disbelieve God and His Prophet. Their newspapers and media spread heresy against God and His Prophet. Other telegrams are sent from the rulers to these clerics, praising them for deceiving the Islamic nation.

The Islamic nation has never been as damaged by a catastrophe like the one that damages them today. In the past, there was imperfection, but it was partial. Today, however, the imperfection touches the entire public because of the communications revolution and because the media enter every home. No home, in [the] city or in [the] desert, was spared this internal strife. None will be spared....

The clerics are the prisoners and hostages of the tyrants. Some of them told me: 'We cannot speak the truth [because we are civil servants]....' Young people must understand the nature of the connection today between civil servants and the ruler. A civil servant is a civil servant.... It is amazing that some object to our linking them with this tyrannical ruler when that is what they are....

The true role of some civil servants is to bear false witness. The role of the Information Minister, for example, is to bear false witness. He and his apparatus deceive the public every day and portray the country as the best country and the ruler as an unparalleled genius. Likewise, the Defense Minister deceives the people and bears false witness, saying that our situation is good and our armed forces are good, while we have been under occupation for over a decade. The whole world knows we are under occupation and that the American planes take off whenever they want, with no prior notification, night or day, and then the Defense Minister comes to us and says: 'We are independent, and no one uses our land without our approval.' This is bearing false witness. God be praised, the people know that they are civil servants. Yet the danger does not come from the Interior Minister and his subordinates, because no matter what they do, they are unable to mislead anyone...because the people know they are lying to them and deceiving them.

The true danger is when the falsehood comes from the *imams* of the religion who bear false witness every morning and evening and lead the Islamic nation astray. This is all the more so when the false witness comes from the house of Al-Haram [the mosque in Mecca] and from the *Ka'ba*....

Bearing false witness is one of the biggest sins on any piece of soil, all the more so when you bear false witness in the house of Al-Haram every Friday and at every opportunity in order to lead an entire nation astray for a handful of coins...How great is the sin of he who does this. They are civil servants to whom no reasonable person can turn [to] on religious matters. The least you can say about them, as Sheikh Muhammad bin Abd al-Wahhab said, the least you can say about the clerics who defend the tyrants, is that they are corrupt. The people must boycott and banish them....

[They are mistaken], those who want to tell people that the religion exists even though the ruler disbelieved God and His Prophet a hundred years ago, ever since he rose through English strength, English support, English weapons, and English gold(1).... It is inconceivable that there be faith, and that the religion will continue to rule, if the ruler is an infidel. This must be clear: If the ruler is an infidel...Islam ceases to exist, and there must be an act that will elevate a [believing] ruler....

(1) The family of Hussein bin Ali, who in World War I conspired against the Ottoman Caliphate with the British.

The region's rulers deceive us and support infidels and then claim they still cling to Islam. What increases this deceit is the establishment of bodies to lead the people astray. People may wonder how it is that bodies engaging in [studying] Islamic law and jurisprudence play this role, whether wittingly or unwittingly. The aim of the regime in putting some [unfaithful] clerics on satellite television and radio stations to issue *fatawa* for the people is not [to spread knowledge of Islamic law]—were this the case, the regime would put the faithful clerics on satellite television and radio; the goal of these authorities [in putting the unfaithful clerics on television and radio] is to [use them] when necessary.

For example, when the regime decided to bring the American Crusader forces into the Land of the Two Sacred Mosques, and the youth raged, these bodies [the unfaithful clerics]...issued *fatawa* and praised the behavior of the ruler, whom they called Wali Amr(2), while in truth he was not really Wali Amr over the Muslims. We must pay attention to this.

People may wonder and ask how it is possible that Sheikh 'So-and-So,' or 'Anonymous,' who is a respected elder Sheikh with great knowledge of religion, could sell out his religion for a meager sum from this world. I say that no man is protected from error. If we examine the history of the Islamic world over the past centuries, we will find that these instances recur.... Many clerics have misled [people] because of threats of beating, imprisonment, or perhaps even death [by the regimes]; only a few stood fast, and one of these, as you know, is Imam Ahmad ibn Hanbal....

The regime appropriates a huge budget for these bodies [the unfaithful clerics] whose role is to grant legitimacy to the regime...Imagine! The offices of the Clerics Authority [in Saudi Arabia] are adjacent to the royal palace, and the building of the *Fatwa* Authority of Al-Azhar is adjacent to Hosni Mubarak's Palace of the Republic.... In such a situation [when even the offices are linked], is it reasonable to ask a civil

---

(2) Men of authority: in accordance with the *Qur'an*ic requirement that believers obey those of authority among them.

servant, who receives his salary from the king? What is the ruling regarding the king, and should the king be regarded as supporting infidels?...

Civil servants don a robe and take for themselves grand titles, but they are in fact civil servants.... We learned from their books, where it says that one of the 10 acts that contradict Islam is supporting infidels. In closed forums, they speak to us candidly, but [in public] they are afraid, and give [other interpretations].

The spirit of martyrdom is our strength and our weapon for the sake of the survival of our religion, and for resistance to any domestic or foreign attempt to distort our religion.

Jihad is the way to attain truth and abolish falsehood. Therefore, the youth...who love the religion and sacrifice [themselves] for God, must pay no attention to these civil servants and to those who refrain [from waging *jihad*].... As a result of the communications revolution and the enormous advances in communication...the young people hear from a young age that Sheikh 'So-and-So' sent a telegram to the king, and the king sent him a telegram in return, and he appears at the king's right hand every Monday, and so on.... The public is misled and says: "If that king were no good, Sheikh 'So-and-So' would not visit him." They disregard the fact that anyone who goes to see the king is a civil servant in the Royal Office or the Interior Ministry [and not an independent, faithful cleric]....

There is nothing of Muhammad's religious law in the religious law of the government clerics and sultans, and they do not understand the nature of the path of God. We must be aware that clinging to the religion requires us to show hostility to the people of falsehood....

The faithful clerics possess characteristics described in the Book of God [*Qur'an*].... The most prominent characteristics are faith and *jihad* for the sake of God.... Those who do *hijra*, and those who support God and His Prophet and wage *jihad* for the sake of God, are the faithful ones.... In contrast, the other clerics [are those who] see [and remain silent when] the rulers support infidels and [do not] rule in accordance with what was sent down by God, who praise the tyrants and ignore the bank towers next to the Al-Haram Mosque, that charge interest [which is forbidden in Islam].... No faithful cleric can claim that interest is not a great sin....

A fundamental and realistic fact is that the Land of the Two Sacred Mosques is occupied—and if it is occupied [by the U.S. military], the greatest commandment, after faith itself, is to repel the aggressive enemy. Their [the rulers of Saudi Arabia] statements attest to their situation. In an interview with some world press agencies, [Saudi] Prince Talal bin Abd al-Aziz said: 'Were we to tell the American forces to leave, they wouldn't.' That is candor. Also, the Qatari Foreign Minister said: 'If we tell the American government and the American forces to leave Qatar, we'll be wiped off the map.'

The land is occupied in the full sense of the word. Yet despite this, people are busy with all sorts of [other] rituals. We must focus on making the starting point *jihad* for the sake of God, guarding against those who refrain [from *jihad*], and *hijra* and *jihad* for God. All these are obligatory in the present situation in order to establish the truth and abolish falsehood.

Source: MEMRI, *Special Dispatch Series*, No. 539, 18 July 2003.

22

American Hell in Afghanistan and Iraq

(10 September 2003)

A 45-minute Al Qaeda video entitled "American Hell in Afghanistan and Iraq" was produced by the Sahab Institute for Media Production and shown on *Al Jazeera* on 10 September 2003. In it Bin Laden praises the men who carried out the 11 September 2001 attacks against the U.S.

Those youths inflicted heavy moral and material losses on the enemy. They also confused the enemy's hostile schemes. Documents have shown that this aggression to occupy and divide the region [the U.S.-led invasion of Iraq] had been preplanned six months ahead of the two conquests [the New York and Washington attacks on 9/11/2001]. The confusion caused to the enemy was sufficient to make people wake up from their slumber and rise for *jihad* for the sake of God.

I had the honor of knowing these men. One is honored by knowing such men. God has honored them and enabled them to champion the cause of Islam. I do not see them except as seeds that God planted in His faith and used in His obedience. May God bless them.

> "These are my forefathers; get me men like them if we are to meet again, O Jarir." [a line of poetry]

He who wants to learn faithfulness, honesty, generosity, and courage to support religion from contemporary persons must draw lessons from Saeed al-Ghamdi, Muhammad Atta, Khalid al-Mihdar, Ziad al-Jarrah, Marwan al-Shehhi, and their brothers, may God have mercy on them. These persons learned from the traditions of our Prophet Muhammad (PBUH), who is the most honest, courageous and generous man.

He [Muhammad] (PBUH) said: "You will never find me to be stingy, a coward, or a liar." These traits are necessary for upholding the faith. Whoever is denied these traits cannot champion or uphold the faith.

Here, I say to those who do not enjoy some of these characteristics and who failed to carry out *jihad*. He who is not convinced of killing should go away and not influence those who are convinced of killing. I say to them: [verses of poetry]

> "He who fears climbing mountains will always live among holes.
> This faithful youth and his brothers are young."

> "Man is judged by the tiniest parts of his body; that is, his heart and tongue." [a *Hadith* by the Prophet Muhammad]

However, they are men with big brains and great resolve. They repeatedly protected their sanity and minds from being trampled underfoot or exposed to danger by the deception of the agent governments and their institutions, which paint vice as virtue and *vice versa*, falsehood as right, and enemies as friends.

This is because these young men are true believers, and believers are not bitten twice from the same hole, as our Prophet (PBUH) says. Those youths knew that the road to eternal damnation is the obstruction of Islamic law and even some of its rulings. They refuse to bootlick even princes and scholars over this. They believe that the integrity of Islamic law enjoys precedence over the safety of men regardless of how great they are.

In God's faith, people are treated as equals. They are guided by the saying of the Prophet (PBUH) which says: "By God, if Fatimah Bint-Muhammad were to steal, I would chop off her hand." These young men have understood the meaning of the phrase "*There is no god except God and Muhammad is the Messenger of God*", which is the core of Islam. It must prevail over our actions, and guide us in all aspects of our life.

Because the facts on the ground are otherwise—as a matter of fact, the rulers' whims and their legislation prevail over people's actions, even though they permit people to perform some rituals—these young men knew that the rulers were in the wrong. As a matter of fact, they are apostates, even if they perform prayers, fast and claim to be Muslims.

These young men refused to stay behind and engage in unimportant things. They set out on *jihad* and hastened to uphold the cause of God and the call of monotheism: "*There is no god except God and Muhammad is the Messenger of God.*" They engaged in *jihad* against the infidels. Their condition is like that of Mu'az Bin-al-Jamuh when he asked Abd al-Rahman Bin-Awf, may they both achieve God's satisfaction, the following question: "O uncle, do you know Abu-Jahl[1]?" Bin-Awf said: "Yes, What for, my nephew?" Bin al-Jamuh said: "I have been told that he called the Messenger of God names. By God, if I see him, I will engage him in a fight until the one who is predestined to die before the other is killed." This is honesty, and this is faith.

Each and every matter has its own reality. The reality of this hero, Saeed al-Ghamidi and his brothers, is that they showed the truthfulness of their faith by offering themselves and their souls for the sake of God. Thus, they gained a status that greatly angered the infidels, and will continue to anger them for a long time, God willing.

This happened when they opted for practical applications and drastic solutions to champion the cause of the faith and shunned the unjust atheistic solutions—the solutions offered by the United Nations, the atheistic parliaments, and the tyrannical rulers, who turned themselves into gods who legislate and shun God's rulings.

Moreover, they did not pay attention to the futile solutions, the solutions of the prevaricators, the Arabs of the desert who failed to join the *mujahideen* who were preoccupied with their money and kindred, and who were deceived by themselves to

---

[1] Amr Bin-Hisham, archenemy of the Prophet Muhammad and Islam in the early years.

the effect that they have been busy preparing for *jihad* for dozens of years.

There is no difference between he who views the fields of preparation and the arenas of *jihad* as a hardship, separation of fathers and sons, and risking one's life and money. Thus, Satan will prevent him from continuing on the road to *jihad* and force him not to go to *jihad* along with those who failed to join the *mujahideen*.

He who views the arenas of *jihad* as being the market of paradise, whose doors are open, fears that they will be closed to him if he is late for an hour or that God is not pleased with him, and so, He will make him lag behind. God says: "*And if they had intended to march out, certainly, they would have made some preparation for it; but God was averse to their being sent forth, so He made them lag behind, and it was said to them: 'Sit you among those who sit* [at home]'" [Qur'an 9:46].

If he does not respond to God's order and fails to go to *jihad* by obeying the Arabs of the desert who failed to join the *mujahideen*, God will come in between him and his heart, and thus he will stray from the right path and be of the sinful ones.

God says: "*O you who believe! Answer God* [by obeying Him] *and His Messenger when he calls you to that which will give you life, and know that God comes in between a person and his heart* [He prevents an evil person to decide anything]" [Qur'an 8:24].

"*And verily, to him you shall all be gathered*" [Common Qur'anic verse].

God also says: "*Say: If your fathers, your sons, your brothers, your wives, your kindred, the wealth that you have gained, the commerce in which you fear a decline, and the dwellings in which you delight are dearer to you than God and His Messenger, and striving hard and fighting in His cause, then wait until God brings about His decision* [torment]" [Qur'an 9:24].

"*And God guides not the people who are rebellious* [disobedient to God]" [Qur'an 5:108].

23

Messages to the Iraqis and the U.S.

(18 October 2003)

Broadcast on *Al Jazeera* on 18 October, two audio tapes, purportedly from Bin Laden, were directed to the Iraqis and the U.S. Vowing more martyrdom attacks inside and outside the U.S. and threatening U.S. allies in Iraq, Bin Laden also urged the Iraqis to wage *jihad* until an Islamic government was set up in Baghdad.

To the Iraqis

Praise be to God, praise be to God, who says: "O *Prophet! Strive hard against the unbelievers and the hypocrites, and be firm against them. Their abode is Hell—an evil refuge indeed*" [Qur'an 9:73]. May God's blessings be upon our Prophet Muhammad, who says: "He who is killed in defense of his property is a martyr; he who is killed in self-defense is a martyr; he who is killed in defense of his religion is a martyr; and he who is killed in defense of his family is a martyr."

This is the second message to our Muslim brothers in Iraq. O grandchildren of Sad, al-Muthanna, Khalid, al-Muanna, and Saladin. May God's peace, mercy, and blessings be upon you. I greet you, your effort, and blessed *jihad*. For you have massacred the enemy and brought joy to the hearts of Muslims, particularly the people of Palestine. May God reward you for that. You are to be thanked for your *jihad*. May God strengthen your positions and guide you to achieve your targets.

You should be pleased, for America has fallen into the quagmires of the Tigris and Euphrates. Bush thought that Iraq and its oil are easy spoils. Now, he is in a critical situation, praise be God. Today, America has started to cry out and crumble before the entire world. Praise be to God, who foiled its plots and made it ask for help from the lowliest people and beg for the mercenary soldiers from the east and the west. No wonder you did these deeds to America and made it suffer in this way, for you are the sons of those great knights, who carried Islam eastward until they reached China.

Let it be known to you that this war is a new Crusader campaign against the Muslim world, and it is a war that is crucial to the entire Islamic nation. Only God knows the extent of its serious repercussions and negative effects on Islam and Muslims. O young people of Islam everywhere, especially in the neighboring countries and in Yemen, you should pursue *jihad* and roll your sleeves up. Follow the right path and be careful not to support the men who follow their whims, those who sat idle, or those who relied on oppressors. For those would seek to shake you and inhibit you from pursuing this blessed *jihad*.

There have been voices in Iraq, as there were in Palestine, Egypt, Jordan, Yemen, and other countries before, calling for a peaceful, democratic solution in dealing with the apostate governments or the Jewish and Crusader invaders instead of fighting for the cause of God. It was thus imperative to draw attention in brief to the seriousness of this wrong, misleading approach, which is against God's law and which inhibits fighting for His sake. For how can you obey, when *jihad* becomes a duty, those who never fought for the sake of God? Will you not learn a lesson? It was those who obstructed the efforts of the honest men of the Islamic nation.

They relied on the whims of people and on democracy—the religion of the pre-Islam era—to join legislative councils. They have gone far astray and misled many people. Why do they join the council of polytheism—the legislative council of representatives, which Islam destroyed—thus destroying the pillars of religion? What was left for them?

They claim that they are on the right path, but they are doing a great wrong. God knows that Islam is innocent of their deeds, for Islam is the religion of God. The legislative councils of representatives are the religion of the pre-Islam era.

He who obeys the leaders or scholars in permitting what God banned, such as joining the legislative councils, or banning what He permitted, such as *jihad* for His sake, would be associating other gods with Him. God is our sole source of strength.

To the American People and U.S. Soldiers Fighting in Iraq

Praise be to God. There is to be no transgression except on the ones that do injustice to others.

From Osama bin Muhammad bin Laden to the American people regarding your aggression on Iraq.

I greet those that follow the guidance of God. O American people, some people pictured you as a great people. It turned out that most of you are riff-raff who do not have any share in great ethics. You elect the evildoers from among you who tell many lies and are impolite. You are being enslaved by those who have the most money, the most influential ones, and those who have the strongest news media, particularly the Jews, who are dragging you behind them under the trick of democracy in order to support the Israelis and their schemes and hostility to our religion and at the expense of our blood and land, as well as at the expense of your blood and economy.

Events have proven this. The fact that you were driven to the Iraqi war, in which you have no interest whatsoever, is evidence of this. Bush came with his hard-booted, hard-hearted gang. This gang is a huge evil on all humanity, its blood, money, environment, and morality. They came to deal strong and consecutive blows to honesty that is the basis of morality, each from the position he holds, until they professionally rendered it dead before the world. With this behavior of theirs, they encouraged hypocrisy, corrupted people, and spread political bribery at the level of heads of state with no shame.

This gang and their leader do not find anything wrong with lying, war, theft, and robbery if it would serve their personal greed. Their fangs drip blood from the corpses of the children of Vietnam and Somalia and the children of Afghanistan and Iraq. They did not care about you, went behind your backs, invaded Iraq once again, and lied to you and the whole world. It has been said: a nation's strength is in its morality; if the morality of the people of any nation was to deteriorate they would cease to exist. Bush has pushed your children into the mouth of the lion so that they will slaughter others and get slaughtered, claiming that this is in defense of international peace and America. In so doing, he hides the true motive.

On the one hand, he implements the demands of the Zionist lobby, which helped him enter the White House, to destroy the military power of Iraq, which neighbors the Jews in occupied Palestine. In so doing, he shows absolute indifference to the repercussions on your blood and economy. On the other hand, he conceals his own greed and the ambitions of this lobby in Iraq and its oil. He is still thinking in the mentality of his ancestors who used to kill the red Indians to seize their lands and loot their wealth.

He thought that the matter would be easy spoils and a short trip that would not end in failure. However, God had those lions waiting for him in Baghdad, the home of the Islamic caliphate, the lions of the desert who believe that the taste of death in their mouths is better than honey. They, praise be God, turned his gains into losses and his joy into sorrow. Bush is now like the one who would be pleased to relinquish the spoils if he comes back safe. Praise be to God who uncovered his lies and exposed his motives and brought more calamities to you under his rule.

I tell Bush that appealing for help from the world around you and begging for mercenary soldiers from everywhere, even from the small countries, has shattered your pride, insulted your prestige, and exposed your powerlessness after you used to defend the world in its entirety. You are now like the one who used to defend people with his own sword, but now he looks for others to defend him.

Let the unjust ones know that we maintain our right to reply, at the appropriate time and place, to all the states that are taking part in this unjust war, particularly Britain, Spain, Australia, Poland, Japan and Italy. The Islamic world's states that are taking part in this war, particularly the Gulf States, mainly Kuwait, the land base for the Crusader forces, will not be excluded from this.

I also tell the U.S. soldiers in Iraq: After the daylight emerged and the biggest liar and his true nature were exposed, your continued presence in Iraq is compound injustice and a great folly. You are selling your life for the sake of others. So, your blood is being shed in order to increase the assets of the White House's gang and their partners of the arms dealers and owners of the conniving big companies. The most stupid person is the one who sells life for the sake of others.

Concluding, I tell the American people: God willing, we will continue to fight you. We will continue the martyrdom operations inside and outside the United States until you end your injustice, abandon your stupidity, and curb your insolent fellows. You should know that we count our killed ones, may God have mercy on their souls, particularly those killed in Palestine at the hands of your allies, the Jews. So, we will punish you for them, God willing, just like what happened on the New York day. Just remember what I told you at the time about our security and your security.

As for Baghdad, the Caliphate house, God willing, you will never take it. We will fight you as long as we have weapons in our hands, and if these weapons fall, our sons will pick them up. Let our mothers be bereaved if we leave any trace of you on our land. How can a person sleep when his main concern is to remove injustice? You will never be able to take Baghdad as long as there is a sword in our hand.

We fight those who fight us and chop off their heads with our swords. There will be no peace until infidelity is defeated. God suffices us, and He is our supporter, and you do not have any supporter.

Source: "Bin Laden tapes addresses Iraqis, Americans, vow more attacks—full text" Al-Jazeera TV, Doha, in Arabic 1602 gmt 18 Oct 03/BBC Monitoring/ ©BBC

24

Message to the Islamic Nation

(4 January 2004)

In this 14-minute long audiotape aired on *Al Jazeera* on 4 January, Bin Laden urged Muslims to continue *jihad* and condemned Gulf Arab leaders for supporting the U.S.-led invasion of Iraq.

Thanksgiving and praise are due to God alone, we seek aid from Him alone; and we beseech forgiveness of our sins from Him only; and consign ourselves to the protection of God against the evils of our souls and against all offenses. Truly, whosoever God guides on the straight path—and He puts him only on the straight path who sincerely desires to walk along that way—no one can lead him astray. And whosoever God deflects—and He deflects only him who yearns to be deflected—no one can put him on the straight path. And I bear witness that "*There is no god except God, and Muhammad is the Messenger of God.*"

> "*O Believers! Fear God, as He should be feared, and do not die except in a state of Islam.*" [Qur'an 3:102}

From Osama bin Laden to his brothers and sisters in the entire Islamic nation. God's peace, mercy and blessings be upon you.

My message to you concerns inciting and continuing to urge *jihad* to repulse the grand plots that have been hatched against our Islamic nation, especially since some of them have appeared clearly, such as the occupation of the Crusaders, with the help of the apostates, of Baghdad, the house of the Caliphate, under the trick of weapons of mass destruction.

There is also the fierce attempt to destroy the Al-Aqsa Mosque and destroy *jihad* and the *mujahideen* in beloved

Palestine by employing the trick of the road map and the Geneva peace initiative. This is in addition to the Crusader media campaigns against the Islamic nation. These campaigns show how malicious are the evils they harbor against the Islamic nation in general and against the people of the Two Holy Mosques in particular. The Americans' intentions have also become clear in statements about the need to change the beliefs, curricula and morals of the Muslims to become more tolerant, as they put it.

In truth, it is a religious-economic war. They want the Muslims to desist from worshipping God so that they can enslave them, occupy their countries, and loot their wealth. It is strange that they want to dictate democracy and Americanize our culture through their jet bombers. Therefore, what is yet to come is even more malicious and devilish.

The occupation of Iraq is a link in the Zionist-Crusader chain of evil. Then comes the full occupation of the rest of the Gulf States to set the stage for controlling and dominating the whole world. For the big powers believe that the Gulf and the Gulf States are the key to global control due to the presence of the largest oil reserves there.

What have we prepared for this? The Zionist-Crusader campaign against the Islamic nation today is the most dangerous and rabid ever, because it threatens the entire Islamic nation, its religion and existence. Did Bush not say that it is a Crusader war? Did he not say that the war will continue for many years and target 60 states? Is the Islamic world not around 60 states? Do you not realize this? Did they not say that they want to change the region's ideology, which vents hatred against the Americans? They mean Islam and its peak after all. They know full well that they will not enjoy our wealth and land as long as we remain *mujahid* Muslims. So, learn this and keep it in your minds.

O Muslims! The situation is serious, and the misfortune is momentous. By God, I am keen on safeguarding your religion and your worldly life. You are my brothers in religion and my family in kinship. An honest person would not cheat his own people. So, lend me your ears and open up your hearts to me so that we may examine these pitch-black misfortunes, and so that we may consider how we can find a way out of these adversities and calamities.

To talk about this, let me tell you what God's messenger Shu'ayb told his people: "*I only desire your betterment to the best of my power; and my success in my task can only come from God. In Him I trust, and unto Him I look*" [Qur'an: 11:88]. In so doing, I seek God's assistance and trust to enforce His will no matter what the consequences are. I seek the truth and fear nobody in championing rightfulness. I am after God's satisfaction, even if this angers some people. Our life terms will come to an end, and our sustenance is predestined by God. So, why should one fear telling the truth and championing rightfulness? No one should desist from championing *jihad* when it becomes obligatory except for those who have lost their direction, humiliated themselves, and deprived themselves of unmatched reward. Therefore, the first step to emerge from this dilemma is to return to Almighty God, pray for His forgiveness, turn in repentance to Him, and follow the path of His great *Qur'an* and the tradition of His faithful Messenger (PBUH).

We should also look for the main reasons that diverted the march from the straight path [guidance] from inside and identify the active forces that caused this deviation. We will find, without much effort, that these reasons are the princes, scholars, and preachers of evil, and those who have done injustice to the Islamic nation, as well as the media persons of these states and those who followed them. The bitter truth is that the princes have managed to seduce many of the individuals of these groups and muffled the voices of those who have refused to join them.

Since telling the truth and differentiating between truth and falsehood are part of the teachings of the *Qur'an* and the Prophet's tradition so that people would not mix falsehood and truth, and thus stray from the right path [guidance], God said: "*And cover not Truth with falsehood, nor conceal the Truth when you know what it is*" [Qur'an 2:42].

To remove any ambiguity, things have to be called by their true names and described with their religious terms, especially when we talk about the forces that influence the Islamic nation's march. This helps us have a clear image of these forces and their actions, and makes it easier for us to deal with them since judging things comes after knowing about them. Therefore, religious terms should be used when describing the ruler who does not follow God's revelations and path, and champions the infidels by extending military facilities to them or implementing the U.N. resolutions against Islam and Muslims. They should be called infidels and renegades. The forces that consciously support tyrants by their own free will are partners in the injustice being done to Muslims. I appeal to the people of the Islamic nation to oust their leaders who supported these tyrants and select strong and honest leaders who can shoulder their duties under the current difficult circumstances and defend the Islamic nation. The media persons who belittle the religious duties, such as *jihad* and other rituals, are atheists and renegades. This is as far as those forces that have diverted the course of our march from inside are concerned.

As to how to resist these enemy forces from outside, we must look back at the previous Crusader wars against our countries to learn lessons that will help us confront this onslaught, understand the most important causes of these attacks, and learn how they were repulsed and resisted.

The West's occupation of our countries is old, yet new. The conflict between us and them began centuries ago and will continue because the conflict between truth and falsehood will continue until Judgment Day. Such a confrontation is good for both the countries and peoples. God says: "*And did not God check one set of people by means of another, the earth would indeed be full of mischief*" [part of *Qur'an* 2:251]. Those who interpret the *Qur'an* say that this verse means that had the believers not fought the infidels, the latter would have defeated the believers and the Earth would have been corrupted by their ill deeds. So, pay attention to the importance of conflict.

There can be no dialogue with occupiers except with weapons. If we look at the nature of the conflict between us and the West, we find that when they invaded our countries more than 2,500 years ago they did not have a sound religion or ethics. Their motive was to steal and plunder. Our ancestors in Bilad al-Sham [Jordan, Syria, Lebanon and Palestine] remained under occupation for more than 10 decades. We defeated them only after the mission of our Prophet Muhammad (PBUH). It was the true commitment to Islam that reshaped the Arab character, liberated it from pre-Islamic concepts, enlightened the hearts and minds, and released energies. Neither the Arabs nor anybody else could stand in the face of the battalions of faith at the time. The Persians, Tatars, Turks, Romans and Berbers collapsed in front of the shouts of 'God is great'. We were the pioneers of the world. We rescued the people from worshipping people to worshipping the God of people (SWT).

When our adherence to our religion weakened and our rulers became corrupt, we became weak and the Romans [Western Christians] returned by waging their infamous Crusader wars. They occupied the Al-Aqsa Mosque, but after 90 years we regained our strength when we returned to our religion. Thus, with the help of God, we regained the Al-Aqsa Mosque at the hands of a wise leader who pursued a sound approach. The leader was Saladin, may God bestow his mercy on him, and the approach was Islam, whose peak is *jihad* in the cause of God. This is what we need today and what we should seek to do. Islamic countries in the past century were not liberated from the Crusaders' military occupation except through *jihad* in the cause of God.

Under the pretext of fighting terrorism, the West today is doing its utmost to tarnish *jihad* and kill anyone seeking *jihad*. The West is supported in this endeavor by hypocrites. This is because they all know that *jihad* is the effective power to foil all their conspiracies. *Jihad* is the path, so seek it. This is because if we seek to deter them by any means other than Islam, we would be like the one who goes round in circles. We would also be like our forefathers, the al-Ghasasinah.[(1)] The

(1) Al-Ghasasinah: an Arab people who lived in a state historically located in the north-west of the Persian empire.

concern of their seniors was to be appointed officers for the Romans and to be named kings in order to safeguard the interests of the Romans by killing their brothers of the peninsula's Arabs. Such is the case of the new al-Ghasasinah; namely, Arab rulers.

Muslims: If you do not punish them for their sins in Jerusalem and Iraq, they shall defeat you because of your failure. They will also rob you of the land of al-Haramain [Mecca and Medina]. Today [they robbed you] of Baghdad, and tomorrow they will rob you of Riyadh and so forth unless God deems otherwise. Sufficient unto us is God.

What then is the means to stop this tremendous onslaught? As you may recall, the Islamic nation made several attempts in the recent decades to resist the Zionist-Crusader alliance to liberate Palestine. The republics and kingdoms embraced several earthly religions in the region, like pan-Arabism, Socialism, Communism, Democracy, and other doctrines. These material forces have proved beyond any shadow of a doubt that they surrendered to the U.S.-led Crusader-Zionist alliance. The people followed these forces for a long time only to find they are still at square one. We have had enough of chasing mirages. Stop manipulating the people's minds.

In such hard times, some reformers maintain that all popular and official forces should unite, and that all government forces should unite with all their peoples. Everyone would do what is needed from him in order to ward off this Crusader-Zionist onslaught. The question strongly raised is: Are the governments in the Islamic world capable of pursuing this duty of defending the faith and Islamic nation and renouncing allegiance to the United States? Let us have an objective look at these governments' history with regard to the Islamic nation's crucial issues to understand their policies so that we will not be led to a dead-end and so that we will not experience what had been experienced for many decades.

1. Their [the governments'] position on the Crusader aggression in World War I: When they [the Crusaders] attacked the Islamic world and sought to topple the Ottoman state, these rulers rose up against the Ottoman state, divided the

Muslims, and made an effective contribution in terms of fighting this state, thus leading to its fall under the Crusader occupation and division into more than 50 countries. The prominent role in this treason was played by King Abd al-Aziz al-Sa'ud and Al-Sharif Husayn and his sons.

2. The Palestine Question: The position of these rulers toward this pivotal issue for nine decades has been based on pledging to the British to allow the Jews to establish a state on the land of Palestine, letting down the people of Palestine, and misleading them on several occasions to lay down their weapons. The most prominent of these attempts was made by King Abd al-Aziz al-Sa'ud. When the Zionist organization, or the so-called United Nations, issued its resolution on dividing Palestine and establishing a Jewish state in it, the Arab rulers stood idly by. They have even remained members in this organization until today. They have done nothing, except for shameful actions, to prevent this from happening. A fabricated war erupted after the Jewish state was established one year after the issuance of the resolution of partitioning [Palestine]. Then, the Arab rulers agreed to sign a temporary truce in response to the request of the United States, which asked them to sign a permanent truce after one year. Thus, they almost buried alive Palestine and its people, but God protected them.

The conspiracies continued, including the Madrid conference and what came after it. The efforts continued to abort the first *Intifada*. In the Sharm al-Shaykh conference in 1416 A.H. [1996], they supported the Jews and Christians against our oppressed people in Palestine. In addition, the Beirut initiative recognized the Jews and a large part of the land they occupied in Palestine. The most recent conspiracy is the road map. In the course of these conspiracies, they give some money to the people of Palestine to throw dust in the eyes. History attests that they have restored nothing of Palestine during the past nine decades.

What is surprising, and disgusting as well, is the position of those rulers toward the families of the *mujahideen* who carried out martyrdom operations. While these families were expecting good deeds from them, they met them with evil.

Not only did they condemn the martyrdom operations, but they also came up with something that is more annoying and distressing. Look at the conditions of these families in Palestine as well as the conditions of our sisters the widows, whose husbands were killed by the Jews. Some of them sacrificed their sons for the sake of Islam and Islamic sanctuaries. After the possessors of thrones and armies abandoned them, the Jewish soldiers came to corrupt the land of Jerusalem, destroy the agricultural lands, and kill the people. They forced the Palestinian widow to leave her house and destroyed its contents, not allowing her to take her precious possessions. She became homeless on roadsides, and tears filled her eyes not knowing where to take her children and those of her son—whom we consider a martyr but God knows best—as a result of her suffering and dire distress.

Thanks to God, some kindhearted people from the Land of the Two Sacred Mosques and other countries were sending alms to the families of those widows and orphans to ease their suffering and distress. Unfortunately, the conceited, arrogant prince, Abdallah Bin Abd al-Aziz, ordered that these well-doers be prevented from sending money to these families so that the martyrdom operations would stop. What kind of heart is that to issue such an order? Is it a heart of a human being, or is it a heart made of stone? What kind of meanness is that to prevent small amounts of money from reaching a widow, an orphan, or a poor person? Can such cruel-hearted people bring us good or defend our countries and peoples? Those hypocrites, worshippers of money, claim that they are our leaders and will defend us.

The calls by some reformers are strange. They say that the path to righteousness and defending our countries comes through these apostate leaders. I tell these people: If you have an excuse preventing you from *jihad*, it does not give you the right to depend on the unjust leaders and thus be responsible for your sins and those of whom you misled. Fear God for your sake and for your Islamic nation's sake. God does not need your flattery and praise for the tyrants for the sake of His religion. Almighty God says: "*So hearken not to those who deny the truth, their desire is that you should be pliant, so would they be pliant*" [Qur'an 68:8-9]. It is better for a person to be at the bottom of right than to be at the peak of wrong.

3. The Gulf States proved their total inability to resist the Iraqi forces. They sought help from the Crusaders, led by the United States, as is well-known. How can these states stand up to the United States and the Iraqi forces, which are being formed these days under the U.S. command? The decision made by Jabir al-Sabah [*Amir* of Kuwait] and his comrades following the Iraqi invasion of Kuwait—when they fled the country—is the same decision that will be made by all the Gulf rulers, unless they reach an agreement with the United States to leave their thrones and be given other jobs to deceive the people and protect U.S. interests, pledging not to ask about oil revenues, as happened with their agents in the transitional Iraqi Governing Council (IGC). What proves their defeatism and submission to the occupier is their acceptance to receive IGC members and cooperate with them. In short, these states came to America's help and backed it in its attack against an Arab state which is bound to them by covenants of joint defense agreements. These covenants were reiterated at the Arab League just a few days before the U.S. attack, only to violate them in full. This shows their positions on the Islamic nation's basic causes.

4. These regimes wavered too much before taking a stand on using force and attacking Iraq. At times they absolutely rejected participation, and at other times they linked this with U.N. agreement. Then they went back to their first option. In fact, the lack of participation was in line with the domestic desire of these states. However, they finally submitted and succumbed to U.S. pressure and opened their air, land and sea bases to contribute toward the U.S. campaign, despite the immense repercussions of this move.

Most important of these repercussions is that this is a sin against one of the Islamic tenets and high treason against the Islamic nation. This move would also stir up popular anger and pave the way for bringing down these treacherous, apostate, and powerless regimes. Most important and dangerous in their view was that they feared that the door would be open for bringing down dictatorial regimes by armed forces from abroad, especially after they had seen the arrest of their former comrade in treason and agentry to the United States when it [U.S.] ordered him [Saddam Hussein] to ignite the First Gulf War against Iran, which had rebelled against it [the U.S.]. The war consumed everything and plunged the area into a maze from which it has not emerged to this day. The wars that followed were repercussions of this war.

They are aware that their turn will come. They do not have the will to make the difficult decision to confront the aggression, in addition to their belief that they do not possess the material resources for that. Indeed, they were prevented from establishing a large military force when they were forced to sign secret pledges and documents long ago.

5. What shows their position toward the Islamic nation's causes is the support they provided to the United States by opening their bases to contribute to its Crusader campaign against Afghanistan. It is an obvious support for the infidels against an Islamic country. This is a cardinal sin that renders one an infidel.

6. One of the obvious facts that showed what kind of position the Gulf rulers were ready to take when they came under U.S. pressure to hand over oil fields to the United States was their collective support for Zayid Initiative, which called on Saddam Hussein to hand over Iraq, its people, and its oil to the United States; to leave power; and to accept to be given political asylum under the pretext of sparing the Iraqi people the bloodshed. Sa'ud al-Faysal repeatedly and shamelessly underlined this principle. Ostensibly, and based on what has been said, this apparently shows that if they come under U.S. pressure and face a U.S. desire to occupy the oil regions, the Gulf rulers, including the Riyadh ruler, will take the same stand.

7. The most obvious reflection of the rulers' stand *vis-à-vis* repulsing the aggression is the stand taken by their leader, which manifested itself when U.S. tanks entered the Arabian Peninsula and its waters were disturbed by the Crusader aircraft

carriers that were carrying the most sophisticated ammunition and weapons to occupy the region. Their leader, who taught them submission, came out to address the public to instill into the nation submission, humiliation, and subjugation, and say: These troop concentrations are not for war. How shameful?

> "If you do not know, that is a calamity. If you do, the calamity is greater." [poetry]

In short, the ruler who believes in some of the above-mentioned deeds cannot defend the country. How can he do so if he believes in all of them and has done that time and again? Those who believe in the principle of supporting the infidels over Muslims and leave the blood, honor and property of their brothers to be easy prey for their enemy in order to remain safe, claiming that they love their brothers but are being forced to take such a path—of course this compulsion cannot be regarded as legitimate from the point of view of Islamic law—are in fact qualified to take the same course against one another in the Gulf States. Indeed, this principle is liable to be embraced within the same state itself.

For example, the Riyadh ruler is capable of abandoning the eastern, central, and other provinces to the Americans. Likewise, he is capable of abandoning the northern province and part of the western province to Jews in exchange for keeping Jazan, Samitah, and Abu Arish. Those who read and understood the history of kings throughout history know that they are capable of committing more than these concessions, except those who enjoyed the mercy of God. Indeed, the rulers have practically started to sell out the sons of the land by pursuing and imprisoning them and by unjustly and wrongly accusing them of becoming like the Al-Khawarij sect[2] who held Muslims to be infidels and went to excess in killing them. We hold them to be martyrs. Sufficient unto them is God.

All of this happened before the Riyadh explosions in Rabi al-Awwal of this year [May 2003], which the regime advances as a pretext. This campaign came within a drive to implement the U.S. orders in the hope that they will win its blessings,

---

(2) Al-Khawarij sect: a rebellious, extremist Islamic group in early Islam.

even though it was the regime which provoked the youths by opening the country for the Crusaders in violation of religion, in disregard for the Muslims' sentiments, and in defiance of the manliness of the men of the Two Holy Mosques. Consequently, it was the regime which really disturbed security. Because this message cannot accommodate all my thoughts in this regard, I discussed this issue in a special message addressed to the Land of the Two Sacred Mosques which I hope will reach you soon.

What sums up the situation of the nation, the ferocious attacks of the enemies against it, the treason of the atheistic rulers, their betrayal of religion, their tyrannical treatment of their peoples, and the failure of Islamic groups to wage *jihad* are the following lines of poetry which are mostly written by Dr. Yusuf Abu-Hilalah, who says:

"The great nation has become a play thing in the hands of the priest and rabbi.

It is like a nation that, in terms of standing, makes no difference regardless of whether it remains idle or stands up.

Now that calamities are eliminating it, its leaders are sitting on their thrones as skeletons and bones.

Jerusalem, woe unto Jerusalem, its chastity has been desecrated, and Muslims have chosen not to engage in *jihad*.

Baghdad, O House of the Caliphate, woe unto you, why has your chastity been defiled by rabble?

Why did those who betrayed their religion yesterday choose to turn a blind eye to the raids on your sanctuaries?

Are you assaulting lions when dealing with peoples, and rabbits and ostriches when it comes to dealing with Jews?

I no longer have a home whose shelter I can seek, for my homeland has been desecrated and set on fire.

> O my nation, I am a bird who has seen a thicket, may I sing? Will I be blamed if I do?
>
> Am I to blame if I present you with a fact; namely, that the rulers are our mortal enemies?
>
> They are unbelievers; yet, they are called the servants and *imams* of Muslims.
>
> They pretend to be our support, when, in point of fact, they are our disease and death.
>
> The Crusaders' army has enveloped the universe, where are the pious, magnanimous, and audacious men?"

Based on the above, the extent of the real danger, which the region in general and the Arabian Peninsula in particular is being exposed to, has appeared. It has become clear that the rulers are not qualified to apply the religion and defend the Muslims. In fact, they have provided evidence that they are implementing the schemes of the enemies of the nation and religion and that they are qualified to abandon the countries and peoples.

Now, after we have known the situation of the rulers, we should examine the policy which they have been pursuing. Anyone who examines the policy of those rulers will easily see that they follow their whims and desires and their personal interests and Crusader loyalties.

Commitment to Islam is not one of the constants in their policies and religious practices. They believe in a part of the Book and reject the rest in conformity with their whims to keep their thrones, which is a grievous act of infidelity, as the Almighty God demonstrates in the following *Qur'an*ic verse: "*Then is it only a part of the Book that you believe in, and do you reject the rest? But what is the reward for those among you who behave like this but disgrace in this life?—and on the Day of Judgment they shall be consigned to the most grievous penalty. For God is not unmindful of what you do*" [Qur'an 7:167].

To them, the only major constant is keeping the seat of power. Therefore, the flaw does not involve a secondary issue, such as personal corruption that is confined to the palace of the ruler. The flaw is in the very approach. This happened when a malicious belief and destructive principle spread in most walks of life, to the effect that absolute supremacy and obedience were due to the ruler and not to the religion of God. This means that slavery is for the ruler and not for Almighty God. This is the important reality that the rulers manipulate even if they use Islam as a cover in some countries, especially after they assigned an army of scholars, preachers, writers, and the entire mass media for about a century to exaggerate the meaning of obedience to the ruler away from the restrictions to this concept stipulated in God's religion. Therefore, the ruler becomes an idol that is worshipped instead of God—as the situation in the Land of the Two Sacred Mosques. If any of the scholars refuses to flatter the rulers, his fate will be prison until he is forced to flatter. In other countries they have used the guise of parliaments and democracy.

Thus, the situation of all Arab countries suffers from great deterioration in all walks of life, in religious and worldly matters. It is enough to know that the economy of all Arab countries is weaker than the economy of one country that had once been part of our Islamic world when we used to truly adhere to Islam. That country is the lost Andalusia. Spain is an infidel country, but its economy is stronger than our economy because the ruler there is accountable. In our countries, there is no accountability or punishment, but there is only obedience to the rulers and prayers of long life for them.

We have reached this miserable situation because many of us lack the correct and comprehensive understanding of the religion of Islam. Many of us understand Islam to mean performing some acts of worship, such as prayer and fasting. Despite the great importance of these rituals, the religion of Islam encompasses all the affairs of life, including religious and worldly affairs, such as economic, military and political affairs, as well as the scales by which we weigh the actions of men—rulers, scholars and others—and how to deal with the ruler in line with the rules set by God for him and which the ruler should not violate.

These rules also include enacting legislation contrary to God's will, allegiance to infidels and supporting them against Muslims, or tampering with, or embezzling huge amounts of the nation's money. Many people think that this is part of the ruler's authority and do not know that these actions by the ruler are some of the cardinal sins in our Islamic law that should not be accepted. Furthermore, enacting legislation contrary to God's will by the ruler and his allegiance to the infidels constitute a greater atheism that drives the person who does them away from faith, which necessitates rising against him after good preparation.

Had they read the *Qur'an* and Prophet Muhammad's traditions and had they learned lessons from them, which is what we should do, this would have become very clear to them in several texts. Among these texts is a *Hadith* by Uday bin-Hatim, who converted to Christianity before Islam, and who thought, as many people think, that following the leaders and scholars in allowing what has been forbidden by God and banning what has been allowed by God is not worship of these leaders and scholars and is not atheism, because this does not mean praying or fasting for them. However, when Bin-Hatim came to the messenger of God (PBUH) while he was reading this *Qur'an*ic verse: "*They take their priests and their anchorites to be their lords in derogation of God*" [Qur'an 9:31], he said that he told the Prophet: "They did not worship them." The Prophet answered: "Yes, but they forbade what is allowed and allowed what has been forbidden and followed them. Therefore, this is what they worship."

Be careful with this verse, because this verse and that *Hadith* clearly show that obedience to the ruler, a scholar, or anyone else in allowing what has been forbidden by God and banning what God has allowed is tantamount to worshipping them rather than God. This is a greater polytheism and drives the person away from faith, may God protect us and you from this.

This is what Almighty God associated Himself of when he says: "*Praise and glory to Him:* [Far is He] *from having the partners they associate* [with Him]" (Qur'an 7:190 & 27:63] after he says: "*Yet they were commanded to worship but one god. There is no god except He*" [Qur'an 9:31]. This shows that issuing legislation concerning what is allowed and what is banned is a type of worship. This is one of the most important traits of God and one of the most important prerequisites for testifying that "*There is no god except God*", the first and most important pillar of Islam. This is a serious warning to those who think that Islam is mere words uttered in which one testifies that "*There is no god except God*", while they do not know that these words have requirements that if they do not heed, they would not be committed to the testimony that there is no god. The gist here is that the absence of a comprehensive understanding of God's religion as a system for all walks of life, including Islam's way of holding the rulers accountable—because if they follow God's religion things become good for the country and the people—is one of the greatest flaws in the Islamic nation at present. We should be fully aware of this issue and start the reform march today in order to follow the right path [guidance], God willing. We should not continue in this wrong path for another century.

One of the beneficial books that explained the previous *Qur'an*ic verse is *Kitab al-Imam* [*The Book of Faith*] by Sheikh Ibn Taymiyah, may God have mercy on his soul; and also the book titled *Fath al-Mujid* by Sheikh Abd al-Rahman bin-Hasan al-Sheikh, may God have mercy on his soul; and the book entitled *Concepts that Should be Corrected* by Sheikh Muhammad Qutb. These showed that the rulers are incapable and traitors, and that they have not followed the right path of Islam but followed their wishes and lusts, and this is the reason for the setbacks in the Islamic nation's march during the past decades. Therefore, it becomes clear to us that the solution lies in adhering to the religion of God, by which God granted us pride in the past centuries and installing a strong and faithful leadership that applies the *Qur'an* among us and raises the true banner of *jihad*.

The honest people who are concerned about this situation, such as the scholars, leaders who are obeyed among their people, dignitaries, notables and merchants should get together and meet in a safe place away from the shadow of these suppressive regimes and form a council for *Ahl al-Hall wa al-Aqd*[(3)] to fill the vacuum caused by the religious invalidation of these regimes and their mental deficiency. The right to appoint a leader is for the Islamic nation. The Islamic nation also has the right to make him correct his course if he deviates from it and to remove him if he does something that warrants this, such as apostasy and treason.

This temporary council should be made up of the minimum number of available personnel, who should be tough on the rest of the Islamic nation, except what the religion allows in case of necessity, until the number is increased when the situation improves, God willing. Their policy should be based on the book of God [*Qur'an*] and the tradition of His Prophet [Muhammad], (PBUH). They should start by directing Muslims to the important priorities at this critical stage and lead them to a safe haven, provided that their top priority should be uniting opinions under the word of monotheism and defending Islam and its people and countries, and urging Muslims to carry out *jihad* and prepare for it.

The people should be given easy access to arms, particularly light weapons; anti-armored rockets, such as RPG's; and tank mines; as well as the declaration of a general mobilization in the Islamic nation to prepare for repulsing the raids of the Romans, which started in Iraq and no-one knows where they will end. God suffices us and He is the best supporter.

My brothers in faith, we should be certain that our success and happiness in this world and in the hereafter lies in implementing Islam and carrying out *jihad*. Our pride and happiness lie in them based on the true Prophet's saying, which was told by Abu Dawud citing Ibn Umar, may God be pleased with them. The Prophet (PBUH) says: "If you practiced *Tabaiya al-Ainiya* [Selling goods to a person for a certain price and then buying them back from him for a far lesser price], followed the tails of cows, satisfied yourselves with agriculture, and abandoned *jihad*, God will cover you with humiliation and will not remove it until you return to your religion."

---

(3) A reference to honest, wise and righteous people who can appoint or remove a ruler in Islamic tradition.

Caliph Umar told Abu Ubaydah, may God be pleased with them: "We are a people whom God made powerful with Islam, and if we seek strength from other sources, God will humiliate us." Therefore, the advocates of reform should know that reforming and uniting the Islamic nation under Islam cannot be achieved through lectures and books only, but there should be a practical plan involving the entire Islamic nation, each according to his own capabilities, beginning with prayer to God and ending with fighting in the cause of God, for fighting in the cause of God is an indivisible part of our religion. In fact, it is the peak of religion. So, how can religion survive without its peak? It is a pressing need for our Islamic nation's life, glory and survival. Although our enemy lies, it tells the truth when it says: You fight, so you exist. This is what they teach their children, but they tell us the contrary. Moreover, fighting is a need for the survival of big powers. Just read history if you want, including the history of America. It [the United States] ignited dozens of wars throughout six decades only. This is because that was one of its most pressing needs. When the United States makes a sincere decision to stop wars in the world, then it knows before anyone else that that day will mark the beginning of its collapse and the disintegration of its states. This day is coming, God willing. So, beware of any call for laying down arms on the pretext of achieving peace. This is because this will be a call for humiliating us. Only a hypocrite or an ignorant person can promote such calls.

Before concluding, I urge the Muslim youths to carry out *jihad*, particularly in Palestine and Iraq. I also call on them to be patient and pious, and to weaken the enemy by inflicting wounds on it, along with protecting Muslims during this. They also should be careful not to expand on applying the law regarding the use of human shields, for this should be left to their honest scholars on a case by case basis. We beseech God to grant us victory through patience and piety. May God make us patient and pious.

Concluding, I would like to say a few words to Muslim youths, words which we heard from your grandfathers who had been tested by events throughout many years in Palestine, and who had been witness to many initiatives, conspiracies, calamities, and calls for peace. I just want to remind you of these words. These are:

My son, they will talk to you about peace, do not listen to such calls, because although I once believed them I am still living in a tent. "*And God has full power and control over His affairs; but most among mankind know it not*" [Qur'an 12:21]. "*Our Lord! Give us good in this world and good in the Hereafter, and defend us from the torment of the Fire!*" [Qur'an 2:201]. O God, I beseech you to strengthen the *mujahideen* everywhere, particularly in Palestine, Iraq, Kashmir, Chechnya, and Afghanistan. We beseech God to grant them success, to strengthen them, to unite their ranks, and to grant them victory over their enemies, especially since no one grants them victory except Almighty God. O God, we beseech you to put this Islamic nation's feet firmly on the right path in order to strengthen those who obey You and to humiliate those who disobey You. "*Praise be to God, the Cherisher and Sustainer of the Worlds*" [Qur'an 1:2]. May God's prayer and peace be on the last of prophets and messengers.

25

A Reconciliation Initiative to Europe

(15 April 2004)

On 15 April, an audiotape from Bin Laden was broadcast by *Al Arabiya* (United Arab Emirates) and *Al Jazeera* (Qatar). Using the phrase *Mubadart Sulh*, Bin Laden offered Europe a reconciliation initiative, while maintaining the U.S. as a legitimate target. It was rejected by the European countries.

Praise be to Almighty God; Peace and prayers be upon our Prophet Muhammad, his family, and Companions. This is a message to our neighbors north of the Mediterranean, containing a reconciliation initiative as a response to their positive reactions. Praise be to God; praise be to God; praise be to God who created heaven and earth with justice and who allowed the oppressed to punish the oppressor in the same way. Peace upon those who followed the right path.

In my hands there is a message to remind you that justice is a duty towards those whom you love and those whom you do not. And people's rights will not be harmed if the opponent speaks out about them. The greatest rule of safety is justice, and stopping injustice and aggression. It was said: Oppression kills the oppressors and the hotbed of injustice is evil. The situation in occupied Palestine is an example. What happened on 11 September [2001] and 11 March [the Madrid train bombings] is your commodity that was returned to you. It is known that security is a pressing necessity for all mankind. We do not agree that you should monopolize it only for yourselves. Also, vigilant people do not allow their politicians to tamper with their security.

Having said this, we would like to inform you that labeling us and our acts as terrorism is also a description of you and of your acts. Reaction comes at the same level as the original action. Our acts are in reaction to your own acts, which are represented by the destruction and killing of our kinfolk in Afghanistan, Iraq and Palestine. The act that horrified the world; that is, the killing of the old, handicapped [Hamas spiritual leader] Sheikh Ahmed Yassin, may God have mercy on him, is sufficient evidence. We pledge to God that we will punish America for him, God willing.

Which religion considers your killed ones innocent and our killed ones worthless? And which principle considers your blood real blood and our blood water? Reciprocal treatment is fair and the one who starts injustice bears greater blame. As for your politicians and those who have followed their path, who insist on ignoring the real problem of occupying the entirety of Palestine and exaggerate lies and falsification regarding our right in defense and resistance, they do not respect themselves. They also disdain the blood and minds of peoples. This is because their falsification increases the shedding of blood instead of sparing it.

Moreover, the examining of the developments that have been taking place, in terms of killings in our countries and your countries, will make clear an important fact; namely, that injustice is inflicted on us and on you by your politicians, who send your sons—although you are opposed to this—to our countries to kill and be killed. Therefore, it is in both sides' interest to curb the plans of those who shed the blood of peoples for their narrow personal interest and subservience to the White House gang.

We must take into consideration that this war brings millions of dollars in profit to the major companies, whether it be those that produce weapons or those that contribute to reconstruction, such as the Halliburton Company, its sisters and daughters. Based on this, it is very clear who is the one benefiting from igniting this war and from the shedding of blood. It is the warlords, the bloodsuckers, who are steering the world policy from behind a curtain.

As for President Bush, the leaders who are revolving in his orbit, the leading media companies and the United Nations, which makes laws for relations between the masters of veto and the slaves of the General Assembly, these are only some of the tools used to deceive and exploit peoples. All these pose a fatal threat to the whole world. The Zionist lobby is one of the most dangerous and most difficult figures of this group. God willing, we are determined to fight them.

Based on the above, and in order to deny war merchants a chance and in response to the positive interaction shown by recent events and opinion polls, which indicate that most European peoples want peace, I ask honest people, especially scholars, preachers and merchants, to form a permanent committee to enlighten European peoples of the justice of our causes, above all Palestine. They can make use of the huge potential of the media.

I also off a reconciliation initiative to them, whose essence is our commitment to stopping operations against every country that commits itself to not attacking Muslims or interfering in their affairs—including the U.S. conspiracy on the greater Muslim world. This reconciliation can be renewed once the period signed by the first government expires and a second government is formed with the consent of both parties. The reconciliation will start with the departure of its last soldier from our country. The door of reconciliation is open for three months of the date of announcing this statement.

For those who reject reconciliation and want war, we are ready. As for those who want reconciliation, we have given them a chance. Stop shedding our blood so as to preserve your blood. It is in your hands to apply this easy, yet difficult, formula. You know that the situation will expand and increase if you delay things. If this happened, do not blame us—blame yourselves.

A rational person does not relinquish his security, money and children to please the liar of the White House. Had he been truthful about his claim for peace, he would not describe the person who ripped open pregnant women in Sabra and Shatila [reference to Israeli Prime Minister Ariel Sharon] and the destroyer of the capitulation process [reference to the Palestinian-Israeli peace process] as a man of peace. He also would not have lied to people and said that we hate freedom and kill for the sake of killing. Reality proves our truthfulness and his lie.

The killing of the Russians was after their invasion of Afghanistan and Chechnya; the killing of Europeans was after their invasion of Iraq and Afghanistan; and the killing of Americans on the day of New York [reference to 11 September] was after their support of the Jews in Palestine and their invasion of the Arabian Peninsula. Also, killing them in Somalia was after their invasion of it in Operation Restore Hope. We made them leave without hope, praise be to God.

It is said that prevention is better than cure. A happy person is he who learns a lesson from the experience of others. Heeding right is better than persisting in falsehood. Peace be upon those who follow guidance.

Source: "Full text: Bin Laden tape." BBC Monitoring Research in English 15 Apr 04/BBC Monitoring/© BBC

26

Message to the Islamic Nation in General and to Our Muslim Brothers in Iraq in Particular

(6 May 2004)

In a 20-minute recorded message, Bin Laden offered gold to anyone killing Paul Bremer, the U.S. administrator in Iraq, or Kofi Annan, the Secretary General of the United Nations. A smaller amount of gold (1 kg) was offered to anyone killing soldiers or civilians from countries that are "possessors of the [U.N. Security Council] veto, such as the Americans or Britons," and half that (500 g) was pledged for the killings of citizens of Japan and Italy who were called "slaves" of the U.N. as a tool of the Crusaders.

Praise be to God, the Cherisher and Sustainer of the worlds, and peace be upon our Prophet Muhammad, his family and his Companions.

This is a message to the Islamic nation in general and to our Muslim brothers in Iraq in particular, God's peace, mercy and blessings be upon you.

I greet our resolute brethren in the heroic land of Iraq, and I greet the *mujahideen* who are there in the way of God. I say to them: You are the heroes of the Arabs and the people who are defending Islam. You cannot be thanked enough or given enough credit by Muslims. A whole year has passed since the [U.S.-led] invasion, and the invaders have not be able to implement their plans, thanks to God and thanks to your *jihad* and the *jihad* of the people who support you. God reward you with the best reward. The enemy has been surprised by the force of the resistance as things have gone against his wishes. On the internal and external fronts the results achieved by this blessed *jihad* are very big and positive on many levels, including the casualties in the enemy's ranks and the huge financial costs for his budget, God be praised. The enemy is still suffering loss after loss, God be praised, He is All-Giving. Here I want to stress some important points:

First, there was a dangerous development of great magnitude which showed everyone how things really are. This was when the occupier [Paul] Bremer [U.S. administrator in Iraq] announced that he would not accept Islam as the source of all legislation, meaning he would not accept Islam as the religion for Iraq. Consequently, the announced constitution came according to his will. On one hand, this has clearly shown that the Iraqi Interim Governing Council (IGC) is but a puppet and a tool in the enemy's hands to implement their plans against an unwary people, and on the other hand, it has shown the extent of their hidden hatred of Islam. This also shows that the struggle is an ideological and religious struggle and the clash is a 'Clash of Civilizations'. They are keen to destroy the Islamic identity of the entire Islamic world. This is their true position regarding us. As for their position regarding other peoples, they can live with all earthly ideologies in the East and in the West, because these ideologies can be changed and manipulated, so they can consume the riches of people, enslave them, and Americanize them as they please. However, in the Islamic world the real challenge for them is an ideological and religious challenge and not primarily an economic and military challenge.

Their primary intention is to destroy Islam because they are completely convinced that their schemes in their various plans—especially the economic, ideological, military and security plans—cannot be implemented in our countries if Islam exists and is in power in the region. This is because the Muslims are the people who have the ideology, the will, and the ability to resist their plans and fight against them and their injustice.

Based on the aforementioned, and after it has become clear to everyone that the U.S. campaign has nothing to do with weapons of mass destruction or alleviating the suffering of the

Iraqi people, but is only a blatant occupation in every sense of the word, *jihad* is a must for all Muslims in northern, central and southern Iraq. Those who follow their religious leaders, using them as an excuse, and are involved with the IGC, do not have any excuse after this Council approved the constitution of the infidel Bremer. It is no secret that the use of any other legislation along with Islamic law is major polytheism and renders one an infidel. This means the members of the IGC, when they approved the constitution, became more infidel than they already were. What is the difference between political leaders like Fahd, Husni, Jabir and Saddam and the rest of the rulers, on one hand, and the religious leaders in the Interim Council of polytheism on the other? The main reason for declaring our rulers infidels is that they do not rule by the law of God in all our affairs, in addition to their alliance with America. They use the pressure the alliance exerts on them as an excuse, and the same excuse is being used by the members of the IGC. Therefore, the same verdict applies to them.

The evidence we mentioned in statement 17, indicating the rulers have forsaken the Islamic nation in that they do not sustain the commitments entailed in saying "*There is no god except God and Muhammad is the Messenger of God*" also applies to the religious leaders in the IGC and any other leadership in any other council in the Islamic world that does what these leaders have done. The most important meaning of "*There is no god except God and Muhammad is the Messenger of God*" is that there is no ruler or legislator but God. Legislation is one of the most essential attributes of God. Whoever knowingly approves of this council and its constitution has forsaken God. A believer is commanded to obey God and His Prophet (PBUH). "*If you do love God, follow me: God will love you*" [Qur'an 3:31]. "*We sent not an apostle, but to be obeyed, in accordance with the will of God*" [Qur'an 4:64]. He who obeys the Prophet (PBUH) obeys God, and he who obeys the ruler or a clergyman, regardless of his nationality, in sanctioning what God has prohibited and prohibiting what God has sanctioned, is an infidel. "*What! Have they key partners* [in the godhead], *who have established for them some religion without the permission of God*" [Qur'an 42:21].

The sincere ones must overcome the infidel leaders. Because reform and liberation need wise leaders and a sound system, and because the Holy *Qur'an* is infallible, thanks to God, and the leaders are the way we have described, then the duty becomes that of the best people to follow in rank and so on. If some of the seniors forsake God or sit idle, then those who should pursue their duty are the ones who follow in rank, even if they are young. This is because justice is greater than everyone. In this case, the sincere ones in the Islamic nation, in general, and in Iraq, in particular, must disavow and abandon the infidel religious and political leaders and exclude the leaders who are not undertaking *jihad* or those who are taking the side of injustice. The sincere ones must also take the initiative, disclose justice, and raise the flag of *jihad* against the Crusaders and infidels. The previously stated entails that whoever supports the infidels against the Muslims, such as supporting the occupation forces and their offshoots, including an interim or permanent government, will have disavowed his Islam, thus sanctioning his money and blood, and sanctioning divorcing his wife from him. Furthermore, *jihad* becomes the individual duty of Iraqis, not only against the Crusaders but also against the infidel government and its supporters. Moreover, every Muslim in the Islamic world or outside it must support this *jihad* with himself or his money, seeking the guidance of trusted people who know the country and the people, until this is enough of the needed support.

Second, the so-called transfer of power to the Iraqis is an exposed ploy intended to sedate the people and abort the armed resistance. The sincere Iraqi *mujahideen* have not fallen for it. Iraq will not be sovereign as long as there is a Crusader soldier on its land and as long as it does not depend on Islam in running its affairs.

Third, Bush, Musaylamat al-Asr[(1)], says that the top front for fighting terrorism is Iraq, which clearly means that the top

---

(1) Reference to Musaylamah who claimed to be a prophet and was fought by the Prophet Muhammad's Companions.

front for fighting Islam is Iraq. This necessitates intensifying efforts to rally Muslims to confront this onslaught. I urge the youth and the honest merchants to seize this chance to carry out a great duty to defend the religion and save the Islamic nation by supporting *jihad* with money and fighting our enemies, especially in Palestine and Iraq.

> "If the wind is favorable, seize it because all wind subsides." [poetry]
>
> "It was also said: If you have an opinion, possess will, for hesitation corrupts opinion." [poetry]

This is a rare and essentially valuable chance in every sense of the word to mobilize the Islamic nation's potential and unchain it in order to take off to the battlefields in Iraq to cut off the head of world infidelity. The youth must be alert to nomads who seek excuses and delude themselves and their brothers into believing that they are guarding a great fortified borderline, when in fact, they stopped guiding the great fortified borderline and have made the country open to Crusaders and infidels, and from whose direction Muslims were attacked. It is time for their sincere brothers to break free to rectify their situation. Caution and liberation from the magic of media is also required so that we will not be mere viewers of catastrophes and events, but rather fight the enemy and make events. This is a decisive war, after which we will either rise and have pride or descend and be humiliated.

We are at a crossroads. This is a great issue that is important for the entire Islamic nation. It is obvious that the great trick being promoted nowadays by the United States, under the pretext of forcing the so-called reform on the greater Islamic world, is a replica of Bremer's plan for Iraq, which provides for excluding religion, plundering wealth, killing men, terrifying people, and transgressing on that which is inviolable, including women in their private rooms or quarters at night. "*There is neither power nor strength except from God.*" Can you not see? Do you not have honor? Do you not have a sense of honor for your religion and sisters? Only a short time separates you from experiencing the ordeal that is being experienced in Iraq. Reflect on the issue thoroughly, and do not be like those who prove to be unintelligent on all occasions. Know that defending the lands of the Muslims, particularly the Land of the Two Sacred Mosques, begins with fighting on the front lines in the lands of Mesopotamia [Iraq].

O Muslims: Wake up and see the magnitude of the danger and the fast pace of events and mobilize for the arenas of *jihad*. The Sheikh of Islam [Ibn Taymiyah], may God have mercy on his soul, said that it is the consensus of the Islamic nation that the paramount duty, after having faith, is to repulse the assaulting enemy. God knows that if I were a student among you, I would shun my studies and mobilize as God has ordained. "*You go forth*, [whether equipped] *lightly or heavily, and strive and struggle, with your goods and your persons, in the cause of God. That is best for you, if you* [but] *knew*" [Qur'an 9:41]. Were I a merchant, I would shun my trade and join the *mujahideen* brigades in response to the following words of the Almighty God: "*O you who believe! Shall I lead you to a bargain that will save you from a grievous penalty? That you believe in God and His Messenger, and that you strive* [your utmost] *in the cause of God, with you property and your persons: That will be best for you, if you but knew*!" [Qur'an 61:10-11].

Were I to talk to you lots of times, I would talk to you about the issue that is of paramount importance; that is, the issue pertaining to the testimony that "*There is no god except God and Muhammad is the Messenger of God*" in terms of meaning and acting upon this meaning, and on *jihad*, the pinnacle of Islam, so that you may mobilize for *jihad* in the cause of God. For the current crisis is not one of knowledge or *Hadith* literature. Thanks to the grace of God, knowledge is widespread. The crisis lies in the failure to act upon what we know due to weakened trust, honesty and certainty. Religion cannot be upheld by crumbs of our funds and time. Rather, it is upheld by standing under the shadows of swords. Blessed be those who understood the issue and emulated the Prophet (PBUH) of mercy and epics, and thus fought and got killed in the cause of God. We beseech God to accept them as martyrs.

The people of Iraq gladdened the Muslims' hearts in the month of Badr[2], and later in Al-Nasiriyah where dozens of the occupation soldiers were killed or wounded, and also in Baghdad, Al-Fallujah, Al-Ramadi, Mosul and Tikrit. They inflicted material losses on the enemy in terms of the aircraft shot down, and caused them to taste some of what the Muslims in Palestine, Iraq, and Afghanistan are tasting, not to mention the adverse impact on their morale.

Greetings of reverence to the people of Samarra, Baqubah, and other cities, who upheld the banner of *jihad*. We would like to address them, saying: Have patience and enjoin each other to patience. If you demonstrate greater patience than Bush, you will get your heart's desire, God willing, for victory is achieved when one demonstrates a measure of patience.

> "I offer my life and what I already have to the knights in whom my trust was not misplaced.
>
> The knights who are not fed up with death even though fierce war rages.
>
> Their valiance does not wear out even if they are roasted in war every now and then.
>
> If the heat of the battle rages, they do not care. They treat madness with madness." [poetry]

Before concluding, I would like to remind you of an anecdote related by the authors of *Al-Siyar* books.[3] The story is as follows: When the Muslims conquered North Africa, the commander of the polytheists offered a prize for whoever would kill the commander of the Muslims. Abdallah Bin al-Zubayr[4] asked the commander of the Muslims, may God be pleased with both of them, to offer the same prize for whoever would kill the commander of the polytheists. A Muslim killed the polytheists' commander. Thus, he received his prize in full.

---

(2) The month of Ramadan, when the battle of Badr took place in the early years of Islam.

(3) These are books that deal with both the internal and external relationships of the state, with subjects, other nations or people.

(4) The son of Al-Zubayr, one of the Prophet Muhammad's most prominent Companions.

You know America has offered great rewards to those who kill the *mujahideen* engaged in *jihad* in God's cause. God willing, we within the Al Qaeda organization are committed to offering a prize amounting to 10,000 grams in gold to whoever kills the occupier Bremer, his deputy, the commander of the U.S. troops, or his deputy in Iraq.

With respect to the U.N., it is merely a Crusader-Zionist tool even though it might seek cover by offering some relief work. Which organization handed over Palestine to the Jews other than the U.N.? Which organization brought about the secession of East Timor other than the U.N.? Which organization justified the Iraq embargo and the killing of more than one million children other than the U.N.?

It is today continuing its [word replaced with asterisks] role against the Islamic nation. Therefore, whoever kills Kofi Annan, the head of his mission to Iraq, or his representatives, like Lakhdar Brahimi, will have the same prize, which is 10,000 grams of gold. There will be a prize of 1,000 grams of gold for whoever kills a military figure or civilian from the veto masters, such as the Americans or British, and 500 grams of gold for whoever kills a military figure or civilian from the slaves of the General Assembly in Iraq, such as Japan and Italy. In view of the security circumstances, the handing over of the prizes will be at the nearest possible opportunity, God willing. Whoever is killed after killing one of the soldiers of occupation, the biggest prize will be for us and for him. We pray that God would grant us martyrdom for His sake. As for the smaller prize [the gold], it will be for his heirs, God willing.

Finally, I address an appeal to the youth of Islam. I say to them: Rise to fight the Crusaders and the Jews. Celebrate the praises of God. By God, the outcome is either victory or martyrdom. None of us will be killed unless thus ordained by God. He would be missed by his family, but his soul, as our Prophet (PBUH) said, will be inside green birds flying wherever they want in Heaven. They will then land on the lamps hanging from the throne of the Merciful.

What a difference between the two neighborhoods, the neighborhood of one's family and the neighborhood of one's

God. So, O young men of Islam everywhere, especially the people of the neighboring countries, where your duty is greater. O young men of Islam in the Arabian Peninsula, the land of Al-Kinanah [Egypt], and Al-Sham [historical Syria], O brave men of Rabi'ah and Mudar [old Arab tribes], the descendants of Saladin, the knights of Muhammad the Conqueror, the *fedayeen* of Umm al-Fida and Aleppo, the great and noble men of Ma'an and Al-Zarqa [Jordan], O dauntless men of Asir [Saudi Arabia], O heroes of Hashid, Mudhaj and Bakil [Yemen], let your assistance continue, to help your brothers in the land of Mesopotamia. The war is underway there, and its fire is raging. The steeds of the Cross have raided them, killing thousands of them and capturing thousands of others. They want to eliminate those people and extinguish the light of their civilization. Praise be to God, they are fighting firmly in the face of the treacherous Romans [Westerners], sacrificing their souls and all their treasured possessions to defend their religion. How capable they are, and how good those who support them are!

They set out in the journey of supporting their mission, sacrificing their souls and money. They fear not death, leaving behind their kith and kin. They left their loved ones at home, and followed the path of Khalid and Bilal [early Islamic heroes].

God, accept our martyrs, heal our wounded, set free our prisoners, help our heroes stand fast and assist them with your might, for only you can provide support for us or them. God, who revealed the Book [the *Qur'an*], who drives forward the clouds and defeated the parties [opposed to the Prophet Muhammad], defeat them and grant us victory over them. "*Our Lord! Give us good in this world and good in the Hereafter, and defend us from the torment of the Fire*" [Qur'an 2:201]. Ordain for this Islamic nation a right guidance, where those who obey you will attain glory, while those who disobey you will reap humiliation. Ordain for this Islamic nation a guidance where what is right is enjoined and what is wrong is forbidden. God, assist the *mujahideen* to prevail over the infidels in Palestine, Iraq, Afghanistan, Kashmir, the Philippines,

Chechnya, Pakistan and everywhere else. You are All-Hearing, always near and ready to answer. Our last word is: Praise be to God, the Lord of the Worlds.

27

Address to the American People

(29 October 2004)

Prior to the U.S. presidential election, about seven minutes of an 18-minute Bin Laden videotaped speech were broadcast by *Al Jazeera*. Below is the full text of the speech produced by the Al-Sahab Institute for Media Production. The U.S. media generally mistranslated the word *ay wilaya* (which means "each U.S. state") to mean a "country" or "nation," while in fact the threat was directed at each individual U.S. state.

> "*The prohibited month for the prohibited month,—and so for all things prohibited,—there is the law of equality. If then any one transgresses the prohibition against you, transgress you likewise against him. But fear God, and know that God is with those who restrain themselves.*" [Qur'an 2:194]

Praise be to God who created the creation for his worship and commanded them to be just and permitted the wronged one to retaliate against the oppressor in kind. To proceed:

Peace be upon he who follows the guidance:

O American people, I address these words to you regarding the best way of avoiding another Manhattan, and regarding the war, its causes, and its consequences. But before this, I say to you: Security is one of the important pillars of human life, and free men do not take their security lightly, contrary to Bush's claim that we hate freedom. Let him explain why we did not attack Sweden, for example. Clearly, those who hate freedom—unlike the 19 [9/11 hijackers], may God have mercy on them—have no self-esteem. We have been fighting you because we are free men who do not remain silent in the face of injustice. We want to restore our Islamic nation's freedom. Just as you violate our security, we violate yours. Whoever toys with the security of others, deluding himself that he will remain secure, is nothing but a foolish thief. One of the most important things rational people do when calamities occur is to look for their causes so as to avoid them.

But I am amazed at you. Although we have entered the fourth year after the events of 9/11, Bush is still practicing distortion and deception against you, and he is still concealing the true cause from you. Consequently, the motives for its reoccurrence still exist. I will tell you about the causes underlying these events, and I will tell you the truth about the moments this decision was taken, to allow you to reflect.

I say to you, as God is my witness: We had not considered attacking the [World Trade Center] towers, but things reached the breaking point when we witnessed the injustice and tyranny of the American-Israeli coalition against our people in Palestine and Lebanon—then I got this idea.

The events that had a direct influence on me occurred in 1982, and the subsequent events, when the U.S. permitted the Israelis to invade Lebanon with the aid of the American Sixth Fleet. They started shelling, and many were killed and wounded, while others were terrorized into fleeing. I still remember those moving scenes—blood, torn limbs, and dead women and children; ruined homes everywhere, and high-rises being demolished on top of their residents; bombs raining down mercilessly on our homes. It was as though a crocodile swallowed a child, and he could do nothing but cry. But does a crocodile understand any language other than arms? The entire world saw and heard, but did not respond.

In those critical moments, I was overwhelmed by ideas that are hard to describe, but they awakened a powerful impulse to reject injustice and gave birth to a firm resolve to punish the oppressors. As I was looking at those destroyed towers in Lebanon, I was struck by the idea of punishing the oppressor in the same manner and destroying towers in the U.S., to give it a taste of what we have tasted and to deter it from killing our children and women. That day I became convinced that iniquity and the premeditated murder of innocent children and women is an established American principle, and that terror is [the real meaning of] 'freedom' and 'democracy,' while they call the resistance 'terrorism' and 'reaction.' America stands for iniquity and for imposing sanctions on millions of people, resulting in the death of many, as Bush Sr. did, causing the mass slaughter of children in Iraq, [the worst] that humanity has ever known. It stands for dropping millions of pounds of bombs and explosives on millions of children in Iraq again, as Bush Jr. did, in order to depose an old agent and to appoint a new agent to help him steal Iraq's oil, and other sorts of horrible things.

It was against the backdrop of these and similar images that 9/11 came in response to these terrible iniquities. Should a man be blamed for protecting his own? And is defending oneself and punishing the wicked an eye for an eye—is that reprehensible terrorism? Even if it is reprehensible terrorism, we have no other choice. This is the message that we have tried to convey to you, in words and in deeds, more than once in the years preceding 9/11. Observe it, if you will, in the interview with Scott in *Time* magazine in 1996[(1)], and with Peter Arnett on *CNN* in 1997, then John Wiener [?] in 1998; observe it, if you will, in the deeds of Nairobi and Tanzania and Aden[(2)], and observe it in my interview with Abd Al-Bari Atwan and in interviews with Robert Fisk. The latter is of your own and of your religious affiliation, and I consider him to be unbiased.

Would those who claim to stand for freedom in the White House and in the TV stations that answer to them, would they conduct an interview with him [Fisk] so that he might convey to the American people what he has understood from us concerning the causes of our fight against you? For if you were to avoid these causes, you would take America in the right

---

(1) Apparently a reference to the article "The Most Wanted Man in the World," to which the reporter Scott MacLeod contributed.

(2) Referring to the bombings of the U.S. embassies in Nairobi, Kenya and Dar es Salaam, Tanzania on 7 August 1998, and the bombing of the USS *Cole* in Aden on 12 October 2000.

path to the security it knew before 9/11. So much for the war and its causes.

As for its results, they are very positive, with God's grace. They surpassed all expectations by all criteria for many reasons, one of the most important of which is that we have had no difficulty dealing with Bush and his administration, because it resembles the regimes in our [Arab] countries, half of which are ruled by the military, and the other half are ruled by the sons of kings and presidents with whom we have had a lot of experience. Among both types, there are many who are known for their conceit, arrogance, greed, and for taking money unrightfully.

This resemblance began with the visit of Bush Sr. to the region. While some of our people were dazzled by the U.S. and hoped that these visits would influence our countries, it was he who was influenced by these monarchic and military regimes. He envied them for remaining in their positions for decades, while embezzling the nation's public funds with no supervision whatsoever. He bequeathed tyranny and the suppression of liberties to his son, and they called it the Patriot Act, under the pretext of a war on terrorism.

Bush Sr. liked the idea of appointing his sons as state [*wilaya*] governors. Similarly, he did not neglect to import to Florida the expertise in falsifying [elections] from the leaders of this region in order to benefit from it in difficult moments.

As previously mentioned, it was easy for us to provoke this administration and to drag it [after us]. It was enough for us to send two jihad fighters to the farthest east to hoist a rag on which 'Al Qaeda' was written—that was enough to cause generals to rush off to this place, thereby causing America human and financial and political losses, without it accomplishing anything worthy of mention, apart from giving business to [the generals'] private corporations. Besides, we gained experience in guerrilla warfare and in conducting a war of attrition in our fight with the iniquitous, great power, that is, when we conducted a war of attrition against Russia with *jihad* fighters for 10 years until they went bankrupt, with God's grace; as a result, they were forced to withdraw in defeat, all praise and thanks to God. We are continuing in the same policy—to make America bleed profusely to the point of bankruptcy, God willing. And that is not too difficult for God.

Whoever says that Al Qaeda has triumphed over the White House administration, or that the White House administration has lost this war—this is not entirely accurate, for if we look carefully at the results, it is impossible to say the Al Qaeda is the only cause for these amazing gains. The White House policy, which strove to open war fronts so as to give business to their various corporations—be they in the field of armament, of oil, or of construction—also helped in accomplishing these astonishing achievements for Al Qaeda. It appeared to some analysts and diplomats as though we and the White House play as one team to score a goal against the United States of America, even though our intentions differ. Such ideas, and some others, were pointed out by a British diplomat in the course of a lecture at the Royal Institute for International Affairs; for example, that Al Qaeda spent $500,000 on the event [9/11] while America lost in the event and its subsequent effects more than $500 billion; that is to say that each of Al Qaeda's dollars defeated one million American dollars, thanks to God's grace. This is in addition to the fact that America lost a large number of jobs, and as for the [federal] deficit, it lost a record number estimated at a trillion dollars.

Even more serious for America is the fact that the *jihad* fighters have recently forced Bush to resort to an emergency budget in order to continue the fighting in Afghanistan and in Iraq, which proves the success of the plan of bleeding [America] to the point of bankruptcy, God willing.

Indeed, all of this makes it clear that Al Qaeda has won gains; but on the other hand, it also makes it clear that the Bush administration has won gains as well, since anyone who looks at the scope of the contracts won by large dubious corporations, like Halliburton and other similar ones that have ties to Bush and to his administration, will become convinced that the losing side is in fact you, the American people, and your economy.

We agreed with the general commander Muhammad Atta, may God have mercy on him, that all operations should be carried out within 20 minutes, before Bush and his administration would become aware. We never imagined that the Commander-in-Chief of the American armed forces would abandon 50,000 of his citizens in the Twin Towers to face this great horror alone when they needed him most. It seemed to him that a girl's story about her goat and its butting was more important than dealing with planes and their 'butting' into skyscrapers. This allowed us three times the amount of time needed for the operations, God be praised.

It should be no secret to you that American thinkers and intellectuals warned Bush before the war: All that you [Bush] need in order to assure America's security by ridding [Iraq] of weapons of mass destruction, assuming there were any, is at your disposal, and all the countries of the world are with you in the matter of carrying out inspections, and the U.S.'s interest does not require you to drive it into an unjustified war, whose end you cannot know.

However, the blackness of black gold blinded his sight and his perception, and he gave preference to private interests over America's public interest. And so there was war and many died. The American economy bled and Bush became embroiled in the quagmire of Iraq, which now threatens his future.

His case is like that [described in the parable]: He is like the ill-tempered goat that dug out of the ground the sharp knife [with which it would be slaughtered].(3)

I say to you: More than 15,000 of our people were killed and tens of thousands were wounded, just as more than 1,000 of you were killed and more than 10,000 wounded, and Bush's hands are sullied with the blood of all of these casualties on both sides, for the sake of oil and to give business to his private companies. You should know that a nation that punishes a weak person if he is instrumental in killing one of that nation's sons for money, while letting go free a high-class man who was instrumental in killing more than 1,000 of its sons,

(3) The parable was put into verse by the famous 9th- century Arab writer Jahiz.

also for money. Similarly your allies in Palestine intimidate women and children, and murder and imprison men. [Inaudible]

Keep in mind that every action has a reaction, and finally you should consider the last wills and testaments of the thousands who left you on 9/11, waving their hands in despair. These are inspiring wills, which deserve to be published and studied thoroughly. One of the most important things I have read regarding their hand-waving signals before they fell is that they were saying, 'We were wrong to let the White House carry out unchecked its aggressive foreign policy against oppressed people.' As though they were telling you, the American people, 'You should call to task those who caused our death.' Happy is he who learns a lesson from the experience of others. A verse that I have read is also relevant to their [last] signals:

Evil kills those who perpetrate it,
And the pastures of iniquity are harmful.

There is a saying: 'A small amount spent on prevention is better than a great amount spent on treatment.' You should know that it is better to return to that which is right than persist in that which is wrong. A rational man would not neglect his security, property, or home for the sake of the liar in the White House.

Your security is not in the hands of Kerry, or Bush, or Al Qaeda. Your security is in your own hands, and any [U.S.] state [*wilaya*] that does not toy with our security automatically guarantees its own security.

God is our guardian but you have none.

Peace be upon whoever follows the true guidance.

Source: MEMRI, *Special Dispatch Series*, No. 811, 5 November 2004.

28

To the Muslims of Saudi Arabia in Particular and to the Muslims in Other Countries in General

(16 December 2004)

In an hour-long audio-cassette message broadcast on Islamist websites on 16 December 2004, Bin Laden laid the blame for the unrest in Saudi Arabia on the kingdom's ruling monarchy. The following are excerpts from the speech.

To the Muslims of Saudi Arabia in particular, and to the Muslims in other countries in general:

This is a message concerning the disagreement and conflict between the rulers of Riyadh and the people of this country, and how to resolve it. There has been much talk in Saudi Arabia about the need to have security and safety and about the inviolability of the blood of Muslims and those who have been granted safe passage, and about the importance of [maintaining] harmonious relations and social cohesion, and the dangers of divisiveness and conflict. It has been claimed that the *mujahideen* are responsible for that which has befallen Saudi Arabia. However, the self-evident truth is that the responsibility falls on the shoulders of the regime, which has neglected the conditions necessary for guaranteeing security, life, harmonious relations, and social cohesion.

It did this by disobeying God and committing grave sins which expose the land to God's warning and punishment. God told us the stories of the disobedient and their punishment so that we might take heed. God said: "*God made an example of a city, which used to be safe and peaceful. Its provisions used to be supplied in abundance from every quarter. But they denied God's favors, so God brought upon them hunger and fear because of what they did*" [Qur'an 16:112]. And God said: "*Those who acted as tyrants in the land and increased corruption in it, your Lord unleashed a scourge upon them. Your Lord is always watching*" [Qur'an 89:11-14].

Similarly, all who help this regime and fawn upon it, as well as those who abstain from denouncing evil—they too are responsible.... The acts of disobedience [against God] committed by the regime are very grave. They are worse than merely grave offenses and mortal sins; they are so serious that those who commit such things are no longer Muslims. It is worse than acting iniquitously with the people and depriving them of their rights, humiliating them, insulting their intelligence and sentiments, and embezzling the funds of the Islamic nation. Each day, millions of people suffer from poverty and deprivation, while millions of Riyals flow into the accounts of the heads of the [Saudi royal] family who wield power. In addition to all this, services are being scaled back, they are stealing lands, they forcibly impose themselves as 'partners' in businesses without giving any compensation, and so forth. The regime has gone beyond all this and has reached actions that clearly remove one from Islam.

[The regime] has allied itself with infidel America and helped it [in its war] against Muslims, and has made itself a counterpart to God by legislating to people both what is permitted and what is forbidden, instead of [leaving this to] God....

That which I just mentioned is one of the important causes of disagreement between the Muslims and the rulers of Riyadh. The solution to this matter is simple and well-known in God's religion, provided that the ruler honestly wants reform, and [indeed] if he wants it at all. As for us, Allah knows that we want reform and strive for it as much as we can. We left our country only because of our love for reform, for we didn't lack any worldly goods, praise and thanks to God....

The prosperity of this Islamic nation will come through that which brought it prosperity in its beginnings. The Arabian

Peninsula [before Islam] was [swept by] crashing waves of aggression and killing, and was flooded with barbaric paganism. But when God sent our Prophet Muhammad (PBUH) and revealed the *Qur'an*, and the people joined him in accepting Islam, then their condition improved and they prospered, and God made them mighty after their having been downtrodden....

The solution to the conflict between the ruler and his subjects is the policy [proposed] by the first *Caliph* [Abu Bakr] to the second *Caliph* [Umar], may God's favor be on them both—namely: 'Be upright, and your subjects will behave properly.' These are the words of the Rightly Guided *Caliph*s.... If a ruler properly observes God's law, the subjects will behave properly, and they will be under obligation, by God's command, to listen and obey him. If, however, the ruler becomes an apostate and abandons God's law, it is incumbent upon the subjects, by God's command, to rebel. Obedience to him is not absolute, but rather is conditional upon his probity....

Thus, if we want to arrive at a proper solution—theoretically and practically—to this conflict [between the ruler and his subjects], we must know its roots and dimensions. For this conflict is partly a local conflict, but in other respects it is a conflict between world heresy—and with it today's apostates—under the leadership of America on the one hand, and on the other, the Islamic nation with the brigades of *mujahideen* in its vanguard. This oppressive [regime] in the region, which at present represses every movement for reform and imposes upon the people policies that contradict both their religion and their worldly interest, is the very same family which helped the Crusaders against the Muslims a century ago. It is doing this on behalf of America and its allies, and this constitutes a continuation of the previous Crusaders' wars against the Islamic world.

When we look at the domestic policies of our country, we can clearly discern the extent of the Crusader-Zionist control over it. As for American interference in domestic affairs, there is no end to what one can say about it. It is impossible to appoint the king or his viceroy without America's consent. This is based on agreements between previous kings and the

American government. The farcical situation of the present government in Saudi Arabia is [maintained] with America's consent, in order to prevent the deterioration of the current situation and the deepening of discord among the princes, especially in these most recent difficult years. History has never witnessed anything like the prevailing condition of the government in Saudi Arabia. It may occur that upon the ruler's death, someone may rule the people in his name, as in the case of Shajarat al-Durr[(1)]. However, that the whole land be governed in the name of a king who for a decade already has no idea what is going on—this is unheard of.

According to Islamic law, he has lost his authority, not only due to his having committed actions which remove one from Islam, but also because of his feebleness of mind and his having lost the mental capacity needed for even the smallest of tasks, let alone for administering the country and the people. His brothers should not charge him with that which he is unable to do. They insist on his staying [on the throne] only because they refuse to see his brother Abdallah become king, for then their powers would be reduced, and he would wield exclusive power without them. For his part, he cannot get around them, since they have control of affairs, especially in the Ministries of Defense and Interior, as well as in Intelligence. What is more important is that they are in control of the Royal Chancery, which enables them to issue a royal edict in the name of the nominal ruler to remove him [Abdallah] and to appoint someone else. This sharp controversy within the royal family, in addition to their oppressing the people, enables America to go far in blackmailing the competing princes into meeting its demands, and particularly Prince Abdallah, since Abdallah knows well that if he does not comply with America's orders then he is destined, in the best of circumstances, to be deposed by his brothers, just as they had previously deposed their brother, King Saud. He also knows that his competitors have previous experience, and they are ready to do worse than depose him, if necessary.

---

(1) Shajarat Al-Durr was a female Ayyubid sultan in Egypt. She ruled Egypt for a period of 80 days following the death of her husband in 1250.

Whoever wants a recent real-life example for the role of America in deciding to depose someone should look at the case of Prince Hassan ibn Talal of Jordan. After he had been viceroy for a number of decades, his brother Hussein returned from America a few days before his death determined to depose his brother, and [indeed] he deposed him. He [Hassan] acquiesced, and became a mere political footnote. It is this [fate] that Prince Abdallah fears [would befall him] should he disobey his protector—America. Thus, it is no secret that those who make decisions about important things are in America.

The proof of the depth of the Crusaders' control over our country is that their agents carry out the changes imposed on them by those who appointed them—even in our school curricula—with the intention of disfiguring the identity of the Islamic nation and westernizing its children. This is an old plan, which began decades ago, with regard to the curricula of Al-Azhar in Egypt.

America has also asked the other agent [Arab] states to change their curricula so as to dry up what it [America] calls: 'The fountainheads of the [Islamic] awakening.'

America demanded from Yemen that it close its scholarly [Islamic] institutes more than two decades ago; likewise, America required the rulers of Riyadh to change the religious curricula, and this was actually done in deference to its [America's] wishes. All this happened more than 15 years before the attacks on New York and Washington.... This Crusader intervention in the changing of the curricula is absolutely the most dangerous intervention in our affairs, because it is, in short, a change in the religion, while the religion is a whole, which is indivisible....

It is evident that the outcome of changing the religious curricula is damaging both to religion and to material interests. As for [the damage to] religion, you already know that it is blatant apostasy, and as for material interests, the [altered curricula] will eventually produce educated slaves in our country, who will be loyal to America, sell the interests of the country and smile in the face of the Americans, while they conquer the land and defile the [Muslims'] honor, under the pretext of liberty, equality, and the laws of the United Nations. This is one example of the American intervention in domestic policy.

As for intervention in foreign policy, the ruling families defer to America and play their role in its treacheries. [The late Jordanian] King Hussein continued in the treacherous course set by his grandfather, Abdallah, son of Sharif Hussein, and his father too, against Palestine. And his [Hussein's] son, Abdallah II, follows this same course. Muhammad VI of Morocco follows the same line of treachery that was followed by his father and his grandfather before him—they continue to implement the Crusader conspiracies. The scope of this support does not permit a complete depiction of it, and so I will only mention some of the most important cases: The government of Riyadh joined a world alliance with the Crusader heresy under the leadership of Bush against Islam and its people, as has happened in Afghanistan, and likewise the conspiracies in Iraq, which have begun and not yet ended. They opened their bases to American forces in order to invade Iraq, which helped them [the Americans] and made it easier for them to conquer Iraq.... And now, they have shown us a new chapter in the series of conspiracies with America, which they call 'the initiative of sending Arab and Muslim forces for peacekeeping in Iraq'.... With this initiative, they seek to legitimize the American occupation....

What makes this matter an even worse tragedy for the people is the fact that many of them had believed, when Prince Abdallah ibn Abd al-Aziz assumed the management of the country, that he would save it from the mire of religious disobedience, corruption in the administration, finance, media, etc., as well as from subservience to America. However, while people were expecting him to do good, he showed them his evil nature.... Indeed, Saddam is a thief and an apostate, but the solution should never have been to transfer Iraq from the indigenous thief to the foreign thief. Helping the infidel to rob Muslims' land and to gain control over them is an act that removes one from Islam.... Prince Talal ibn Abd al-Aziz publicly revealed that his father was receiving money from the English....

Here, intelligent people must stop to reflect upon the behavior of these rulers, for the dimension of the fault is immense and Muslims cannot accept such people as their rulers.

Those intelligent people who seek reform, and want to achieve it through these [rulers, should ask themselves]: How can they [these rulers] carry out reform while swimming in a stormy sea of reprehensible qualities? It is impossible, for they are bound to drown, and no intelligent person should agree to have someone with such qualities as a partner in any action....

Twenty years ago, I gave good advice [for reform] to the government, through senior scholars—but things have not changed. Then, fifteen years ago, I gave my advice directly to the Deputy Interior Minister, and told him about the grave sins from which the state should desist and the danger of continuing in them, but to no avail.... What I told him about their sins—they know that these things are prohibited in God's religion, but they do not want anyone to denounce them for a simple reason: Because it is not prohibited by the religion of kingly rule....

Whoever is given the gift of true sight by God, and reflects upon the acts of the regime, will clearly see this truth in both domestic and foreign affairs, namely, that people obey the king's orders over God's orders, so that what the king declares permissible, becomes permissible, and what he declares forbidden, becomes forbidden. In their view, he has the sovereign right to permit something one year, and to prohibit it another. For example: it is well-known that usury is strictly forbidden, for God said: "*God has permitted trading and made usury unlawful*" [Qur'an 2:275]. However, the regime issued decrees and legislations, which make it [usury] lawful, and support it, and set penalties for whoever wants to oppose it or avoids paying what they deceitfully call 'profit.' It is well-known, however, that to take usury is a grave sin, and it is one of the acts that removes one from Islam.

The second example is allying one's self with the infidels. For example: The Jordanian regime is a pagan-infidel regime. Nevertheless, the rulers of Riyadh were allied with King Hussein, and if a [Saudi] preacher or writer described him [Hussein] as an agent of the Jews, he would be subject to penalty on the part of the Riyadh regime, through laws that were legislated specifically for this purpose. However, when King Hussein entered an alliance with Saddam, when he [Saddam] invaded Kuwait, King Fahd washed his hands of his former ally, and the Riyadh newspapers filled up with documents and pictures proving that Hussein ibn Talal was an agent of the Jews—which was true, for he was indeed that. On the other hand, the Jordanian newspapers filled with documents and pictures proving that the rulers of Riyadh were agents of the English, and subsequently, of America, which is true, for they are indeed that.

Therefore, despite our grave misfortune caused by the rulers of the region, who are agents [of foreign powers], we suffer greater misfortune because of some of the leaders of the Muslim world, who insist on describing these tyrants as legitimate rulers. Some people, therefore, believe that they are the lifeboat, whereas, in fact, they are the drowning boat.... The honest people of these [Islamic] associations should purge the Islamic activities of them [the tyrants].... Such is also the case with Abd al-Nasser, Sadat, Qaddafi, and Saddam. Abd al-Nasser was in conflict with them [the Saudi regime], so they declared him an infidel from the pulpit of the holy mosque of Mecca, and indeed he was one. However, when he made peace with them, he became a Muslim again. The same with Qaddafi: When he reviled them for three decades, he was an infidel, but when this heretic made peace with them, he became a Muslim, and they let him enter the sacred *Ka'ba*. And Sadat: When he signed the capitulation initiative with the Jews, the rulers of Riyadh, along with the rest of the Arab countries, accused him of treason and of being a foreign agent, which indeed he was, and their papers cursed and reviled him vehemently. Then, when Prince Abdallah acted in the same treacherous manner as a foreign agent in the Beirut initiative, the hypocrites praised him and supported him. The false scholars and mercenary writers turn wherever the ruler turns, and they fall in with him wherever he falls in for the sake of money, and [yet] they still claim religious knowledge and wisdom and guidance and uprightness.

From all this it becomes clear that the ruler believes in another religion, but he trades with the religion of Islam and deceives people with it.... The conflict is a conflict between two ways, and a deep struggle between two beliefs: A conflict between the divine, perfect way, submitting full authority to God in all matters...and the grossly secular way....

After this has become clear, then the solution to improve the conditions is, as has been made clear by [Islamic] law, to depose the ruler; and if he resists and refuses to go, it is obligatory to start an armed uprising against him and to depose him. This is the dictate of [Islamic] law, which preserves both the religion and the earthly interests of the people.... How can any intelligent person, while seeing the apostate ruler and his troops armed to the teeth, claim that he [the ruler] desires reform and peaceful solution?... And we are not talking here about a ruler guilty of some depravity and debauchery, but rather, about apostasy and serving as an agent of infidels. Just as there is no difference between [Paul] Bremer, the former American ruler in Baghdad, and Allawi, the present ruler, with regard to carrying out American policies in Iraq, so there is no difference between Bremer and the rest of the rulers of the region in carrying out America's policies.... The doctrine of rebelling against an apostate ruler is not a doctrine that I invented, but rather, it is a doctrine held by the consensus of all the great religious scholars. Such is the dictate of religious law in a situation such as ours. Therefore, it is obligatory for all Muslims to take action for reform, taking into consideration the dimension of the conflict and the fact that these regimes are nothing but a part of the system of global heresy.

Reform should be [carried out] according to the law of God, otherwise it is a deviation from the law of God and a waste of time and effort....

Those [clerics] who are opposed to the people of the land conducting armed dialogue with the governments in order to regain their rights—those [clerics] practice gross deception.... Their approach is extremely dangerous for two reasons: first... because they let their capricious ideas compete with God's law, which is a grave sin, as is well-known.... Second, because they participate in stopping people from following God's course and they mislead them about their religion, by preventing them from taking their rights in the ways prescribed by God. This pushes the hypocrites and the ignorant to consider adopting the course of the Northern Alliance [in Afghanistan] and of others like them, such as Allawi and his followers. This is absolutely forbidden.

Before ending, let me respond to some of the accusations of the regime.... They have accused the *mujahideen* of following the Kharijite sect[2], but they know that we have absolutely nothing to do with that school [of thought]. Both our messages and our actual behavior attest to this.... We do not declare [Muslim] people collectively to be infidels and do not consider the killing of Muslims to be permissible. If some Muslims are killed during the operations of the *mujahideen*, we pray for God's mercy upon them. This is to be considered accidental manslaughter, and we ask God to forgive us for it, and we bear responsibility for it....

But I say to the ruler of Riyadh: If you wish, I'll tell you about the murder of Muslims...and I shall tell you about the one who declared Muslims collectively to be unbelievers and considered it permissible to kill Muslims—it is your father, Abd al-Aziz, who went to war and helped the English against the Ottoman state and their [the Ottomans'] deputy, Ibn al-Rashid, in Ha'il.... You yourselves rebelled with arms against your brother King Saud...and your clerics did not call you and your father Kharijites[3]....

Is any Muslim ignorant of the fact that assisting infidels against Muslims is prohibited, or that legalizing the taking of interest is prohibited? This is obviously well-known in religion, just as one knows that drinking wine and promiscuity are prohibited....

You permit that which God prohibits and you prohibit that which God allows, and you issue certificates of absolution

---

(2) Kharijite sect: an early Islamic sect known for extremism.

(3) Here bin Laden reviles the Saudis for the slaughter of other Muslims by King Abd al-Aziz Aal Sa'ud in Ta'if, when he fought against the supporters of Sharif Hussein of Mecca in 1924 and defeated them.

to whomever you want, and you accuse the young people [who oppose you] of holding erroneous ideas and being a corrupt gang. But who [in fact] are those who hold erroneous ideas? Are they the ones who follow the order of the Prophet (PBUH) [stating] that it is obligatory to banish the Jews and Christians from the Arabian Peninsula, or those who scoff at the traditions of the Prophet (PBUH)?.... Are we those who hold erroneous ideas, or is it those who betrayed the Islamic nation and abandoned Muhammad's [Arabian] peninsula to the Jews and the Christians, enabling them to take control of it and giving them military bases in it? That is in addition to betraying Iraq, [bearing in mind that] it is forbidden to betray even an infidel....

Who are those who have erroneous ideas and who are a corrupt gang? Are they those who defend the Muslims and their honor and property in Iraq, Palestine, Afghanistan, Kashmir, and Chechnya, or are they those who joined the global alliance of heresy against the Muslims, in addition to robbing the public funds of the Islamic nation?... [Here Bin Laden criticizes the Saudi government for wasting money on an arms deal instead of spending the funds on the unemployed, and for seizing private property and wasting public funds on the building of extravagant palaces. He also criticizes King Fahd (then Crown Prince) for violating the sanctity of the *Ka'ba* in Mecca when he violently quashed a Wahhabi fundamentalist revolt in November 1979.]

Who are those who have erroneous ideas and who are a corrupt gang? Are they the *mujahideen*, or are they those who cooperated with America in murdering more than one million children within a few years, during their wicked embargo on Iraq, in what was the biggest massacre of children known to humanity?...

It is extremely incredible and preposterous that the [Saudi] regime accuses the [Islamist] youth of the sins of which the regime itself is guilty, as when they claim that Zionism stands behind the *mujahideen*. However, both Muslims and infidels, all over the world, know that the *jihad* youth are Zionism's worst enemy, yet the regime accuses us of their own [sins]....

Weren't you [Crown Prince Abdallah] the author of the Beirut initiative, in which you granted recognition to the Zionists and their conquest of Palestine?[4] How have you lost your mind and your honor, you, the commander of the National Guard, to the extent that you lance such false and vile accusations against the *mujahideen*?...

I ask all the Muslims to curse the Zionists and their agents, and I ask of you [Crown Prince Abdallah], if you are sincere, that you and those who obey you pronounce the following supplication in the mosques of Mecca and Medina and in all the other mosques [in Saudi Arabia]: 'O God, turn against the American-Zionist coalition, their allies, and their agents. O God, destroy them and break them; remove them from power and disperse them and scatter them; make their wives widows and turn them against one another. Seek out their weak spots just as they seek out the *mujahideen*'s weak spots. Shame them before all humanity. Rid us of them however, you wish'....

We ask God to give His grace to the *mujahideen* who stormed the American consulate in Jeddah.[5] How can they [the Americans] expect to enjoy security while they bring death and destruction upon our people in Palestine and in Iraq? They do not deserve to be secure anywhere in the world. As for their presence in Saudi Arabia—or rather in all of the Arabia Peninsula—it is prohibited by Islamic law.... And I say to our brethren and our people...continue in your path, and do not fear difficulties. Do not relent in purifying and cleansing the Arabian Peninsula of polytheists, heretics, and apostates....

You, the *mujahideen*: there is now a rare and golden opportunity to make America bleed in Iraq, both economically and in terms of human losses and morale. Don't miss out on this opportunity, lest you regret it. One of the main causes of our enemies' gaining hegemony over our country is their stealing our oil; therefore, you should make every effort in your power to stop the greatest theft in history of the natural resources of

---

(4) This is a reference is to the 2002 Saudi peace initiative.

(5) The attack on the American consulate in Jeddah, Saudi Arabia occurred on 6 December 2004.

both present and future generations, which is being carried out through collaboration between foreigners and [native] agents.... Focus your operations on it [oil production], especially in Iraq and the Gulf area, since this [lack of oil] will cause them to die off [on their own].

In conclusion, I address a brief message to the rulers of Riyadh, and another to those who wield influence. I say to them [the rulers of Riyadh]: Leadership is a contract between the sovereign and his subjects, and both have rights and obligations that derive from the contract. There are also things which nullify it, one of which is when the sovereign betrays his religion and nation—and this is what you did....

It is no secret to you now that the [Saudi] people have awakened from their apathy...and the Muslims in Saudi Arabia now insist in reclaiming their stolen rights, no matter what it takes. Therefore, you have to choose between paths. The first is to return the trust to its owners in a peaceful manner and to let the people of the country choose a Muslim ruler so that he might rule them according to God's Book [*Qur'an*] and His Prophet's tradition. The second is to refuse to return the people's rights...and to recruit some of them with money from the public money of the Islamic nation to beat up and kill their own brothers and cousins who reject your authority. You should know, however...that when peoples rise up to demand their rights, they cannot be stopped by security apparatuses. You should bear in mind the fate of the Shah of Iran, despite the reputation and the power and the experience of his security apparatus, and likewise the fate of Ceausescu in Romania....

You know that we in the Al Qaeda organization are not fighting you over worldly affairs; what offends us rather is that you commit acts which remove you from Islam—among them, ruling by [laws] other than those which God has revealed, and making alliances with the infidels.

I now address the influential people among the honest scholars, the leaders, the dignitaries and notables, and the businessmen. The message is: Take action before it's too late.... Do everything you can to defuse the crisis, as you know that the *mujahideen* in Saudi Arabia have not yet launched the war against the regime—for had they launched it in fact, the top priority would have been to get rid of the local leaders of heresy—namely the rulers of Riyadh. However, what is currently going on is merely an extension of the war against the Crusader-American coalition, which is fighting us everywhere, and whom we fight everywhere, including Saudi Arabia. We strive to expel them from it [Saudi Arabia], God willing. You, the people of influence: Fear God, for your own sake and for the sake of your nation. Let those of you who can do so emigrate from the country, thus freeing themselves from the imaginary shackles and the psychological pressure that the regime has put on them....

Source: MEMRI, *Special Dispatch Series*, No. 838, 30 December 2004.

29

To the Muslims in Iraq in Particular and the Islamic Nation in General

(27 December 2004)

On 27 December, Al Jazeera aired a few minutes of an hour long tape produced by the Al-Sahab Institute for Media Productions. The following are excerpts of this Bin Laden speech.

[The conflict with the West is] a fateful war between unbelief and Islam, between the army of Muhammad (PBUH), the army of belief, and the people of the Cross.... The important, tremendous, and dangerous issue today in the entire world is this Third World War, started by the Crusader-Zionist coalition against the Islamic nation.

What is the difference between the massacre by the tyrant Saddam [Hussein] at Halabja and the massacre by Bush at Fallujah? If Saddam killed there [at Halabja] a few thousand of our Kurdish brothers in the name of the odious nationalism, the pharaoh of this era [George Bush] killed only at Fallujah a few thousand, and wounded and crippled twice as many, in addition to expelling and terrifying hundreds of thousands—and all this in the name of the bloodthirsty Zionist Crusade.

...[The UN is] an organization of infidel [countries] that shapes the nature of the relations between the lords of the veto, headed by America, and the slaves of the General Assembly, and then speaks mendaciously and distortingly of justice, equality and freedom.

...The *jihad* in Palestine and Iraq is a personal duty incumbent upon the residents of the two countries [alone]—[but] if they are unable to carry it out, [this duty] is incumbent upon [the residents of the] adjacent [countries], and so on and so forth, until the circle includes all the Muslim countries....

When there is blatant helplessness in Palestine and Iraq, *jihad* [becomes] a personal duty incumbent upon those around them, such as the residents of Saudi Arabia, Syria, Jordan, Turkey, Iran, and Kuwait, and if [they are also] unable to carry it out, the duty is incumbent upon those around them.... Refraining from personal *jihad* is the most salient trait of the hypocrites.

Aiding America, or the Allawi government [in Iraq] which is apostate, or the Karzai government [in Afghanistan], or the Mahmoud Abbas government [the Palestinian Authority] which is apostate, or the other apostate governments in their war against the Muslims, is the greatest apostasy of all, and amounts to abandonment of the Muslim community.

[This category] includes owners and employees of companies that transfer petroleum, weapons, supplies, or other commodities. Anyone who aids them in any way is an apostate and he must be fought....

The Iraqi who wages *jihad* against the infidel Americans or against the apostate Allawi government is our brother and ally—whether he is Persian, Kurdish, or Turkmen. [In contrast], the Iraqi who joins this apostate government [Allawi government] and fights the *jihad* warriors and those resisting the [foreign] occupation is considered an apostate and an infidel, even if he belongs to the [ancient] Arab tribes of Rabi'ah or Mudar.

Personnel of the [Iraqi] military, security apparatuses, and National Guard...their blood is permitted. They are apostates who should not be prayed over upon their deaths. They cannot inherit, and they must not be inherited from [after their deaths]. Their wives are divorced from them, and they must not be buried in Muslim cemeteries....

Muslims must beware these kinds of elections of princes or presidents are "the right of the Islamic nation." However, this right is limited to particular circumstances, the most important of which is that "the prince [elected] is a Muslim, and he will institute Islam, that is, Islam is the only source of the rulings and laws....

The land [Palestine] is under occupation, the constitution of the land is a *jahili* [pre-Islamic constitution] made by man...the candidate Mahmoud Abbas is a Bahai who was brought in...under the Oslo Accords....

The warrior commander [and] honored comrade Abu Mus'ab al-Zarqawi and the groups who joined him are the best of the Islamic nation that is fighting for the sake of the word of God. Their courageous operations against the Americans and against the apostate Allawi government have gladdened us....

We in the Al Qaeda organization very much welcome their union with us. This is a tremendous step on the path to the unification of the efforts fighting for the establishment of a State of Truth and for the uprooting of the State of the Lie....

Know that the warrior comrade Abu Mus'ab al-Zarqawi is the commander of the Al Qaeda organization in the land of the Tigris and the Euphrates, and the comrades in the organization there must obey him....

I call upon you to attack reinforcement lines and oil [pipe]lines, to sow powerful mines...and to assassinate the owners of companies aiding the needs of the enemy, whether in Riyadh, Kuwait, Jordan, Turkey, or other [countries].

Source: MEMRI, *Special Dispatch Series*, no. 837, 30 December 2004.

30

Offers to Accept a Truce

(19 January 2006)

In an audio speech broadcast by *Al Jazeera* on 19 January 2006, Bin Laden threatened further attacks on the U.S. Contrary to many translations in the Western media, he did not offer a truce, but said he would accept a truce if the U.S. offered it.

In the name of God, most Gracious, most Merciful, my message to you refers to the war in Iraq and Afghanistan, and how to end it. I did not intend to speak with you about this subject because for us this issue is already decided—only iron can defeat iron. Our situation, God be praised, is improving, becoming better and better, while your situation is the opposite.

What brought me to speak out are the repeated deceitful words by your President Bush. In his comment on the results of U.S. public opinion polls, which showed the overwhelming majority of you want the withdrawal of U.S. forces from Iraq, Bush opposed this and stated the withdrawal of troops will convey the wrong message to the enemy. He said: It is better to fight them on their ground rather than they fight us on our ground.

In response to these deceitful words, I say: The war in Iraq is raging without cessation and military operations in Afghanistan are escalating in our favor, God be praised. The Pentagon's numbers indicate an ongoing rise in the number of your dead and wounded, let alone the huge material losses and the collapse of the morale of the soldiers there and the increase in the cases of suicide among them.

Imagine the state of psychological breakdown that afflicts a soldier while collecting the remains of his comrades' dead bodies after they stepped on the mines that tore them apart. Following such a situation, the soldier is between two fires. If he refuses to go out of his barracks on patrol, he will face the penalties of the Vietnam butcher [Sec. of Defense Rumsfeld], and if he goes out, he will face the danger of mines. So, he is between two distasteful situations—fear and humiliation. Moreover, his superiors ignore him. Therefore, he has no choice but to commit suicide.

What you hear about him and his suicide is a strong message to you, which he wrote with his blood and soul while pain and bitterness ate him up, to save what you can save from this hell. The situation is in your hands if you care about him.

The news of our *mujahideen* brothers is quite different from what is published by the Pentagon. What is published in the media is not the truth or the reality on the ground. What increases doubts is the information leaked out about the White House administration's targeting of the news media that carry some facts about the real situation.

Documents have recently surfaced that show the butcher of freedom in the world [President Bush] had planned to bomb the head office of *Al Jazeera* in Qatar after bombing its offices in Kabul and Baghdad. Even though and despite its defects, *Al Jazeera* is one of your creations.

Jihad is continuing, praise be to God, despite all the atrocities committed by the U.S. army and its agents—to the point where there is no significant difference between these crimes and those of Saddam. These crimes include the raping of women and taking them hostage, instead of their husbands. *There is neither power nor strength except from God.* As for the torturing of men, they have used burning chemical acids and electric drills on their joints. And when they give up on [interrogating] them, they use the drills on their heads until they die. Read, if you will, the humanitarian reports of the atrocities and crimes in Abu Ghraib, Guantanamo and Bagram prisons.

I say that despite all these barbaric methods, they have failed to break the sharp blade of the resistance or the *mujahideen*, praise be to God. Instead, the resistance is growing stronger. In fact, reports show the defeat and devastating failure of the ill-omened plan of the cursed quartet—Bush, Cheney, Rumsfeld and Wolfowitz. This defeat is only a matter of time, which is to some extent linked to the awareness of the American people of the magnitude of this tragedy.

The wise among you know that Bush has no plan to achieve his alleged victory in Iraq. If you compare the small number of the dead when Bush made that fake and stupid show-like announcement from an aircraft carrier—the end of the major operations—with the tenfold number of killed and injured who fell in minor operations, you will know the truth in what I say. Bush and his administration do not have either the will or the ability to withdraw from Iraq for their own private, dubious reasons.

To return to where I started, I say that the poll results please sensible people and that Bush's rejection of the results is a mistake. Reality shows that the war against America and its allies has not remained confined to Iraq, as Bush claims. In fact, Iraq has become a point of attraction and restorer of [our] energies. At the same time, the *mujahideen*, with God's help, have repeatedly managed to breach all the security measures taken by the unjust nations of the coalition. Evidence of this is the bombings you have witnessed in the capitals of the most important European countries of this hostile coalition.

As for the delay in carrying out similar operations in America, this has not been due to the inability to breach your security measures. Operations are being prepared, and you will immediately see them in your own homeland upon completion of their preparation, God willing.

Based on the above, it can be clearly seen that Bush's words are false, but what he refrained from saying—and this is the essence of the poll results, which favor troop withdrawal—is that it is better not to fight the Muslims on their own land and for them not fight us on our land.

We have no objection to accepting a long-term cease-fire under fair conditions which we will uphold. We are a nation forbidden by God to betray and lie. In this cease-fire both sides will enjoy security and stability, and we will build Iraq and Afghanistan, which have been destroyed in the war. There is nothing wrong with this solution, except that it will prevent the flow of hundreds of billions [dollars] to influential individuals and the war merchants in America who supported Bush's election with billions of dollars. Consequently, we understand the insistence by Bush and his gang to continue the war.

If you [Americans] are sincere in your desire for peace and security, we have answered you. If Bush decides to continue with his lies and oppression, it would be useful for you to read the book "The Rogue State", the introduction of which states: "If I were president, I would halt the attacks against the United States. First, I would apologize to all the widows and orphans and those who were tortured. Then I would announce that U.S. interference in the nations of the world has ended forever."

Finally, I tell you that the victory in this war is either ours or yours. If we win, you will be defeated and disgraced forever, and this is the direction it is headed, with God's help. And if you win, you should read history. We are a nation that does not tolerate injustice, and we will seek revenge forever. Days and nights will not pass until we take revenge, as we did on 11 September, God willing, and you will continue to live in disgrace and fear, and in the end you will be defeated.

As for us, we have nothing to lose. He who swims in the sea does not fear the rain. You have occupied our land, defiled our honor, violated our dignity, spilled our blood, stolen our wealth, destroyed our homes, and shattered our security. We will treat you in the same way.

You have tried to prevent us from living with dignity, but you won't be able to prevent us from dying with dignity. Refraining from performing *jihad*, which is sanctioned by our religion, is a great sin that we fear. Dying under the shadows of the swords is the best that we wish for. Do not be deluded by your power and your modern weapons. Although they win some battles, they will lose the war. Patience and steadfastness are better than them. You should be watching for the finish line.

For 10 years we patiently fought the Soviet Union with our few weapons, and we depleted their economy till they became history, with God's help. You should take a lesson from that. We will remain patient in fighting you, God willing, until the one whose time has come dies first. We will not leave the fight as long as we hold our weapons in our hands. I swore not to die but a free man, even if I taste the bitterness of death.

Peace be upon those who follow the guidance.

31

Speech to the Muslim Nation on the Zionist-Crusader War Against Islam

(23 April 2006)

In a 51-minute audio speech, excerpts of which were broadcast on *Al Jazeera* on 23 April 2006, Bin Laden talked about the Danish cartoons that insulted the Prophet Muhammad, impious Muslims (*zendiq*), Darfur, Hamas, Kashmir, Pakistan, Chechnya and Iraq. He emphasized that anyone who mocked the Prophet or ridiculed Islam should be killed. The complete audio tape with English subtitles was released by As-Sahab, an Al Qaeda production company, on 26 April.

Praise be to God, Lord of the Worlds, and may peace and prayers be upon our Prophet Muhammad, and on all his family and Companions. To the Islamic nation in general: peace be upon you and the mercy of God and His blessings.

This speech is directed to you [the Muslim nation], urging you to come to the aid of the Prophet Muhammad (PBUH) and punish those responsible for the heinous crime committed by some journalists among the Crusaders or *zendiq*.[(1)] They have insulted the Prophet Muhammad (PBUH), master of the forefathers and the successors.

The sacred verses [of the *Qur'an*] and the noble Prophetic traditions [*Hadith*] have made clear our duty to the Messenger of God (PBUH) in terms of loving, honoring, following and exalting him. God, the Exalted, has forbidden offending

---

(1) *Zendiq*: one who goes so far into innovated and deviant beliefs and philosophizing without sticking to the truth found in the *Qur'an* and the way Muhammad lived his life to such an extreme extent that he/she leaves Islam altogether.

him, saying in the Exalted *Qur'an*: "*Those who offend God and His Messenger, God has cursed them in this world and in the Hereafter, and has prepared for them a humiliating punishment*" [Qur'an 33:57].

And God said: "O *you who believe! Raise not your voices above the voice of the Prophet, nor speak aloud to him in talk, as you may speak aloud to one another, lest your deeds become vain and you perceive not*" [Qur'an 49:2]. It has been authenticated that our Prophet (PBUH) said, "By Him in whose hand my life is, none of you will have faith until he loves me more than his father, children and all mankind combined."

The Muslim nation has reached a consensus that anyone who maligns or belittles the Messenger (PBUH) should be killed. Such offence is regarded as infidelity. Sheikh al-Islam Ibn Taymiyah[(2)] said, "The cursing and defamation of the Messengers—peace be upon them—is the source of all types of impiety, and combines all types of misguidance, and every [act of] impiety is a branch of it."

Qadi Iyaad [famous Muslim jurist] said, "He who likens the Messenger of God (PBUH) to something by way of insulting and scorning him, or belittling his status and significance, or disparaging him or finding fault in him, has cursed him and the ruling regarding him is that of the curser." And Imam Ahmad[(3)], may God have mercy upon him, said, "Whoever curses the Prophet (PBUH) or belittles him, whether Muslim or infidel, is to be killed."

The case and law concerning the *zendiq* and heretics who defame Islam and slander and insult our noble Prophet (PBUH) have been clarified by Imam Ibn al-Qayyim.[(4)] He made it clear that the crime of the *zendiq* is the worst of crimes. The evil of his staying alive among Muslims is among the greatest of evils.

---

(2) Sheikh al-Islam ibn Taymiyah: see Ibn Taymiyah in Terms at the end of the book.

(3) Refers to Ahmad ibn Hanbal (d. 855), the author of a well-known *hadith* collection.

(4) Muhammad ibn Abu Bakr (d. 1350), known as Ibn Qayyim al-Jawziyya, was Ibn Taymiyah's most eminent disciple.

He is to be killed, and his repentance is not to be accepted. Said the Imam, "So this is the constant habit of the *zendiq*, and were his repentance to be accepted, it would mean allowing him to remain impious and a heretic who, whenever he is captured, professes Islam only to return to what he was doing. And why not? He knows that he will be saved from death by outwardly professing Islam, so he is not prevented by fear from public display of heresy, defamation of Islam, and maligning God and His Messenger (PBUH). Thus, his aggression toward Islam is only suppressed by killing him. Also, the one who maligns God and His Messenger (PBUH) is waging war against God and His Messenger (PBUH) and sowing corruption on earth, so the standard for his punishment is death, and the standards are not cancelled out by repentance after capture, as agreed upon by all."

I remind myself as well as you of the actions of the pure and righteous, the first soldiers of Islam, the noble Companions, God be pleased with them, so that we might imitate them in spreading Islam and succeed in imitating them.

The compilers of the way the Prophet Muhammad (PBUH) lived his life as well as the writings of the Companions of the Prophet (PBUH) have related the story of Ka'b bin al-Ashraf's[5] poetry in which he attacked the Prophet (PBUH), and when that reached the Prophet (PBUH), he said, "Who will go for me for Ka'b bin al-Ashraf, for he has maligned God and His Messenger?" Immediately, Muhammad ibn Maslamah arose, saying, "I, oh Messenger of God! Would you like me to kill him?" He replied, "Yes."

God is great, God is great! How quickly they came to the aid of God and of His Messenger! God is great! How great was their faith and conviction, and how knowledgeable and perceptive they were! He, God be pleased with him, knew that the medicine for those who malign God and His Messenger (PBUH) is death, without introduction, unlike the defeatist

---

(5) Ka'b ibn al-Ashraf was a leader of the Jewish tribe of Abu Nadhir. He was killed on Muhammad's orders (ca. 625), according to Islamic sources, for composing poetry calling people to fight against Muhammad and slandering Muslim women.

preachers of today who didn't go to the Crusaders as warriors but instead went as interlocutors. People like these dissolve Islam, so beware of them. Yes, their methodology is contrary to the correct methodology. The methodology of the Messenger of God (PBUH) is that he loves the killing of Ka'b bin al-Ashraf and loves the killing of all who malign God and His Messenger (PBUH). Yes, their killing is something loved by God and His Messenger (PBUH), and God has ordered it and His Messenger (PBUH) has encouraged it. God said, "*But if they violate their oaths after their covenant, and taunt you for your Faith, you fight the chiefs of impiety: for their oaths are nothing to them, that thus they may be restrained*" [Qur'an 9:12]. So when they are fought, they cease to slander Islam.

Ibn al-Qayyim said about this verse, "Whoever defames our religion is a leader of impiety." Many are the leaders of impiety today in the Muslim lands, and many are the followers of Ka'b bin al-Ashraf in the Arabian Peninsula. Many of them are writers in the press, actors and broadcasters in the media. Here it is incumbent that we warn that it is not permissible for a Muslim to listen to any program that includes discussion with the *zendiq*, or any show that mocks Islam or religious Muslims, for that is one of the greatest of sins. How numerous are the *zendiq* who are [government] ministers! Foremost among them is the labor minister in the Land of the Two Sacred Mosques, Ghazi al-Qusaybi. Whoever wants to see the official *fatwa* proclaiming him guilty of impiety and apostasy—such a *fatwa* was issued by former Grand *Mufti* Abd al-Aziz bin Baz, just as he issued a *fatwa* on the impiety and apostasy of the *zendiq* Shamlaan al-Issa in Kuwait.(6) Among these impious is Ahmad al-Baghdadi(7), also in Kuwait, and Turki al-Hamad(8) in the Land of the Two Sacred Mosques—a *fatwa* concerning the latter was issued by Sheikh Hamud al-Uqla—and many others like them. The book *Modernity in the Balance of*

(6) Shamian al-Issa is a political science lecturer at Kuwait University.

(7) Ahmad al-Baghdadi is a Kuwaiti intellectual.

(8) Turki al-Hamad is a reformist Saudi intellectual.

Islam[9] includes many of their names. Sheikh Sa'id al-Ghamdi has also warned against them in his audio tapes.

Now let us return to finish our story. Muhammad ibn Maslamah took with him some of the Companions, and they went and killed the enemy of God, Ka'b bin al-Ashraf. The Jews and those pagans with them were terrified by this and came to the Prophet (PBUH) in the morning, and said, "Our companion was struck tonight, and he is one of our chiefs. He was assassinated, and we know of no crime or incident." The Messenger of God (PBUH) replied, "Had he remained peaceful like others who share his opinion, he would not have been assassinated. But he offended us and satirized us in verse, and anyone of you who does the same will be put to the sword." Yes, this is the ruling of our Messenger (PBUH), concerning all who satirize him and all who belittle Islam and mock it. So, to the youth of Islam: follow the order of God and His Messenger (PBUH) by killing them, and take as your role-model Muhammad ibn Maslamah and his companions, for better the belly of the earth than its back while the *zendiq* are among us, mocking our religion and our Prophet (PBUH). So, respect God in yourselves, and please your Lord. Don't consult anyone in killing these *zendiq*, and seek help in carrying out your tasks through secrecy. This is as far as the apostate *zendiq* are concerned, and we shall now begin talking about the slanderers of Islam among the original *zendiq*.

The sons of the Muslim nation from East to West have risen up to condemn that greatest of crimes, so may God reward well every denouncer of those impious acts. We ask God to accept as martyrs those of them who have been killed, and we promise God that we will take revenge for them on the governments which spilled their blood.

Some voices have been raised in our Muslim nation asking the infidel wrongdoers in the West to clearly and honestly apologize in order to end the crisis—or so they said. But the fact is, the matter is too great and serious for it to be ended

(9) Written in 1988 by the Saudi fundamentalist preacher Awadh al-Qarni, the book lists over 200 Arab writers, academics and journalists and accuses them of heresy—thus making their killing legal.

by mere regret or apology, assuming that they will even apologize in the first place. Rather, the criminals must be punished along with all who sheltered them or stood by them.

Dealing with this crime as a separate incident that is isolated from the general framework only hurts the proper conception needed to know the animosity the West holds toward us and the true nature of the Crusade being waged against our Muslim nation. Because rendering judgment on anything stems from its conception, it is necessary that this crime be placed in the greater context of the aggression being perpetrated against our Muslim nation throughout the past years and decades. By doing so, it becomes easy for us to know the true size of this incident.

Anyone who considers the events which have occurred throughout the past few years and decades clearly sees the ugliness of the West's face and the greatness of its hatred of our Muslim nation. So, it was in this context that the incident occurred, and the repercussions came one after another. Among the most prominent was the Danish government's refusal to even apologize, much less punish the criminals, and its refusal to take steps to prevent the repeat of this type of crime, and then the solidarity shown to it by America and the European Union.

These events, along with what has happened since the Manhattan raid, have confirmed previous truths, but this time with severe clarity and starkness. Despite the media clamor and the huge propaganda about human rights, justice and freedom, it now has become clear from previous events that these pretty notions have very shallow roots in the West. Indeed, they have no roots at all if the matter concerns Muslims; in fact, they are like a feather blown by the wind searching for a place of refuge as it flees from the West, lest the West strangle and trample upon those concepts in its name!

These events, along with what preceded them, have confirmed that the West is incapable of acknowledging others and their rights, much less respecting their beliefs and feelings, and that the West is still living with the complex of racial superiority, and views others with contempt and believes it is superior to others. This view of people as inferior dominates them, and the residues and shadows of past centuries, when the Sun didn't set on what were called their colonies, during which their gluttonous armies occupied our countries, sucked the peoples' treasures and enslaved them. These residues and shadows continue to dominate them. Thus, people, as they see them, are white—they are the masters—and colored—they are the slaves—which is why the West created organizations and made laws which preserve and protect its doctrine of the enslavement of the peoples. It created the United Nations for this purpose, and the right of veto is nothing but glaring proof of this, nothing but the sanctification of the defense of this tyrannical, dictatorial doctrine which considers *jihad* in the path of God and the defense of one's self and homeland to be terrorism.

America and Europe consider the *mujahid* groups in Palestine, Chechnya, Iraq, and Afghanistan to be terrorist groups. So, how can there possibly be dialogue and understanding with them without weapons? The rulers of our region consider America and Europe to be friends and allies, and also consider the *mujahid* groups fighting the Crusaders in Iraq and Afghanistan to be terrorist groups. So, how can there possibly be dialogue and understanding with them without weapons? The essence of what these and those who deny us our right to defend our religion and ourselves all say is that we must surrender, abandon *jihad* and be their satisfied slaves. This is impossible, with God's permission.

Among the greatest of the issues which clearly demonstrates these concepts is Palestine. What oppression, assault and hatred could be more blatant than the Zionist-Crusader alliance deciding to hand over Palestine to the Jews, for it to be their state, after carrying out massacres there and displacing many of its people, then bringing the Jews from various countries to settle them in Palestine? This aggression and oppression have continued for more than nine decades and continue to this very day. All attempts to regain our rights, demand justice and take revenge on the Israeli oppressor have been thwarted by the leadership of the Zionist-Crusader alliance by using what is called the right of veto.

Among the things which display this as well is their rejection of the fairly-elected HAMAS government, although we emphasize what Sheikh Ayman al-Zawahiri indicated regarding the impermissibility of entering the polytheistic councils. Their rejection of HAMAS confirms that it is a Zionist-Crusader war against Muslims.

I say, clarifying their domination of the Security Council, the International Crusade and pagan Buddhism own the five permanent seats and what is called the veto power in what is called the Security Council. America and Britain represent the Protestant Christians, Russia represents the Orthodox Christians, France represents the Catholic Christians, while China represents the Buddhists and pagans of the world. As for the Islamic world, it is represented by 57 countries, and comprises one-fifth of the world's people, and more than one-fourth of the U.N. membership. One province of one Islamic state, like the Punjab in Pakistan, has a population larger than that of France and Britain; moreover, one province of one Islamic state, like Darfur in Sudan, has a land area larger than Britain and close to that of France, yet it has no seat in the Security Council. Here I am not asking for this [seat], because it is wrong, but I am simply describing the facts of the matter. The U.N. is an infidel organization, and whoever accepts its laws is an infidel. It is a tool used to implement the Zionist-Crusader resolutions, including the declarations of war against us and the division and occupation of our lands. It is a Zionist-Crusader war against Muslims.

What did it mean when the Ottoman state, the remnant of the Caliphate, despite its flaws, was destroyed, toppled and divided into dozens of states and mini-states? Soon after, Britain came and separated Sudan from Egypt, then turned once more towards Sudan, seeking to separate its south. It formed an army of southerners, backing them with money, weapons and expertise, and directed them to demand separation from Sudan. Then America adopted this army with moral and material support, and through its international instruments like the U.N., put pressure on the Khartoum government to sign an oppressive agreement permitting the south to separate six years after the signing of the treaty. Let Bashir [President of Sudan] and Bush know that this treaty isn't worth the price of the ink with which it was written, binds us to nothing, and that it isn't the place of anyone—whoever he might be—to give up a hand span of Islamic land. The south shall remain an inseparable part of the land of Islam, with God's permission, even if the wars continue for decades to come.

Even then, the U.S. didn't stop all these subversions and crimes, but stirred up more sedition and strife, among the worst of which is that in the western Sudan, where it has exploited differences between the local tribes and turned that into an all-out war between them which is devouring everything, as a prelude for sending Crusader troops to occupy the region and steal its oil, under the cover of keeping the peace. It is a continuing Zionist-Crusader war against Muslims.

In this regard, I call upon the *mujahideen* and their helpers in general and especially those in Sudan and its environs—including the Arabian Peninsula—to ready all that is necessary to undertake a long-term war against the Crusader thieves in the western Sudan. Our goal is clear: to defend Islam and its people and land, and not to defend the Khartoum government, even if our interests overlap. Our differences with it are great, and it is enough that it failed to apply Islamic law and threw away the south. I encourage the *mujahideen* to acquaint themselves with the land and tribes of Darfur province and its vicinity, for it is said, "The one who knows a land kills it, and a land kills the one uninformed about it." Keeping in mind that the region is about to enter a season when the rains usually increase, impeding movement and cutting the dirt roads, which is one of the main reasons for delaying the occupation until after the coming six months. So, it is imperative to be swift and take advantage of the time factor while taking the greatest possible care, especially in terms of providing huge numbers of mines, sniper rifles and anti-tank artillery like the RPG.

Then, what does it mean when the weapon is forbidden for the defenseless in Bosnia and the Serbian Army is left to slaughter Muslims and spill their blood and violate their rights for several years under the cover and veil of the U.N.? It is a

Zionist-Crusader war against Muslims. What does it mean when the Crusader states apply pressure to Indonesia until they separated East Timor from it in only 24 hours, also with a threat from the U.N.? It is a Zionist-Crusader war against Muslims.

On the other hand, a blind eye has been turned to the U.N. resolution passed over a half-century ago giving Muslim Kashmir the freedom to choose what it wants and choose independence from India. In the same way, the atrocious Hindu massacres of Indian and Kashmiri Muslims have been winked at during the same period, to the extent that Bush, the leader of this Crusade, declared a few days ago that he will order his apostate agent Pervez Musharraf [President of Pakistan] to close the camps of the Kashmiri *mujahideen*. With this he proves and confirms that it is a Zionist-Crusader-Hindu war against Muslims.

In regard to Pakistan: some of the Muslims have done well in helping their brothers who were affected by the earthquake. May God reward them well, but it is also imperative that they help the independent Muslim Pushtun tribes whose houses were destroyed to please America by the earthquake of the Pakistani Army in the Waziristan region. We ask God to accept those killed among the martyrs, and to heal their wounded and bless them, their families and their wealth. I ask God, the One beside whom there is no god, the Living, the Eternal, to punish Bush and Pervez and their troops with what they deserve, and that He make use of one of the lions of Islam to kill Bush's slave boy in Pakistan. He is the custodian of this and able to do it. God said, "*For Pharaoh and Haman and (all) their hosts were men of sin*" [Qur'an 28:8].

What does it mean when there is silence about the atrocities and crimes of the Russians in Chechnya and the dragging of Muslims and tearing apart of their bodies by tying them between tracked vehicles, and what is called the civilized world blesses all of this, and indeed, backs it secretly? It is a Zionist-Crusader war.

What does it mean when the Muslims in Somalia are humiliated and 13,000 of our Muslim brothers are killed, and the greatness of their civilization and their hatred is displayed as they roast our brothers over the fires? *There is neither power nor strength except from God*. It is a Zionist-Crusader war. I remind Muslims to respect God in themselves, and I urge them to avert from their brothers on the African continent the famine which has befallen them, for this is the least they can do for them.

What does the destruction of Iraq's infrastructure mean? What will convey to you what Iraq is and what tragedies have occurred there? What does it mean when depleted uranium is used and Iraq is placed under embargo for several years, during which over a million children died, shocking and distressing all who visited Iraq, including the Westerners themselves? It is a hateful Crusade. What does it mean when Iraq is reoccupied through deception and lies, and grotesque acts are committed there, including bombing, destruction, murder, displacement, and imprisonment and torture, and massive military bases are set up to tighten their control of the entire region. So, pay attention to what is being said to you. It is a Zionist-Crusader war against Muslims.

What does the continuation of the cunning, malevolent media and cultural invasion mean, when controlled TV channels and radio stations are set up, in addition to the Voice of America, BBC and the rest, to continue the ideological invasion of our Muslim nation and make war on its beliefs and change its values and spread obscenity and depravity? Indeed, they have gone so far as to interfere with the curricula—especially the religious curricula—and change them. It is a Zionist-Crusader war.

How are we to interpret France's stance toward the *hijab* [scarf that covers a Muslim woman's hair], and its banning in schools, and France's excessive harshness in dealing with Muslim communities, and then its resolving to set up a TV channel in the Maghrib countries to combat the Islamic renaissance there? It is a Zionist-Crusader war.

After the *zendiq* Salman Rushdie wrote his book, in which he attacked Islam's sacred tenets, the Prime Minister of Britain received him, in a challenge to and mockery of the Muslims and their feelings, and then the former U.S. President received him in the White House, not to mention what you have heard about the intentional desecration of the noble *Qur'an* in Guantanamo prison. So, how can we interpret these actions as anything other than encouraging the mocking of Islam and its Prophet (PBUH) and encouraging the hatred of his followers? The insulting drawings which we denounce today are nothing but the fruit of this aggressive attitude in the West, which is found from the highest levels on down. What it publishes about the caricatures reflects the public opinion of its people and what seethes in their hearts. It is a Zionist-Crusader war.

This is just a small part of something much greater—a little from a lot. Every one of these acts on its own indicates that it is a Zionist-Crusader war against our Muslim nation. How much more so when these acts and others are combined against us!

It takes the people lightly and shows contempt for them when their sacred tenets are mocked and you demonstrate your solidarity with the mocker, and then call for dialogue and calm. It also makes a mockery of the people and scorns them when your aircraft and tanks destroy houses over the heads of our families and children in Palestine, Iraq, Afghanistan, Chechnya and Pakistan. Then you smile in our faces and say, "We aren't opposed to Islam but are opposed to the terrorists only, and we call for peaceful coexistence and dialogue instead of a clash of civilizations."

The facts betray you. The West's politicians only want dialogue for the sake of dialogue, to gain time by anesthetizing us and taking advantage of our carelessness. They are only interested in a cease-fire from our side alone. You are aware of our recent response to their opinion polls, where we offered to accept a truce between us and them after the pullout of their armies and the ending of their harassment of us. All of this was rejected by them. They are bent on continuing their Crusades against us and occupying our countries, plundering our resources and enslaving us, so don't be deceived by what they say or what is said by the hypocrites and apostates from our compatriots or by the rebellious ones, deserters, demoralizers and rumormongers and alarmists, all of whose voices have been raised recently. After the Muslim nation rose up in condemnation of this insult, voices were raised demanding a boycott of their goods and animosity increased towards them.

Bush, the head of the Crusade, announced in front of everyone his demand that his agents in the region—especially the rulers—do their best to calm the people and deal with the reaction. The Arab rulers and those media personnel, evil scholars and preachers of evil who revolve around them responded and raced to calm things down. The one known as the *mufti* of the Americans arose and announced in front of everyone that the regret of the Danish journalist is a sufficient apology, even though everyone knows that they are resolute in their injustice. Neither did they punish these criminals nor did they take any steps to prevent a reoccurrence. After this misled and misleading *fatwa*, some preachers of evil stood up and promoted the restriction of the boycott to Denmark, while everyone knows that many papers all over Europe and America have printed these insults and that they have shown solidarity with Denmark.

These preachers for the rulers justify their neglect and desertion of God's Messenger (PBUH) and their position that they are not obligated to even call for a boycott of their goods with baseless arguments, like their saying that there are trade pacts with them. They pretend to forget that the love of God and His Messenger (PBUH) and *jihad* in the path of God is greater than the love of wealth and trade, and that God has threatened whoever does not see it like that and deprived him of guidance and ruled him rebellious. God said: "*Say: if it be that your fathers, your sons, your brothers, your mates, or your kindred; the wealth that you have gained; the commerce in which you fear a decline; or the dwellings in which you delight—are dearer to you than God, or His Messenger, or jihad in His cause—then wait until God brings about His decision: and God guides not the rebellious*" [Qur'an 9:24].

After this, the most senior of the Arab rulers appeared to guide them to the path of righteousness, or so he claimed, and said at the Jenadriyyah cultural festival that the Muslim nation is suffering an attack which targets its Islamic law and symbols, in reference to the drawings which insult our Prophet (PBUH). The people were delighted to hear this and sat attentively to listen to him remind them of their duty. Some of them expected him to mobilize the Muslim nation to come to the aid of its religion and the Prophet (PBUH) with all it possesses and to stand up to rebuff this assault, but it escaped them that this conflicts with the orders and instructions of America, which state that he must play the same role he played before the invasion of Iraq, when, as you will recall, he lied to the people and said that there is no war, in order to spread submissiveness, humiliation and shame in the Muslim nation.

Today, Iraq is paying the price of that deception, falsehood and war. So, he took the same approach with this issue, and said exactly as follows, "It is the duty of the sons of the Muslim nation and especially its thinkers to emphasize the real face of the Muslim nation, the face of tolerance, equity and balance." Then he came back and said in an unambiguous way that he was against all action to confront this aggression and take revenge on the perpetrators of this crime. He said that he condemns the concept of a clash of civilizations, and called for it to be replaced by the concept of constructive, peaceful coexistence.

I say that these fallacies are major and great. The clash between truth and falsehood will continue until the Hour happens, and from it is the clash which has been going on for nine decades—their civilization against ours. If not, then what does it mean when Palestine has been kept all this time under the occupation of first the British, then the Israelis? Then those who have betrayed God and His Messenger (PBUH) and have betrayed their trust, nations and the Muslim nation demand that we avoid a clash with those who clash with us night and day. May God give them what they deserve. So, disown them and beware of them, and beware of all who revolve around them, and know that there is no way to repel injustice other than by fighting and defending. God said, "*And were it not that God checks one set of people by means of another, the earth would indeed be full of mischief*" [Qur'an 2:251]. And God said, "*Never will the Jews or the Christians be satisfied with you unless you follow their form of religion*" [Qur'an 2:120]. And God said, "*Nor will they cease fighting you until they turn you back from your faith if they can*" [Qur'an 2:217].

So, our stance toward these mockers of our Prophet (PBUH), those who insulted him in those drawings, is that we demand that their government hand them over to us, for them to be judged according to the Law of God, as long as they are saying that it is freedom of expression and the government is not responsible, and that instead the responsibility falls on the newspaper itself. This request of ours is from the category of treating in kind. We say to you, if you have forgotten, let us remind you that when you announced that Osama bin Laden was accused of striking at American interests, you issued a Security Council resolution which was passed unanimously, declaring the extradition of Osama to be mandatory, despite no evidence being provided. Therefore, extradite to us those who have been proven to have committed this act. Or, is it that if the accused is Muslim, no regard is paid to morals or reason, whereas if the accused is American or European, you make excuses for him and justify his outrageous behavior as freedom of expression and the like, and that you have the right to take Muslim citizens for trial in your countries, whereas we have no right to take your citizens for trial in our countries? Should you refuse, you are affirming that you are another race, above man and above reckoning, and that it is your right to enslave others.

We also remind you that after the blessed raid on New York, America declared that it would attack Afghanistan, and Bush said at the time, "I want Osama, dead or alive," and the tyrannical military campaign commenced, before the appearance of any evidence of our carrying out that act, and before we stated that. So, who is it that gave you the right to attack a sovereign state without any proof?

When the media campaign increased in intensity, and the warships began to move, the Afghan foreign minister Mutawakkil rushed to declare his readiness to hand over Osama, and your only response was to say, "Even if you were to hand Osama over to us, we still must attack Afghanistan." This shows with blinding clarity that the attack wasn't merely because of the presence of Al Qaeda in Afghanistan, but was a brazen attack on Islam and destruction of the nascent Islamic state. You went after all its leaders by chasing, imprisoning and killing them, which conclusively proves that it is a Zionist-Crusader war against Muslims.

Indeed, if Bush found at the time enough reasons to justify to his heedless, ignorant people the invasion of Muslim Afghanistan, by virtue of their country being the one that was hit—and you know, as we mentioned previously, that we only struck them in self-defense and to aid our brothers in Palestine, Lebanon and elsewhere—then what business do the people of Europe have with this war which made them race to unite under Bush's banner? They haven't merely failed to criticize him or restrain him; on the contrary, the number of European troops under NATO has increased in Afghanistan. So, what is their concern? If we hypothesized that the one behind the Manhattan raid was an individual from Germany or France, would you have agreed to put him on trial before the appearance of the evidence, and would you have joined Bush and his gang if they had taken a stance like the one they took in the war on Afghanistan to strike Germany or France? The answer is emphatically no, and this confirms the double standards, confirms your hatred of Islam and that it is a Crusade against Muslims. This is what we wanted to prove.

Then I say: the war is a joint responsibility of the peoples and their governments. The war goes on, and the peoples renew their allegiance to their rulers and politicians, send their sons to the armies to fight us, and continue the material and moral support. Our countries are burned, our houses bombed and our people killed, and no one cares about us. A sufficient example for you of the brazen violation of our nation, brothers and countries is what your ally Israel did when it raided and demolished the Jericho prison in collusion with America and Britain.

So, the conclusion is: the war is under way to harm God's Messenger (PBUH), his religion and the Muslim nation.

Therefore, it is imperative that the readiness of the Muslims, their *jihad* and actions correspond to these events. So, what is the duty of our Muslim nation towards this fierce, multi-pivoted new Crusade?

I say: our duty is to make every effort to aid God's Messenger (PBUH), his religion and the Muslim nation with everything in our power and on all levels. Despite the large number of Zionist and Crusader attacks on our Muslim nation—among them military, economic, moral and cultural attacks—by far the most important and serious of them are their attacks on our Prophet (PBUH), religion and methodology of our Islamic law.

The epicenter of this war is located in Baghdad, home of the Caliphate, and they say over and over again that success in Baghdad is success for America and that their failure in Baghdad is failure for America. Thus, if their will is broken there, it means the breaking of all their wars and various attacks against our Muslim nation, with God's permission, and the beginning of the ebb of the Zionist-Crusader surge against us. Your sons and brothers, the *mujahideen* in Iraq, have, by God's grace, taught America and its allies lessons they will never forget. Now the fourth year since the beginning of the Crusader invasion draws near, and your brothers there are steadfast, patient and at their stations. Every day they exacerbate the enemy's wounds and decimate his troops, killing and injuring them. They have upset his plans and crippled his designs, and their condition is going from good to better, and their steps toward the unification of their efforts under the Word of Monotheism are continuing. We ask God to bestow on them and the war His blessings. They have raised the banner of Islam high. May God reward them well and recompense them generously.

It is obligatory upon the Muslim nation, with all its groups and sections, and its men and women, young and old, to provide of themselves, their wealth, their expertise, and all types of moral and material support what suffices to carry on *jihad* in the fields of *jihad*, especially those in Iraq, Palestine, Afghanistan, Sudan, Kashmir and Chechnya. God knows that *jihad* is today an individual obligation and the duty of every Muslim. The Muslim nation is sinful if it doesn't provide what is necessary, and the necessities can be met with only a few of our sons and a little of our wealth and expertise, if we respect God.

Oh people of Islam, don't be terrified by the enemy and his large number of men and equipment, for victory comes from God. The enemy is, by God's grace, in a severe predicament, and your *mujahid* sons' engagements with the American enemy in Afghanistan and Iraq have broken his prestige, weakened his strength, bled his power, and defied him, which has made him tarry and blunder in taking any significant decision about attacking the countries which free themselves from his domination and rule. He has become like the owner of a tank which has run out of ammunition and scares only the fool with its roar.

Oh followers of Muhammad (PBUH), be patient, exhort to patience and stand your ground, for happy is he who stands to defend the banner of Monotheism, and happy is he who makes a shield out of himself and his chest as he defends the religion of God. Make certain that God sees you where He loves to see you. God said, "*Truly God loves those who fight in His Cause in battle array, as if they were a solid cemented structure*" [Qur'an 61:4].

Oh Muslims, whoever is incapable of performing *jihad* by himself shouldn't be stingy with himself in performing *jihad* with his wealth, pen and tongue, for this is a decisive war. This is our Prophet (PBUH), our beloved master, role model and example, suffering harm from the Crusaders and apostates, and you see it and hear about it, and all the states and rulers have deserted him. The boycott should include the countries of America and Europe and the countries in solidarity with them, who all showed solidarity with Denmark, and the boycott should continue, even though, as we noted, that alone is insufficient.

Know that this world is a place of trial and tribulation, and that God is testing you with these events. Will you continue to defend His religion and Prophet (PBUH), or will you take a seat? "*That those who died might die after a clear Sign* (*had been given*), *and those who lived might live after a clear Sign* (*had been given*). *And verily God is He who hears and knows* (*all things*)" [Qur'an 8:42].

The people in relation to this event are three parties: a party which sheltered the perpetrators who insulted the Prophet (PBUH) and showed solidarity with them, and it comprises Europe, America and those who rode with them; another party which sat with those who sat, and deserted God's Messenger (PBUH), and God is looking at us, so it is incumbent upon the Muslim to see which party he is from; and a third party which arose to aid God's Messenger (PBUH), each in his own way, and the best of them was he who aided him with his body, wealth, pen, spear and tongue.

Oh worshippers of God, prepare the answer for the Day of Accounting, because today deeds without accounting, and tomorrow accounting without deeds. As for the *mujahideen*, we, with God's help, promise Him that we will aid Him and His Messenger (PBUH), and His religion and the Muslim nation, until victory is complete or we perish before that.

So, respect God in aiding God's Messenger (PBUH), and don't let God's Messenger (PBUH) and His religion be attacked from your flank and beware. Don't let the *mujahideen* who aid the Messenger of God (PBUH) and His religion be attacked from your flank and beware.

Before I conclude, I encourage myself and my brothers, the *mujahideen*, with these verses from the *mujahid* Sheikh Abu Mansoor al-Shami, in which he says:

The darkness of night is dispersed by the dawn.... And the shame of the face is erased by the weapon
Whoever grazes in the pasture of tyranny one day.... Is punished by the swords and spears
And the oppressed has a right which he demands.... Even if the wounds pierce his neck
And however much the Taghut attempts to plot.... Against God's Deen, he rushes to fight them
Rome has in mind a plot against Islam.... And Rome thinks we are fair game

They think that the knights are in a coma.... And that the lions are frightened by barking

We left you fallen at Yarmuk.... For the eagles and wolves to fight over you

Mutasim and Harun raided you.... And Salahudin demolished you at Hattin

In the Russian tyrants there is a good admonition.... And it is permitted to take a lesson from them

We tore their bonds so they became.... Like grass scattered by the wind

And we pulled down palaces in America.... Did you deny it, and can the Sun disappear?

We raided you with wings of death.... And the ruin never crossed your minds

On their backs rode knights of glory.... Who saw that in embracing death is relief

So they embraced the towers in an embrace of fury.... And the flood overran them and down they came

We flattened them by the grace of God.... And death and wounds flowed through you

The center of your wars became rubble.... And we broke your nose and the pride fell

If you saw Bush when he learned about.... The unadulterated horror and humiliation

You have been faced with a hurricane which.... If the winds were to face, they would fail

As for the spotted snake, it tasted.... Our courage in London and the wails rose

And we confronted your ranks in combat.... In Baghdad, and success cheated you

We have harvested thousands of you, and no matter.... What you hide, your disgrace is unmistakable

And should you one day come to the Sudan.... The lions of God have a habit of combat

We shall reap you with mines and snipers.... And the armor shall rise above your heads

The destiny of Unbelief is loss and then Fire.... And the destiny of those who sacrifice is success

O God, our Lord, give us in this world good and in the next good, and save us from the punishment of the Fire. O God, show us truth as truth and guide us to follow it, and show us falsehood as falsehood and guide us to avoid it. O God, unite the hearts of the Muslims, combine their strength, unify their ranks, have mercy on their weakness and mend their cracks. O God, approve for our Muslim nation a righteous rule in which those who obey You are honored, and those who disobey You are disgraced, and in which good is enjoined and evil forbidden. O God, make faith dear to us and beautify it in our hearts, and make disbelief, rebellion and disobedience hateful to us. O God, open the hearts of our young men and women to the observance of Your religion, and grant us guidance, piety, virtuousness and prosperity. O God, steady our feet on the Day on which the feet slip. O God, steady us and steady the *mujahideen* everywhere, and especially in Palestine, Iraq, Sudan, the Land of the Two Sacred Mosques, Kashmir, Chechnya, Nigeria, Indonesia, and Afghanistan. O God, guide their fire, bind their hearts, and aid them with Your aid. Give them victory against Your enemy and theirs, for neither us nor them have any helper other than You, O Powerful, O Mighty. God is victorious in His affair, but most of the people know not.

Our final prayer is that all praise is due to God, Lord of the Worlds, and may peace and prayers be upon our Prophet Muhammad and all his family and Companions.

Terms

A.H.: after *Hijra* (622 A.D.); Muslim calendar begins on this year, marking Muhammad's flight from Mecca to Medina.

Al-Aqsa Mosque: located in Jerusalem.

Al-Bukhari (810-870 A.D.): author of the most generally accepted collection of *Hadith*.

Amir: a commander, ruler, prince.

Ansar: "helpers"—Muhammad's early supporters in Medina.

Caliph: a successor to the Prophet Muhammad after his death; first four caliphs were Abu Bakr, Umar, Uthman and Ali Caliphate: Islamic government under a *Caliph*.

Companions: Muhammad's followers, seen as examples of righteousness.

Emirate: from the Arabic *imarah*, "right to rule," the rule or jurisdiction of an *Amir Fatwa*: a binding religious ruling made on the basis of Islamic law by a qualified Islamic scholar or jurist.

Fatawa: plural of *fatwa*.

Fiqh: Islamic jurisprudence.

God: *Allah*—a contraction of the Arabic *al-ilah*, "The God."

Hadith: "saying," or "report," a literary form that communicates a "custom" or "tradition" of the Prophet Muhammad Hanbal, Ahmad ibn (780-855 A.D.): a Muslim scholar famous for his collection of *Hadith*.

Hijra: in Islamist terms it signifies leaving an area ruled by an impious government, in emulation of the Prophet Muhammad's emigration (622 A.D.) from his native town of Mecca to Medina.

Hubal: an ancient Meccan idol worshipped by pagans before the advent of Islam; the name is commonly used among Islamists to denote the U.S.

Ibn Taymiyah (1263-1328 A.D.): known as the Sheikh al-Islam, an important religious scholar; Islamists see him as a great religious authority, especially with respect to *jihad*.

Imam: person who leads Muslim congregational prayers, also means Islamic leader.

Intifada: Palestinian "uprising" from 1987-1993; a second uprising began in September 2000.

Jihad: "striving in God's cause to achieve spiritual excellence," for militant Muslim fundamentalists used frequently for holy war.

Ka'ba: literally "cube," the main Islamic sanctuary in Mecca.

Land of the Two Sacred Mosques: Saudi Arabia—Land of Harramain—the entire Arabian Peninsula.

Land of the Two Rivers: Iraq.

Messenger of God: Muhammad.

Mufti: Islamic scholar who is an interpreter of Islamic law, can also issue a *fatwa*.

Muhajirun: those who emigrated with Muhammad from Mecca to Medina in 622 A.D.

Mujahid: singular, one who strives for spiritual excellence; also used to describe one who takes part in *jihad*; plural: *Mujahideen*.

Mujahideen: plural of *Mujahid*, for militant Muslim fundamentalists means warriors fighting for Islam.

Muslim ibn al-Hajjaj (821-875 A.D.): compiled one of the most famous collections of *Hadith*.

PBUH: [God's] Peace and blessings be upon him [Muhammad]

The Prophet: Muhammad.

Qibla: the direction Muslims face during prayer; facing the *Ka'ba*.

Qur'an: "Recitation," the holy scripture of Islam.

Salat: the five daily, ritual prayers.

Sheikh al-Islam: see Ibn Taymiyah.

SWT: *subhannahu wa ta 'aala* means 'Be He [God] glorified'; follows God's name.

"*There is neither power nor strength except from God.*": a phrase used to express resignation to God's will in the face of disaster or hardship or indignation at some outrageous evil.

"*There is no god except God.*": first half of the profession of faith.

"*There is no god except God and Muhammad is the Messenger of God.*": core of Muslim profession of faith; is known as the *shahada*.